RENAISSANCE

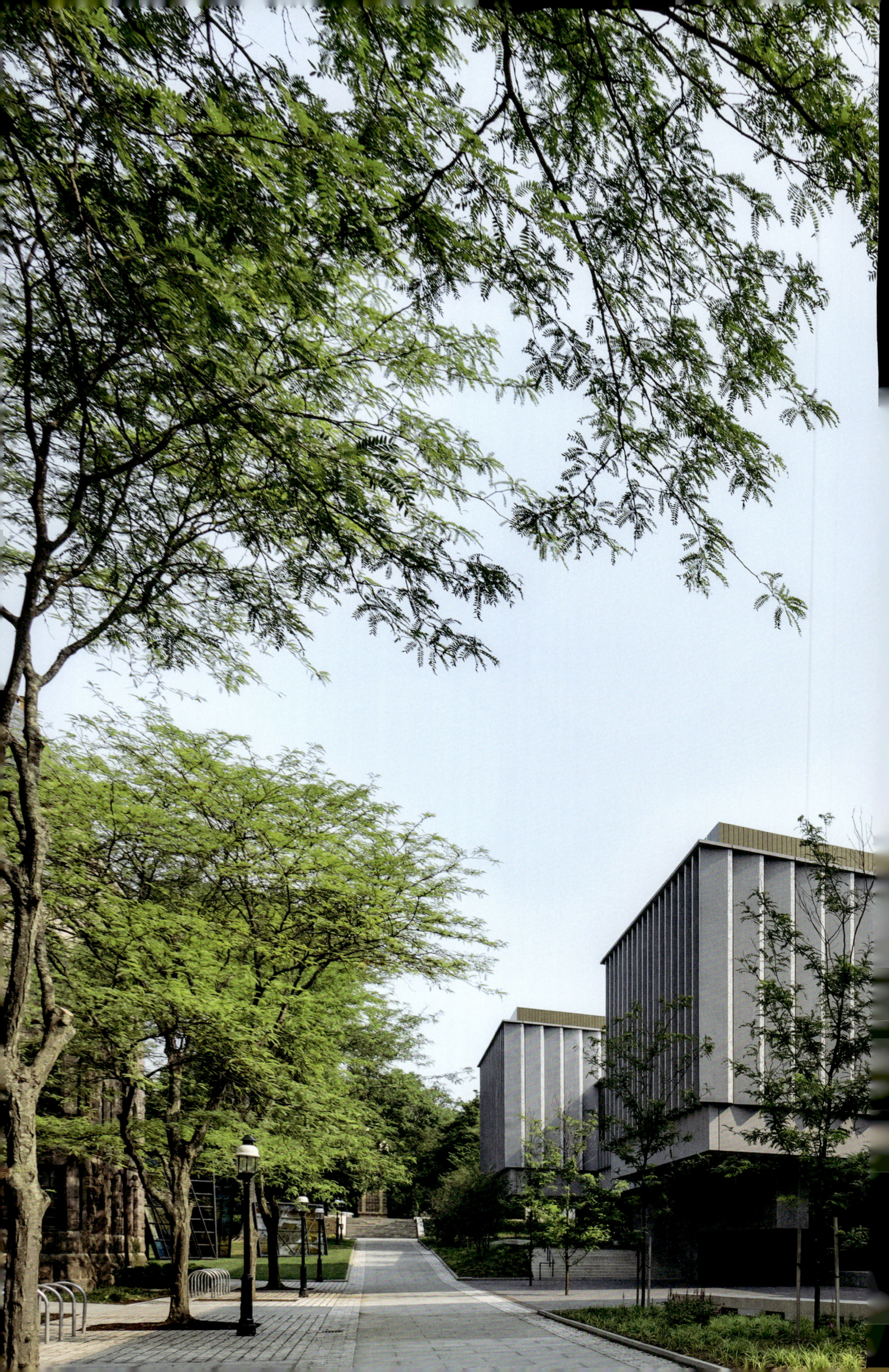

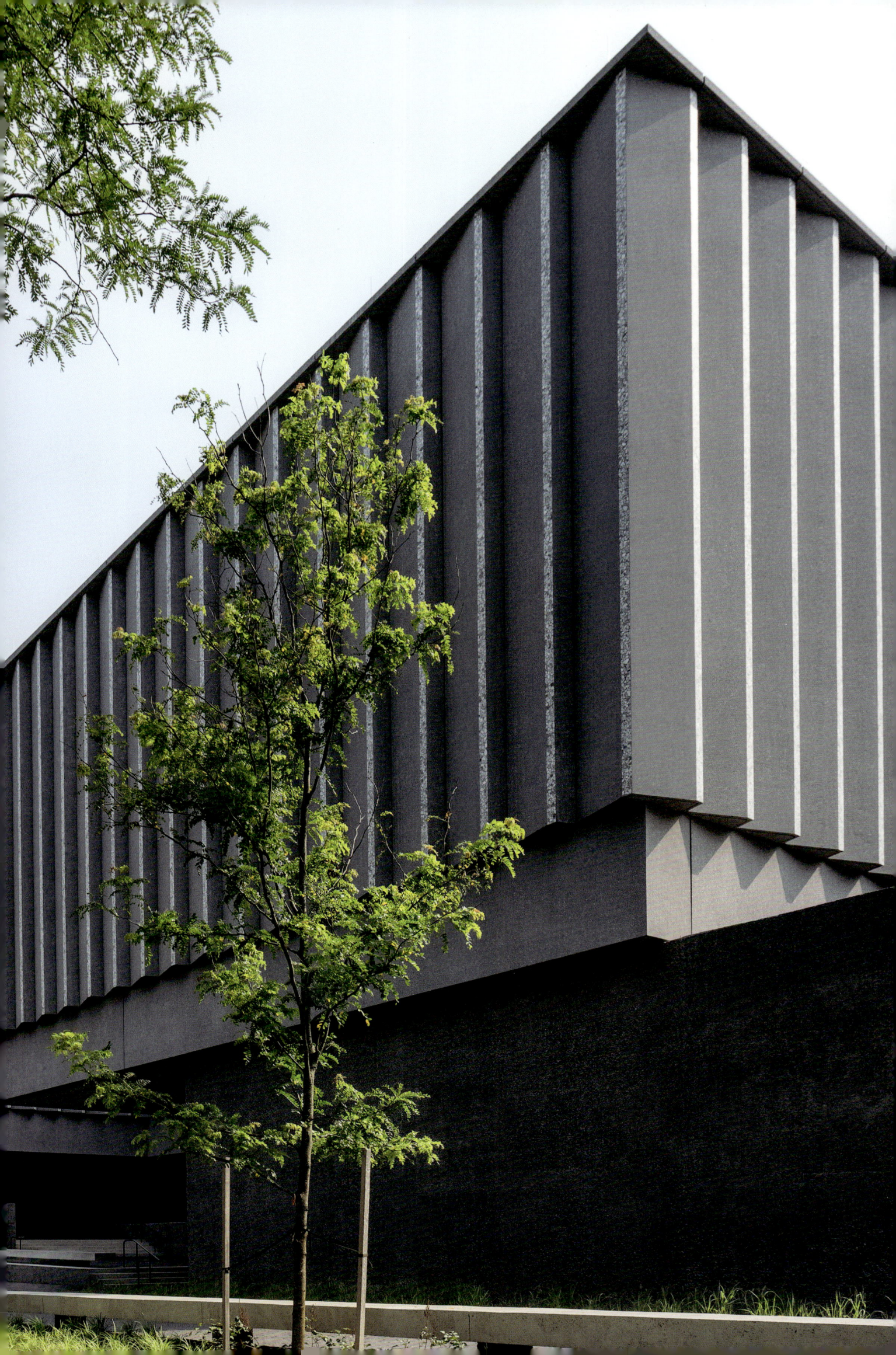

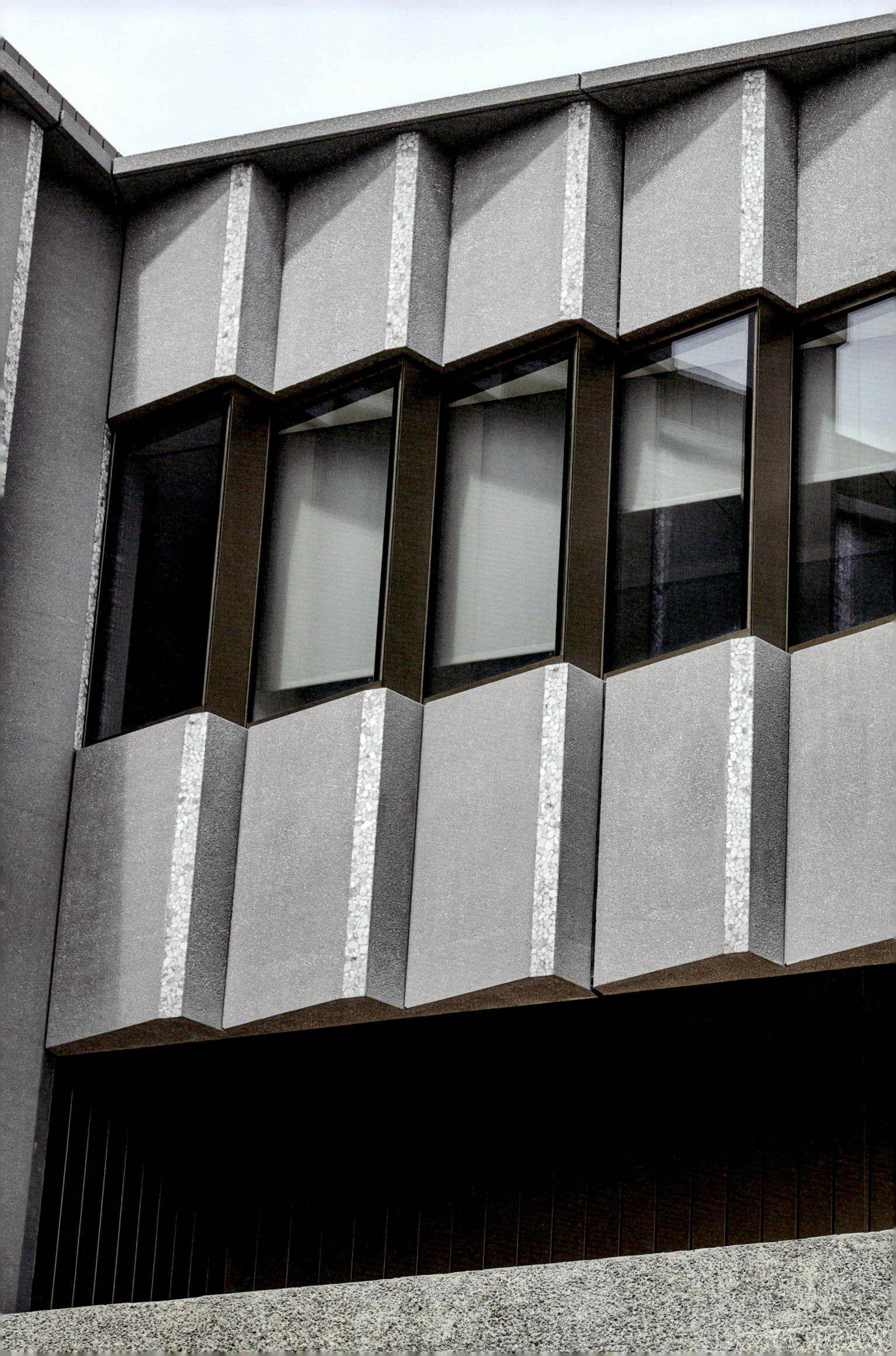

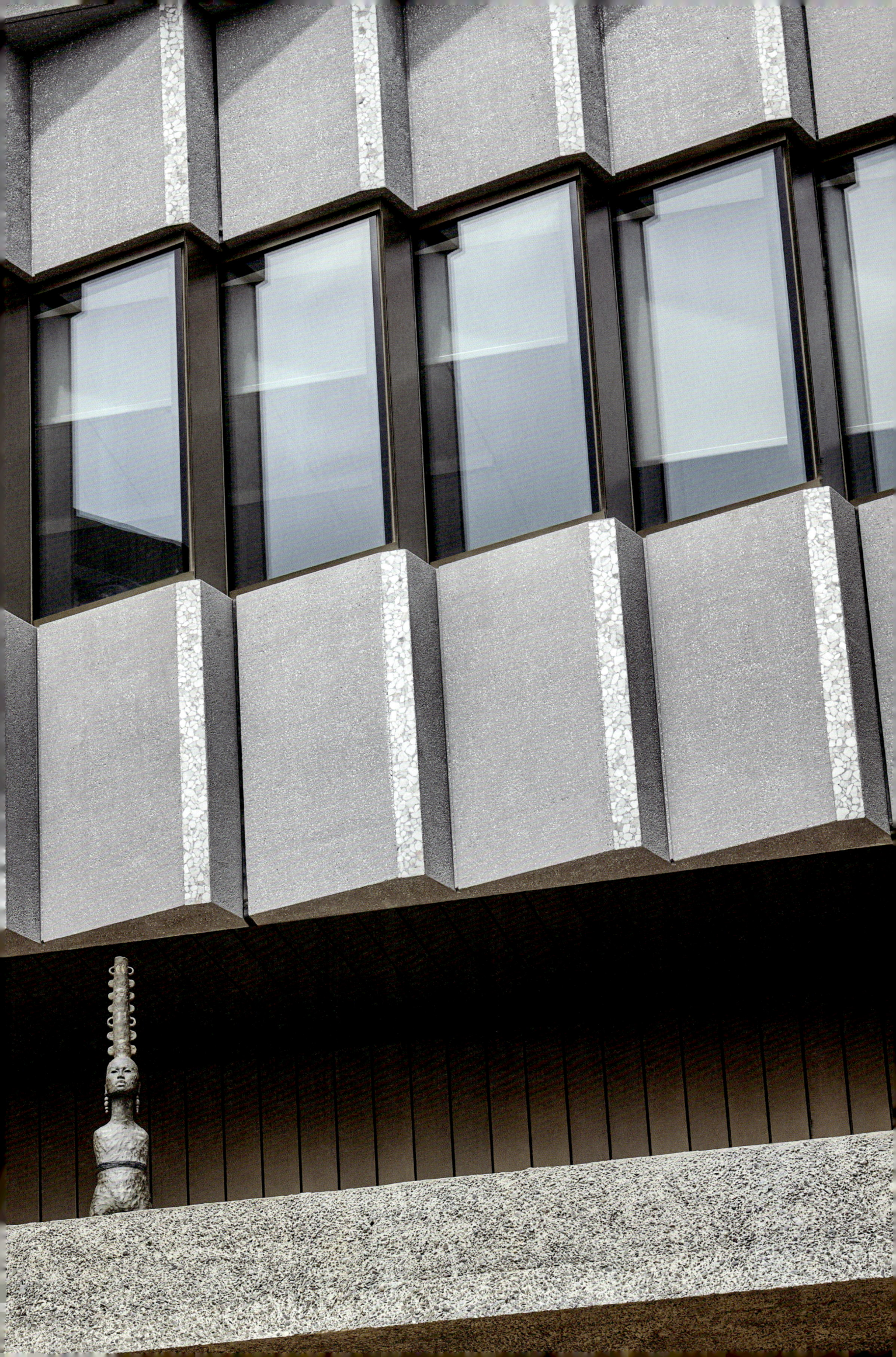

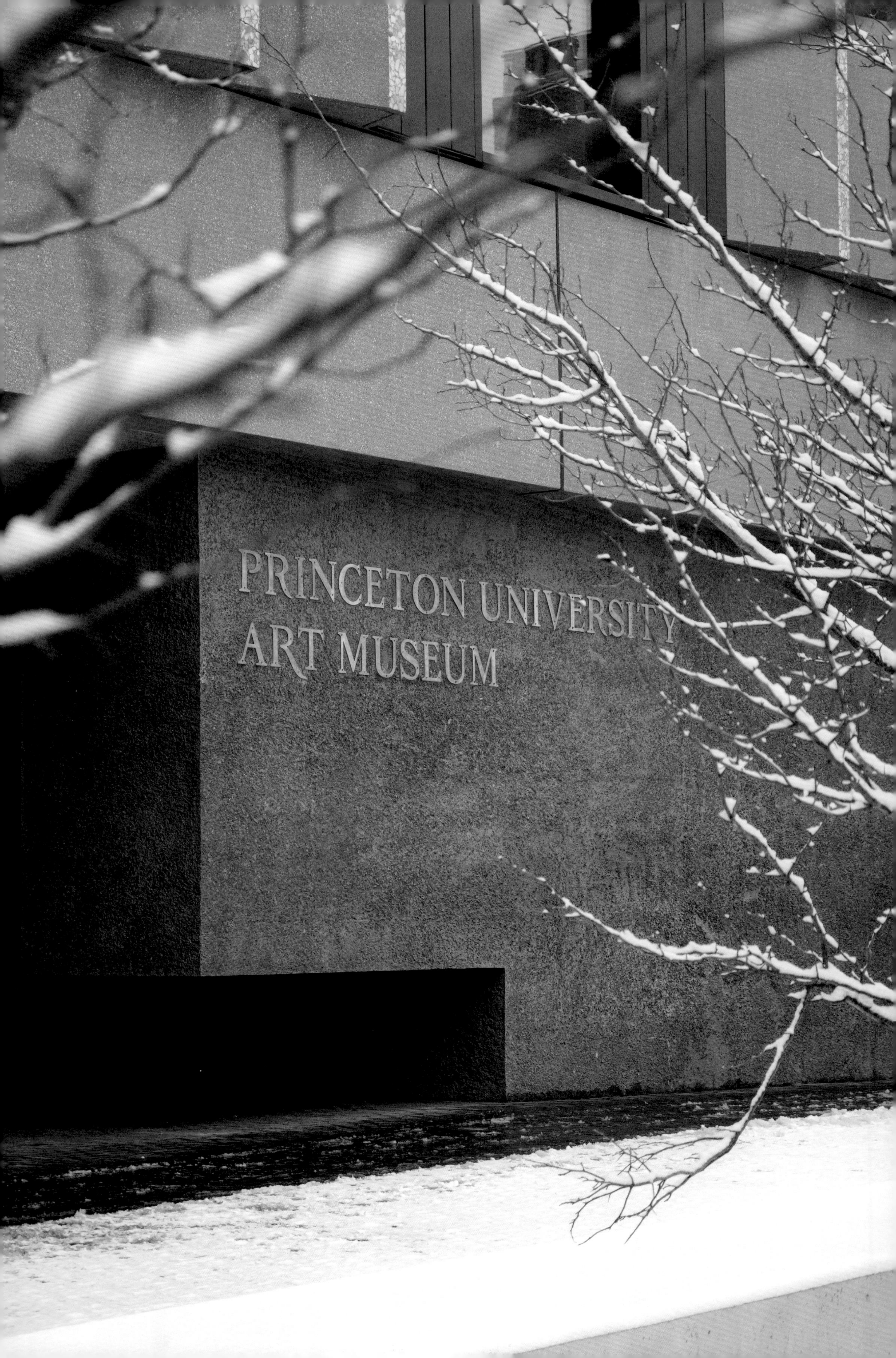
PRINCETON UNIVERSITY
ART MUSEUM

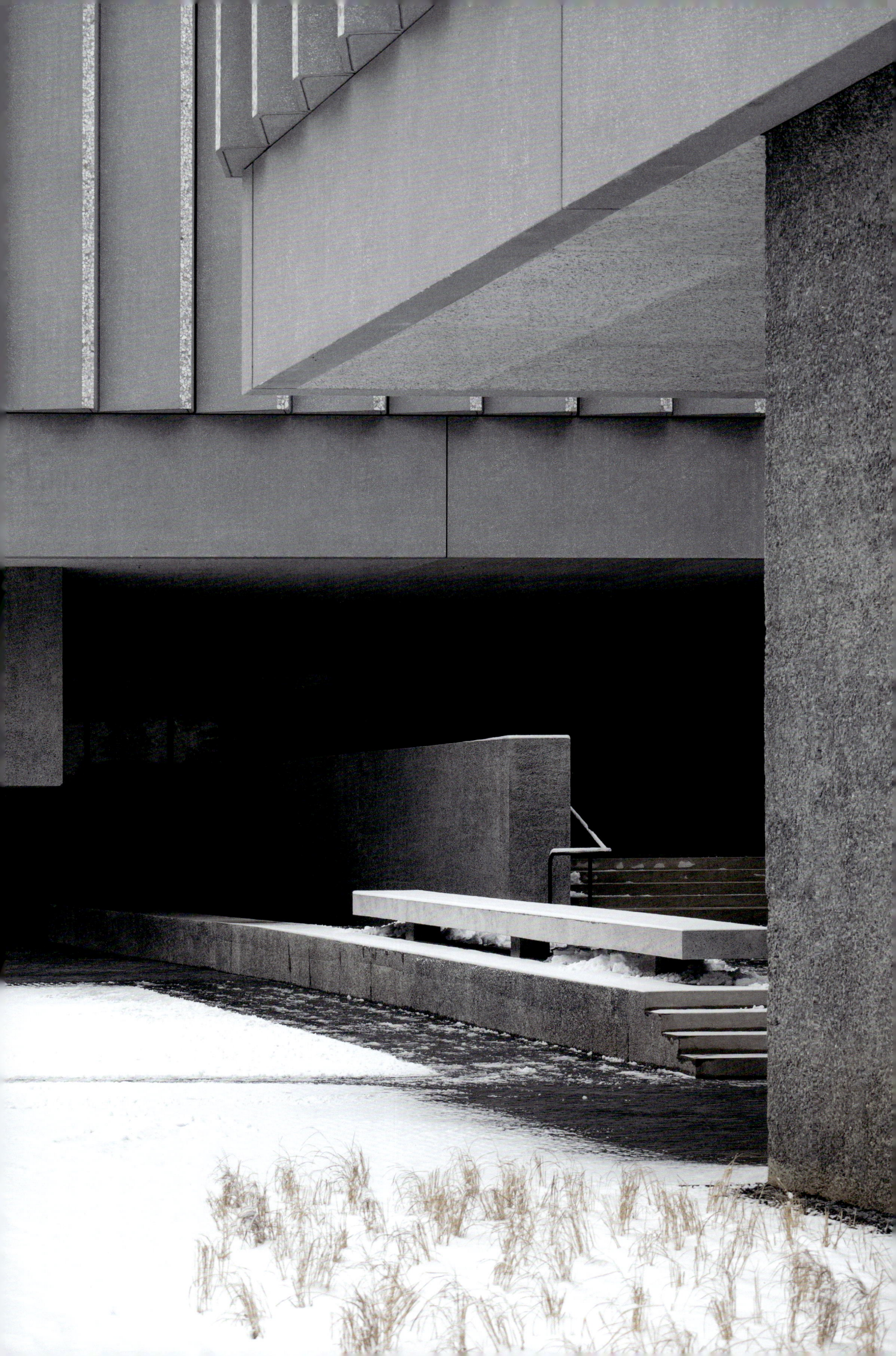

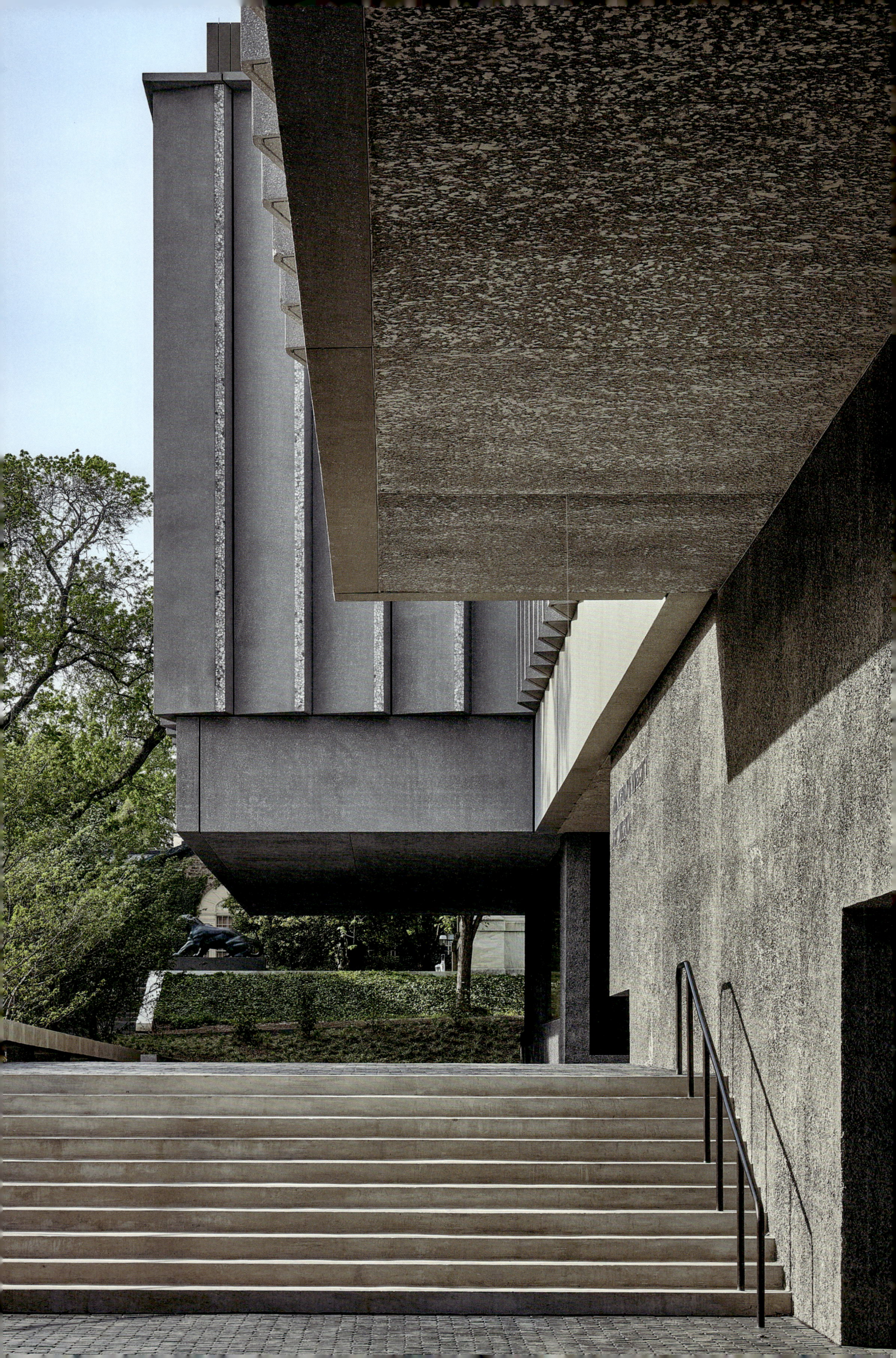

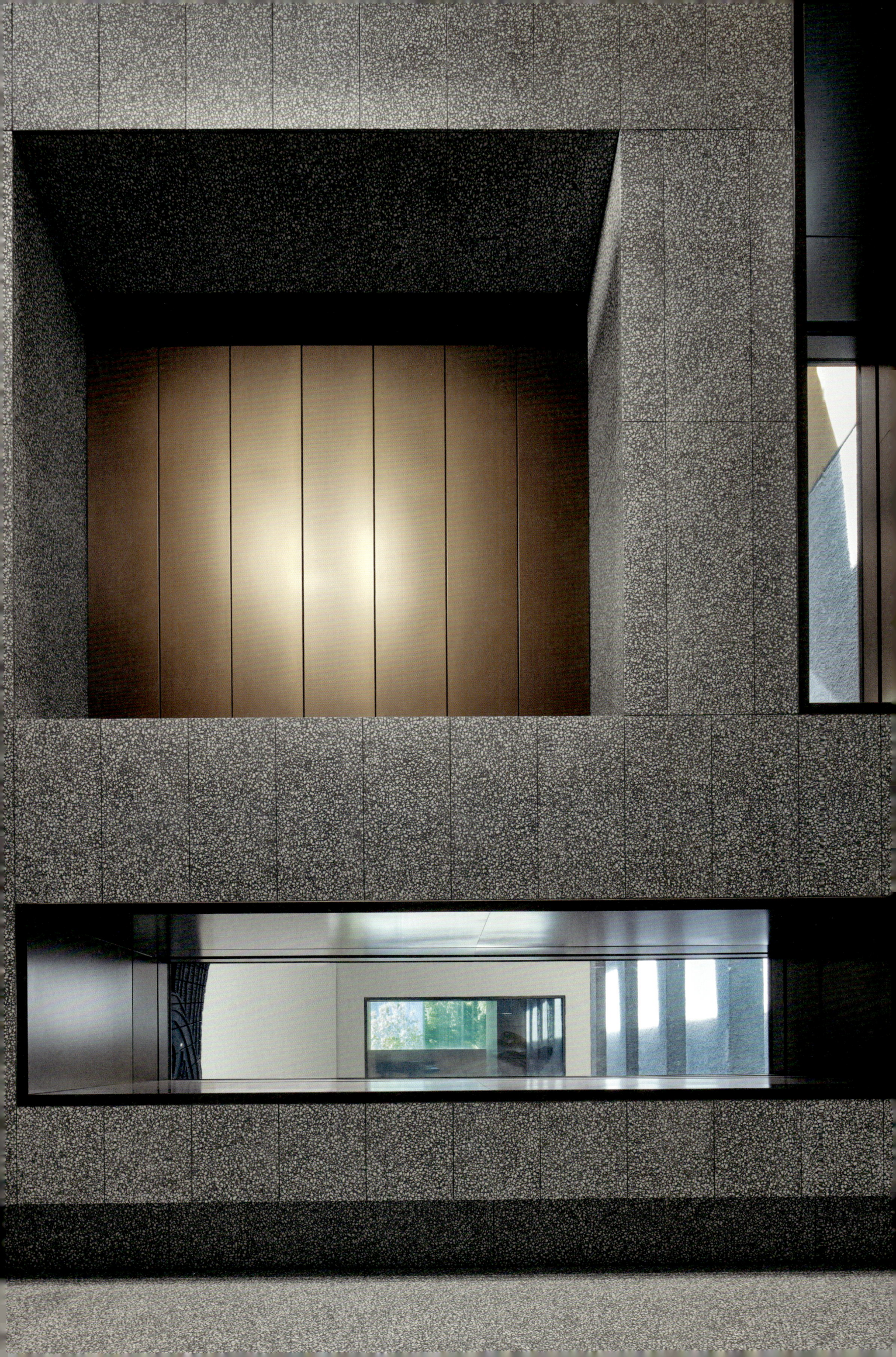

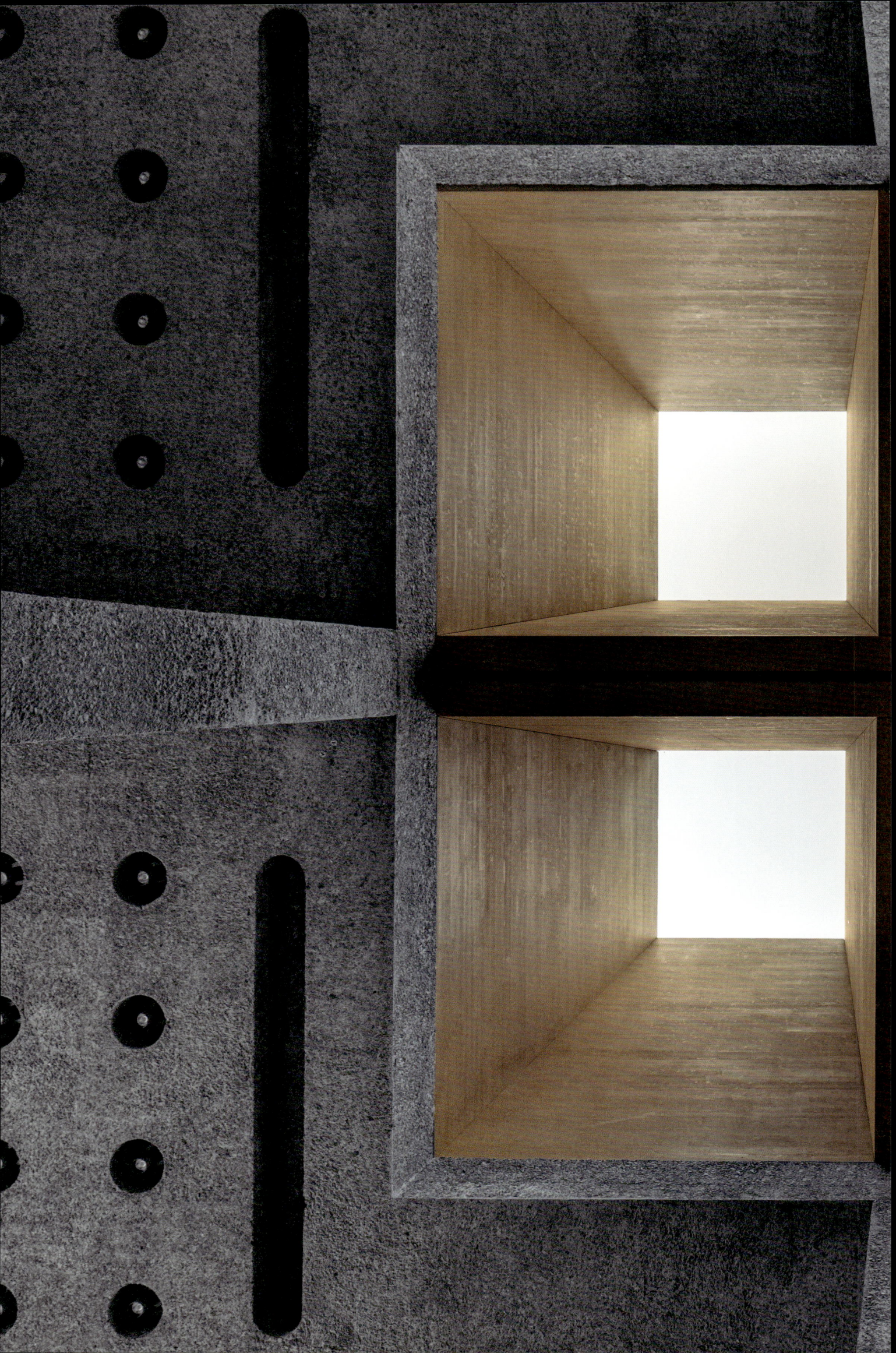

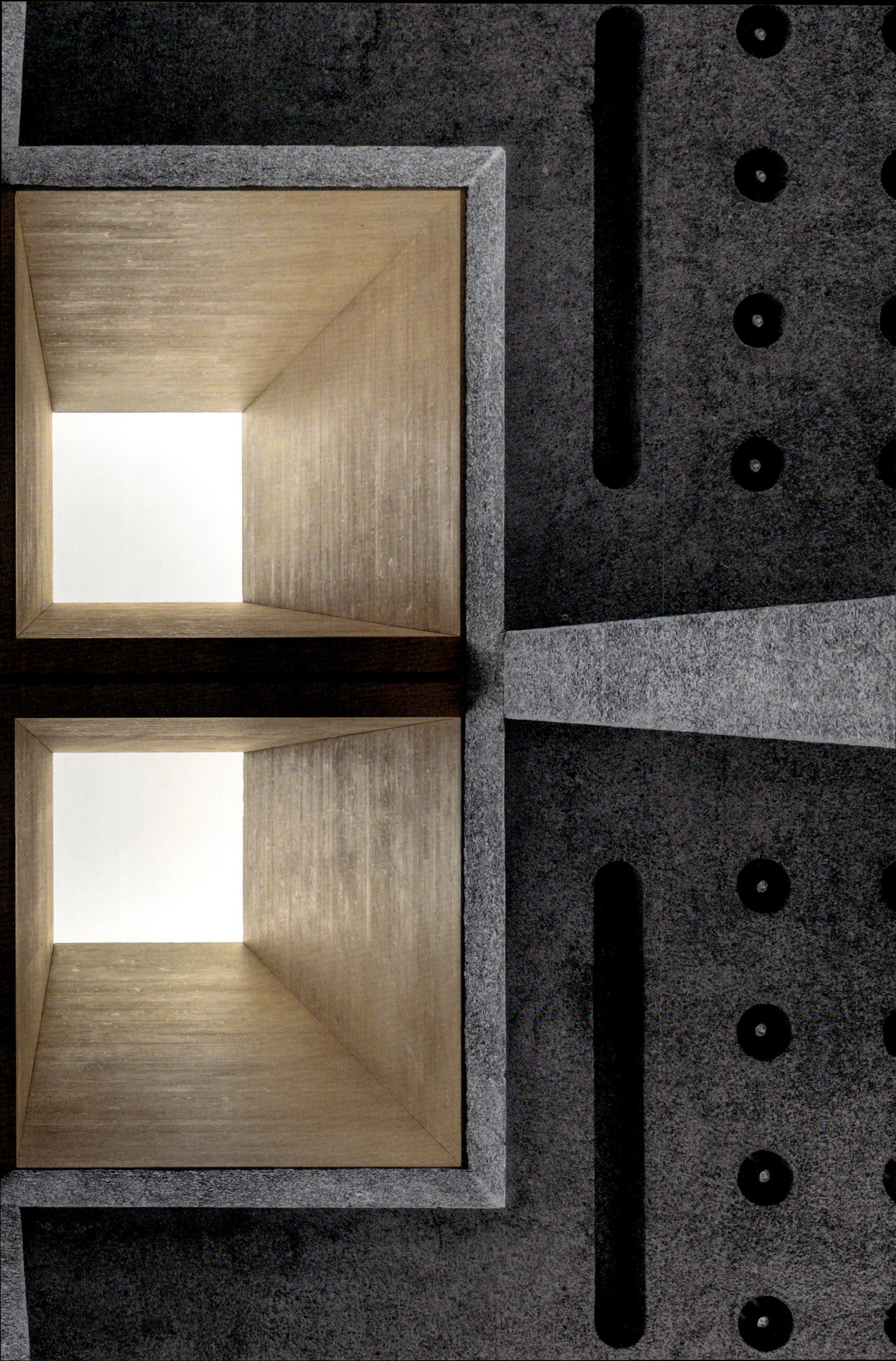

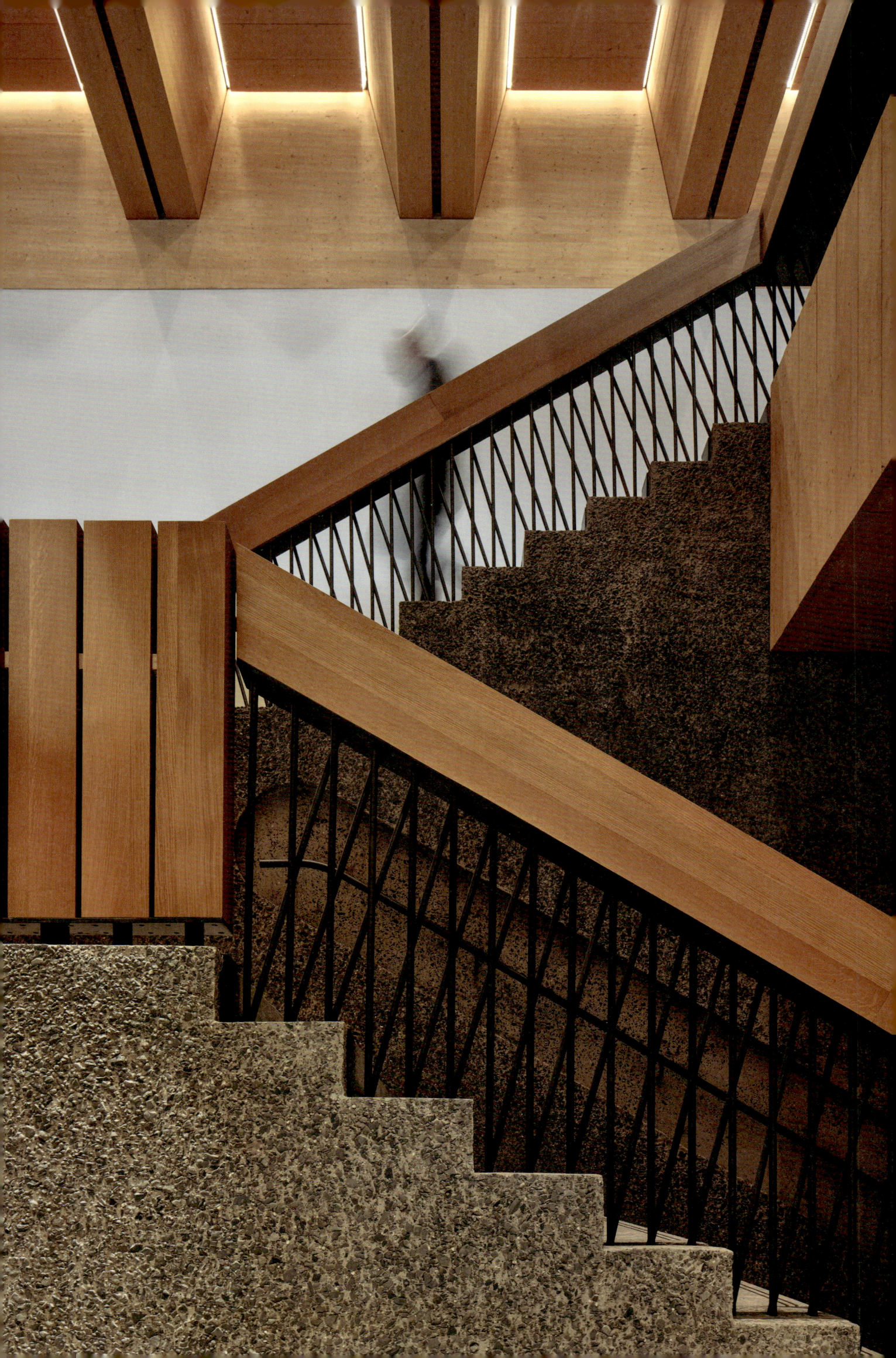

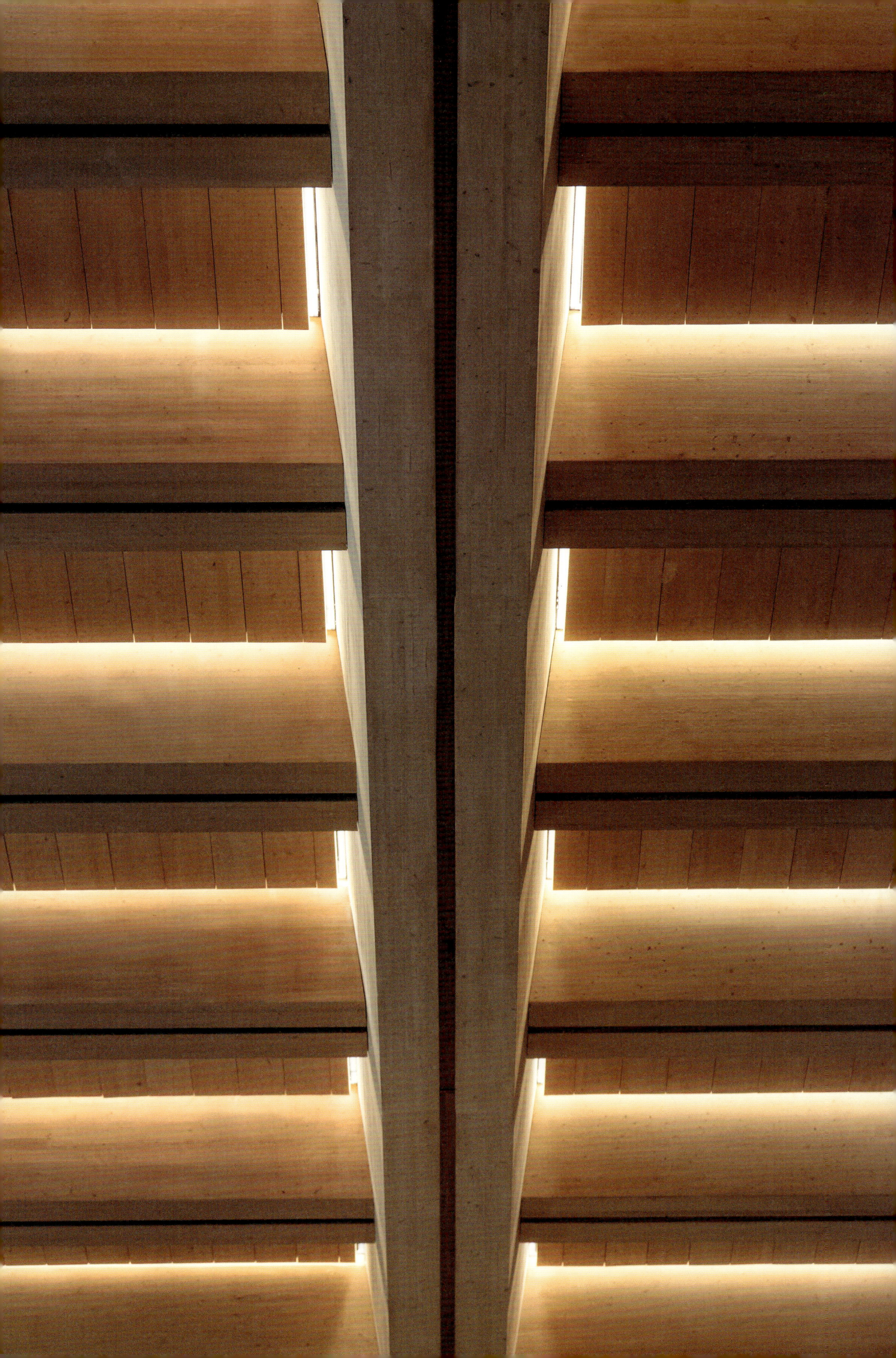

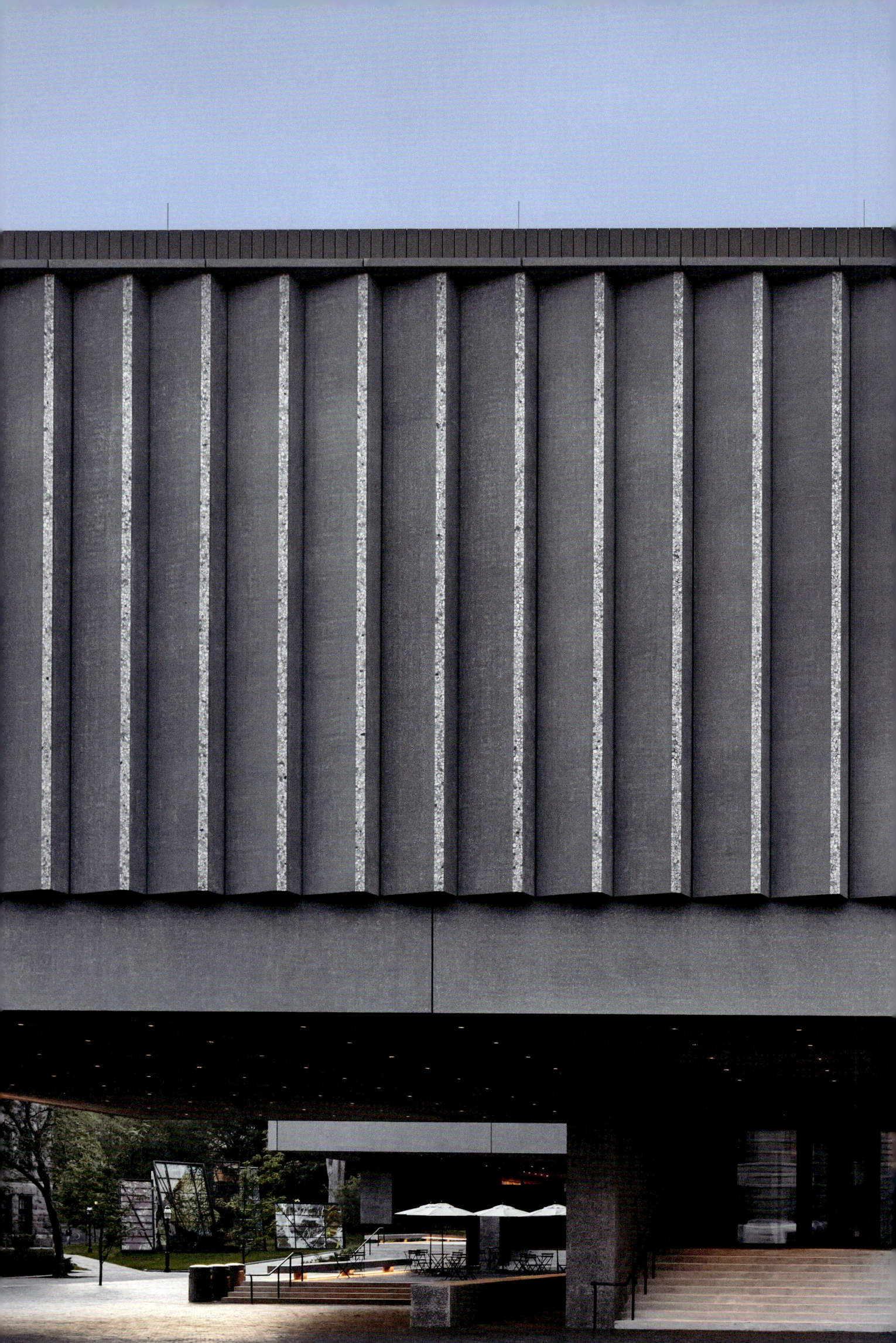

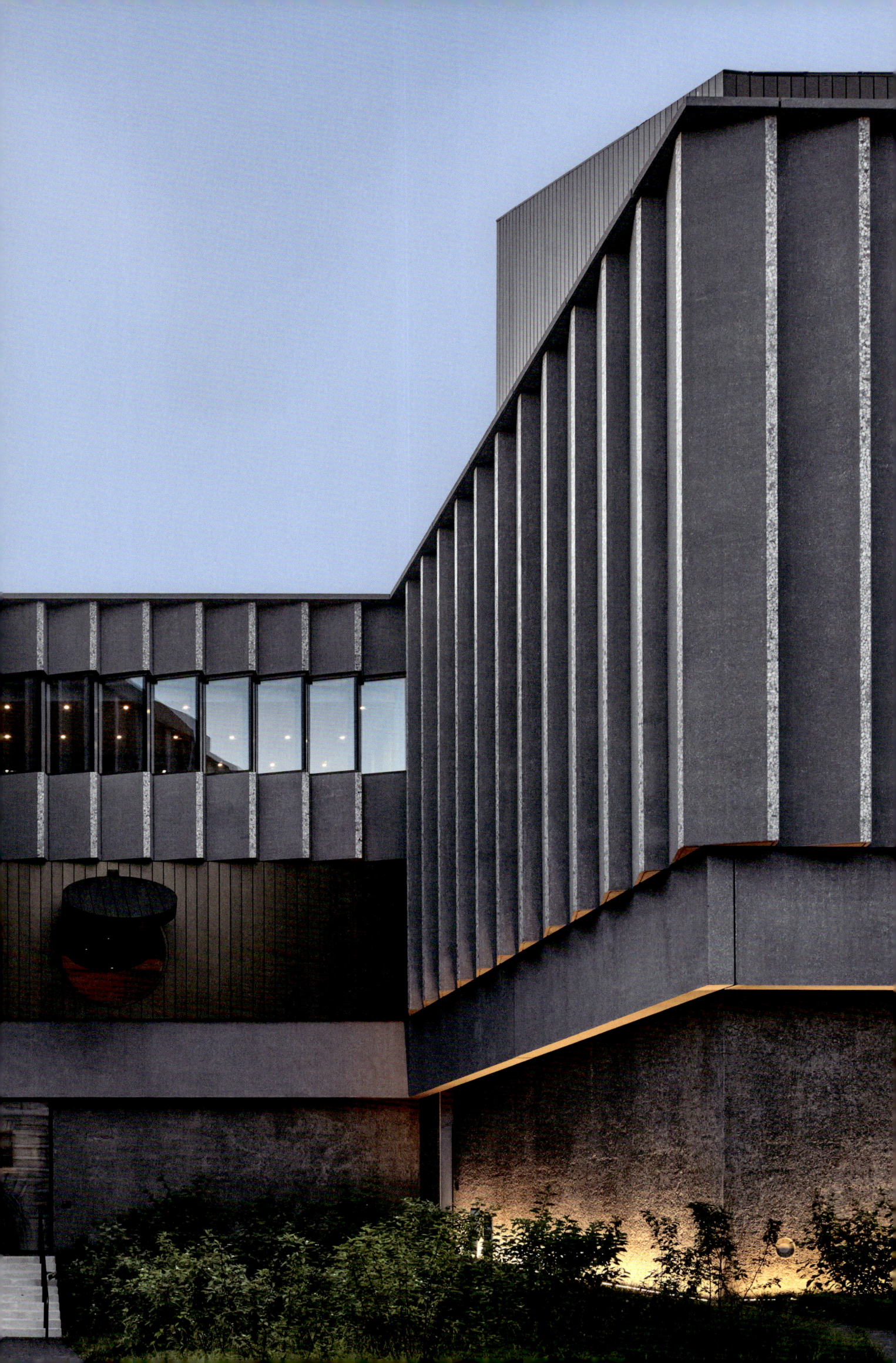

RENAISSANCE

A NEW MUSEUM FOR PRINCETON

JAMES CHRISTEN STEWARD

With contributions by
Paul Goldberger, Ron McCoy, Mark Stevens,
and Susan Stewart

Principal photography by
Richard Barnes

Princeton University Art Museum
Distributed by Princeton University Press,
Princeton and Oxford

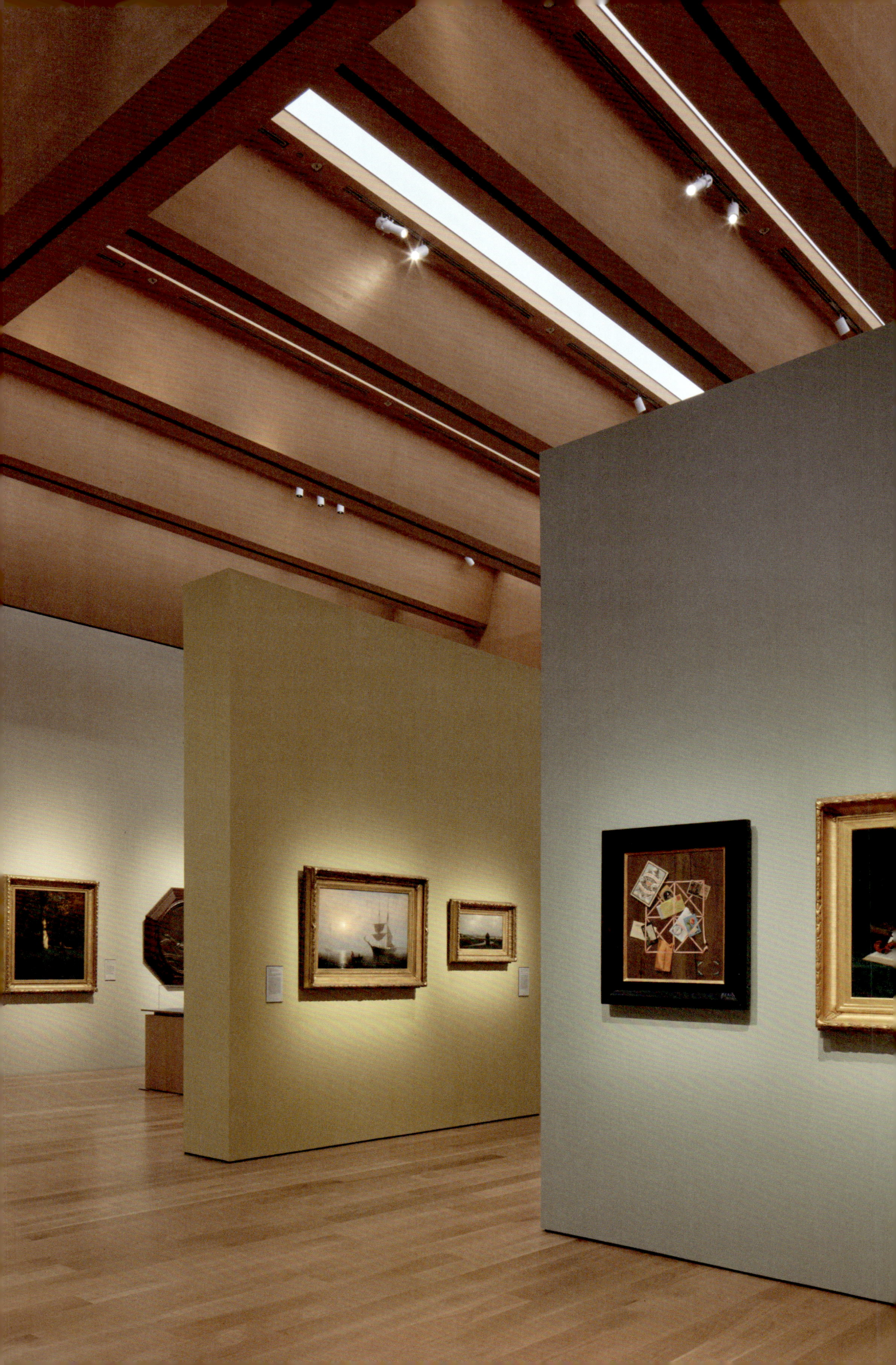

FOREWORD

The new Princeton University Art Museum realizes a dream that originated more than 125 years ago, when college leaders envisioned a museum that would engage students, catalyze humanistic teaching and scholarship, and become an integral part of Princeton's liberal arts education.

In his book *The Making of Princeton University*, the American historian James Axtell characterizes the Museum as "The Tiger's Eye." He describes its founding as a response to a certain kind of myopia, both figurative and literal. In the late nineteenth century, according to Axtell, "students who moved on to college found their academic experience narrowed to the printed world of books and the spoken word of lectures." In this system of education, college students used their eyes mainly for squinting at dense text in dimly lit rooms. Perhaps for that reason, Axtell muses, many collegians in the late nineteenth and early twentieth centuries purchased their first pair of glasses soon after beginning their studies.[1]

When James McCosh took office as president of the College of New Jersey (as Princeton was then called) in 1868, he observed that its students were "sorely lacking in visual skills."[2] McCosh, unlike Axtell, meant the complaint in purely figurative terms: McCosh could not restore students' eyes, but he could educate them, and he set out to do exactly that. He believed that study of the arts was an indispensable element of a liberal arts education. In 1882 he sought and obtained a report urging Princeton to create a department of art and archaeology. Its authors were an unlikely pair: William C. Prime and George B. McClellan. Prime was a distinguished figure in the art world and a suitable founder for this University's extraordinary museum. He was an 1843 graduate of Princeton, a founding trustee and acting president of the Metropolitan Museum of Art, and a major collector of porcelain and pottery. McClellan, by contrast, was perhaps best known as the excessively cautious commander of the Union army who, after Abraham Lincoln relieved him of his post, ran against Lincoln in the 1864 presidential election. McClellan later served as New Jersey's governor from 1878 to 1881.[3]

The report by Prime and McClellan led to the founding of both the Department of Art and Archaeology and the Museum in 1883.[4] They conceived of the two entities as inseparable: "The foundations of any system of education in Historic Art must obviously be in object study. A museum of objects is so necessary to the system that without it we are of [the] opinion that it would be of small utility to introduce the proposed department."[5]

President McCosh appointed Prime and Allan Marquand as the University's first professors of art and archaeology. Marquand directed the Museum until 1922, when Frank Mather succeeded him. Mather was quite clear about what was needed to bring the Museum to the requisite level of distinction: he said that the Princeton museum would get the finest objects "when our collecting friends and alumni realize that to give Princeton a fine work of art is to assure it worthy and permanent exhibition in best company."[6]

Princeton now has one of the greatest university museums in the world, and as Mather predicted, it does so by virtue of the generosity of its "collecting friends and alumni." Throughout its history the Museum has remained faithful to the insights that McCosh, McClellan, and Prime expressed at its creation: namely, that the scholarly study of art depends on encounters with artistic objects and that the foremost purpose of a university museum is to support teaching, scholarship, and research.

These principles guided planning for the new Museum. They dictated that it be a capacious and suitable home for a world-class collection, that it be closely connected to the Department of Art & Archaeology, and that it remain at the center of the campus, where it would draw students and facilitate connection with academic departments throughout the University. A museum at Princeton's heart could become a hub for humanistic scholarship and teaching, whereas a splendid but peripheral facility might attract tourists and other visitors but would not serve the University nearly so well.

These mission-driven principles created architectural challenges. The new Museum would have to be significantly larger than its predecessors, and it would be surrounded by historic buildings and walkways. In a community that venerates tradition, the design solution would inevitably be controversial. I believe that the new building is a beautiful enhancement to the campus, but I have no doubt that Princetonians will continue to debate its merits, as we do so many other things about our beloved University. In the past undergraduates might pass the Museum (as I confess I did) without wondering what lay inside; now that will be impossible. Anyone who enters will find a marvelous collection, one augmented by gifts from collectors newly confident that their donations will have a setting that enables them to be fully enjoyed, appreciated, and studied.

If the Museum's birth came at a time when students used their eyes principally to squint at required texts, its rebirth occurs in a moment dominated by transient imagery flashing across smartphone screens. In this day, as in President McCosh's, liberal arts education benefits tremendously from a museum that cultivates in students a "taste and sensibility which can appreciate beauty and sublimity," manifested by objects from across continents, cultures, and centuries and displayed with expert curatorial judgment and wisdom.[7] Princeton has that museum at last.

Christopher L. Eisgruber
President, Princeton University

Portions of this text were adapted from remarks previously delivered by the author at the celebration of the Princeton University Art Museum's 125th anniversary, February 23, 2008.

1   James Axtell, *The Making of Princeton University: From Woodrow Wilson to the Present* (Princeton University Press, 2006), 487.

2   McCosh, quoted in Marilyn Aronberg Lavin, *The Eye of the Tiger: The Founding and Development of the Department of Art and Archaeology, 1883–1923, Princeton University* (Dept. of Art and Archaeology and the Art Museum, Princeton University, 1983), 8.

3   Axtell, *Making of Princeton University*, 488–89; Lavin, *Eye of the Tiger*, 10; and James McPherson, *Battle Cry of Freedom: The Civil War Era* (Oxford University Press, 1988), 570.

4   Lavin, *Eye of the Tiger*, 12.

5   Prime and McClellan, quoted in Jill Guthrie, ed., *Princeton University Art Museum: Handbook of the Collections* (Princeton University Art Museum; Yale University Press, 2007), xi.

6   Mather, quoted in Axtell, *Making of Princeton University*, 500.

7   McCosh, quoted in Axtell, *Making of Princeton University*, 488.

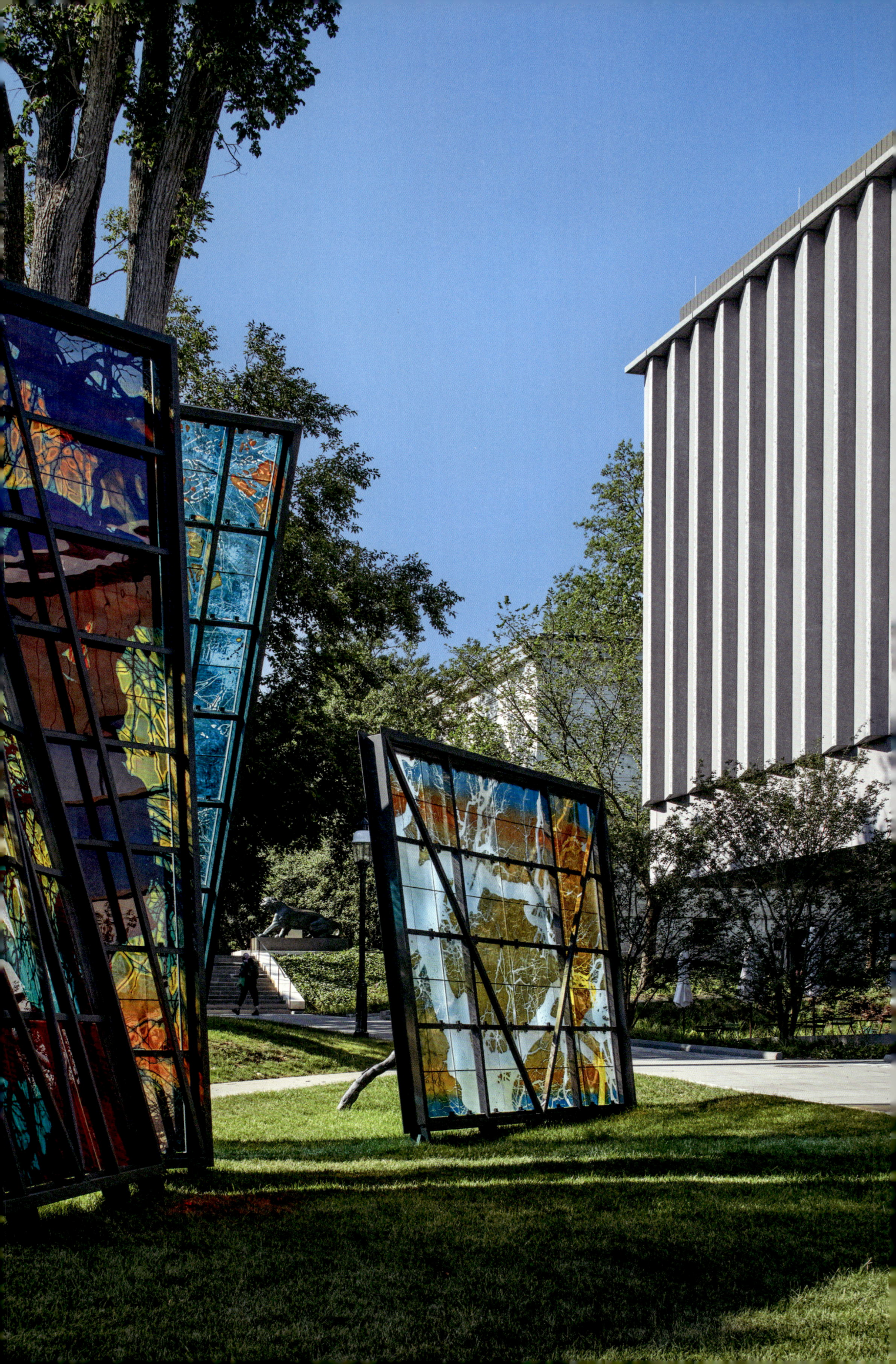

PREFACE

Today's university museums play a vital role in education and public engagement, often presenting exhibitions and collections installations that engage diverse publics and incorporate fresh and varied perspectives on their collections and on the history of art. They do so in ways that civic museums often cannot. The Museum I joined in the spring of 2009 was one of rich, globe-spanning collections but also one whose galleries had become largely static and were substantially devoid of interpretive support, an impediment to less expert visitors who might have been left bewildered about the context or meaning of many of the works of art on view. Attendance had hovered stably at around one hundred thousand annual visitors for as many as twenty years. Ironically abetted by the Great Recession, which put dreams of capital projects on hold, our focus pivoted to academic and operational areas, refreshing the galleries, shaping new modes of gallery interpretation, extending public hours, and other strategies seeking to place the Museum's august collections into dialogue with its diverse and growing communities, including the more than one million visitors who come to the Princeton campus each year.

Dreams of making an entirely new museum facility date back at least to the 1980s, when the last in a series of expansions was carried out that was immediately seen by some as another temporary fix to a long-term problem. Ideas of creating a multivenue museum emerged in the first decade of this century, only to founder in the face of financial crisis—in my view for the better, since such a plan carried untested pedagogical and operational risks. Building on growth in attendance, participation, staffing, and indeed the collections themselves, about ten years ago the Museum was asked to evaluate what kind of space would be required to meet our needs for at least the next thirty years. That study, carried out in partnership with Frederick Fisher and Partners, led to the recommendations that a new facility of approximately twice the size of the existing one would be required, that such a facility could be thoughtfully inserted in the heart of the University campus but only if the former facility was substantially demolished, and that such placement was far preferable to potential "edge" locations because of adjacencies to the University's humanities departments, student residence halls, and downtown Princeton. What we initially termed a fundraising feasibility study followed that led to significant early philanthropic commitments, which in turn led the University to feel it was time to engage the services of a design architect.

That this publication commemorating the opening of the new Museum facility should appear betrays the fact that ultimately bold decisions were made by the University's leadership to undertake such a project. With sufficient philanthropic commitments in hand and a major pledge of support from the University's own assets, the design team of Adjaye Associates—in partnership with executive architects Cooper Robertson, University Architect Ron McCoy and his team, the University's Office of Capital Projects, and the Museum's leadership team—moved forward with design planning, enabling the emptying out of the old Museum to begin in fall 2020 and demolition to begin in 2021. The building we open in fall 2025 is the result after five long years of disruption.

For most of the twentieth century, our many predecessors at the Museum argued that more space or a better building would act as a catalyst to new donations of art or to new purchases that the then-current facility could not have supported. In the same spirit we have sought to capitalize on the new facility by launching what we have informally termed a "campaign for art" over the past four years. This strategic effort to secure gifts or promised gifts of works of art that would build on strengths or fill in gaps has led to more than one thousand new works entering the collections on the occasion of the opening of the new building, without considering the nearly one thousand works of art in the photographic archive of Emmet Gowin, acquired by the Museum in 2023. Highlights from this effort range from extraordinary works of twentieth-century abstract art—including the Museum's first paintings by Mark Rothko, Helen Frankenthaler, Joan Mitchell, and Gerhard Richter, thanks to the remarkable generosity of Preston Haskell III, Class of 1960—to exceptional gifts of photographs, Chinese art, African art, Native North American pots, Inuit art, prints and drawings, and much more. Five galleries in the new building will, when it opens, reveal some of the most striking of these additions in often surprising juxtapositions.

The *New York Times* art critic Holland Cotter has notably praised the academic museum, including in a 2009 article titled "Why University Museums Matter." He wrote: "The august public museum gave us fabulousness. The tucked away university gallery gave us life: organic, intimate and as fresh as news." While I find the dichotomy articulated here a bit artificial—university galleries might also give us fabulousness and are clearly often no longer "tucked away"— I continue to embrace the goal that what we do within these university spaces should be organic, sometimes intimate, and often fresh. The essays in this volume, each in their own way, seek to examine how this can operate, from Paul Goldberger's investigation of the academic museum as an architectural type, to Ron McCoy's study of how our new museum contributes to placemaking on the beloved Princeton campus, to Mark Stevens's rumination on the meanings of having such a museum at Princeton, and my own analysis of how a history of building and rebuilding alongside a tradition of collecting that is now more than 270 years old has shaped this singular institution.

Having cut my teeth in university museums in the 1990s, when museums were taking new attitudes toward their communities and inviting them in as never before, when academic museums in particular were struggling to figure out how to be more welcoming and engaging without losing their commitment to scholarship, and when we were already worrying about what the digital age would mean for the appreciation of works of art in the original, I still take it as an article of faith, as I once wrote in *Inside Higher Ed*, that the study of works of art in the original remains essential to deep critical engagement, close looking, technical analysis, and thus to teaching, research, and layered learning. As Cotter put it sixteen years ago, in words that seem remarkably relevant today: "But at least one good idea seems to be gaining ground. In a bleak economy, when our big public museums threaten to sink under budget-busting excesses, the university museum offers a model for small, intensely researched, collection-based, convention-challenging exhibitions that could get museums through a bumpy present and carry them, lighter and brighter, into the future."

At their advent in the seventeenth century with the founding of the Ashmolean at the University of Oxford, academic museums were repositories for objects from enormously disparate traditions and vehicles for organizing the information that such objects contained and revealed. The holdings of today's academic museums, including ours at Princeton, tend to be more specialized, but these institutions are almost by definition instruments of diversity and diversification. At once classroom, laboratory, entertainment venue, meditative space, third space, and spiritual gymnasium, we build on four hundred years of tradition and innovation to shape spaces and experiences that are desperately needed in the twenty-first century, when democracy itself is challenged, the skills and tools of good citizenship are too infrequently taught, and the power of institutions is regarded with at best skepticism if not distrust and even hostility.

At Princeton we build on a tradition that dates to the 1750s of looking at objects and considering what they can mean to our institutions and to our individual lives. I am proud that our museum, like the Ashmolean, has always welcomed not only students and faculty but also the wider public—even if, in the nineteenth century, unanticipated visitors had to apply to the janitor in East Pyne for the key—just as I am proud that we have never, not even for temporary exhibitions, imposed an admission fee. With the advent of the new Princeton University Art Museum, I am excited to see what possibilities emerge and what impact these can have on the lives of our students, our teachers, and our communities.

James Christen Steward
Nancy A. Nasher–David J. Haemisegger, Class of 1976, Director
Princeton University Art Museum

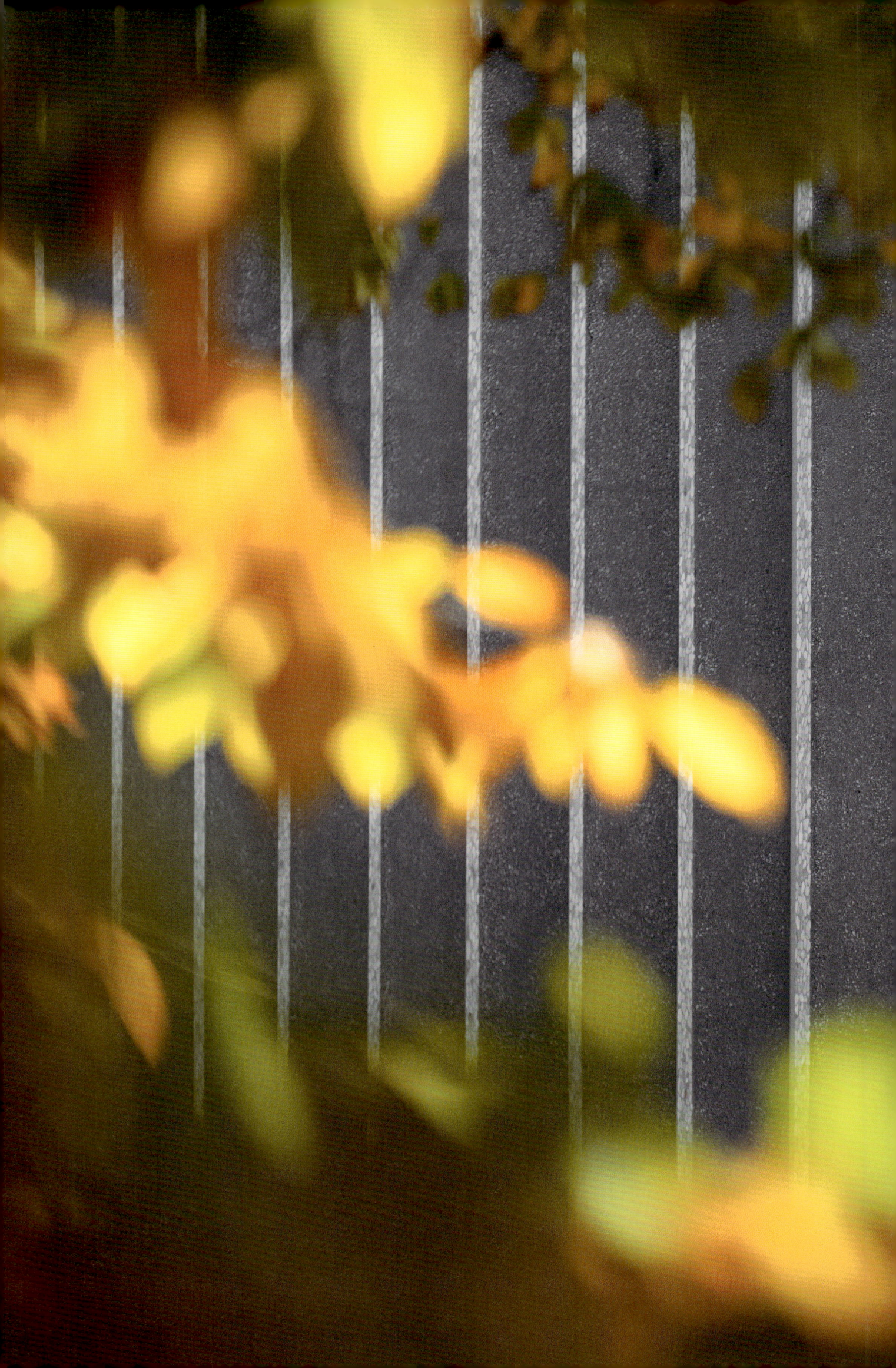

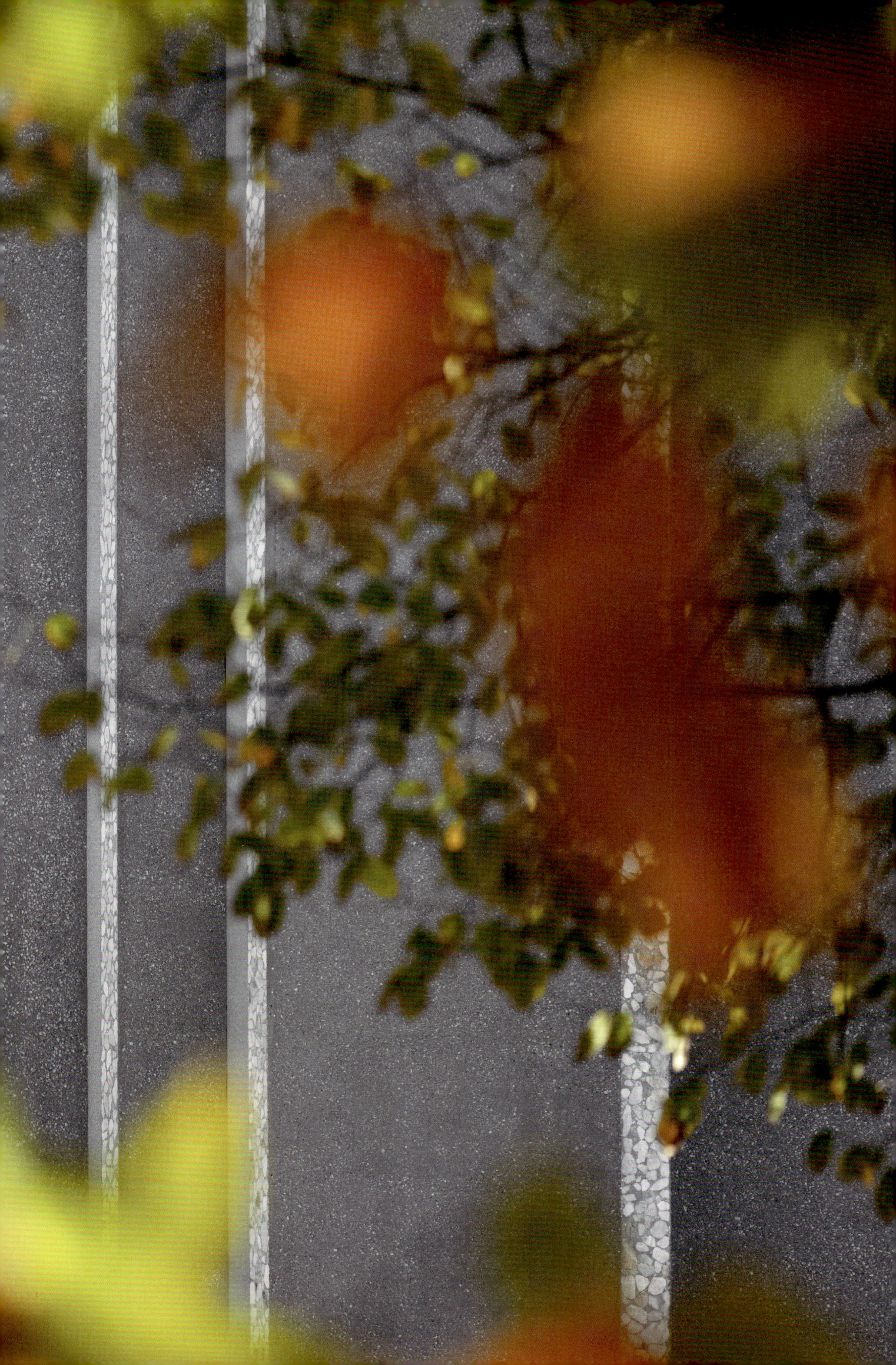

OPENING HOURS

They look to us in their two and three dimensions,
figure and ground, glaze and blue-veined
stone. So like us, though, unfinished
ourselves, we wander on, our attention as

fleeting as life—which is ours, while they remain.
Their shape in the hand, so far from the hands that made
them. Still, they have their names, their scenes
an endless elsewhere, sited between focus and fade.

They carry clouds, and smallest, everlasting, flowers—
their colors are the colors we dream. Seven in
the rainbow, seven continents, seven seas, numbers with

ciphers unknown. In temples you can kneel
and rise and kneel, calling forever for
inspiration. Better here to picture, to frame:

the uprooted elms and beeches, too,
now stand before us again.

—Susan Stewart

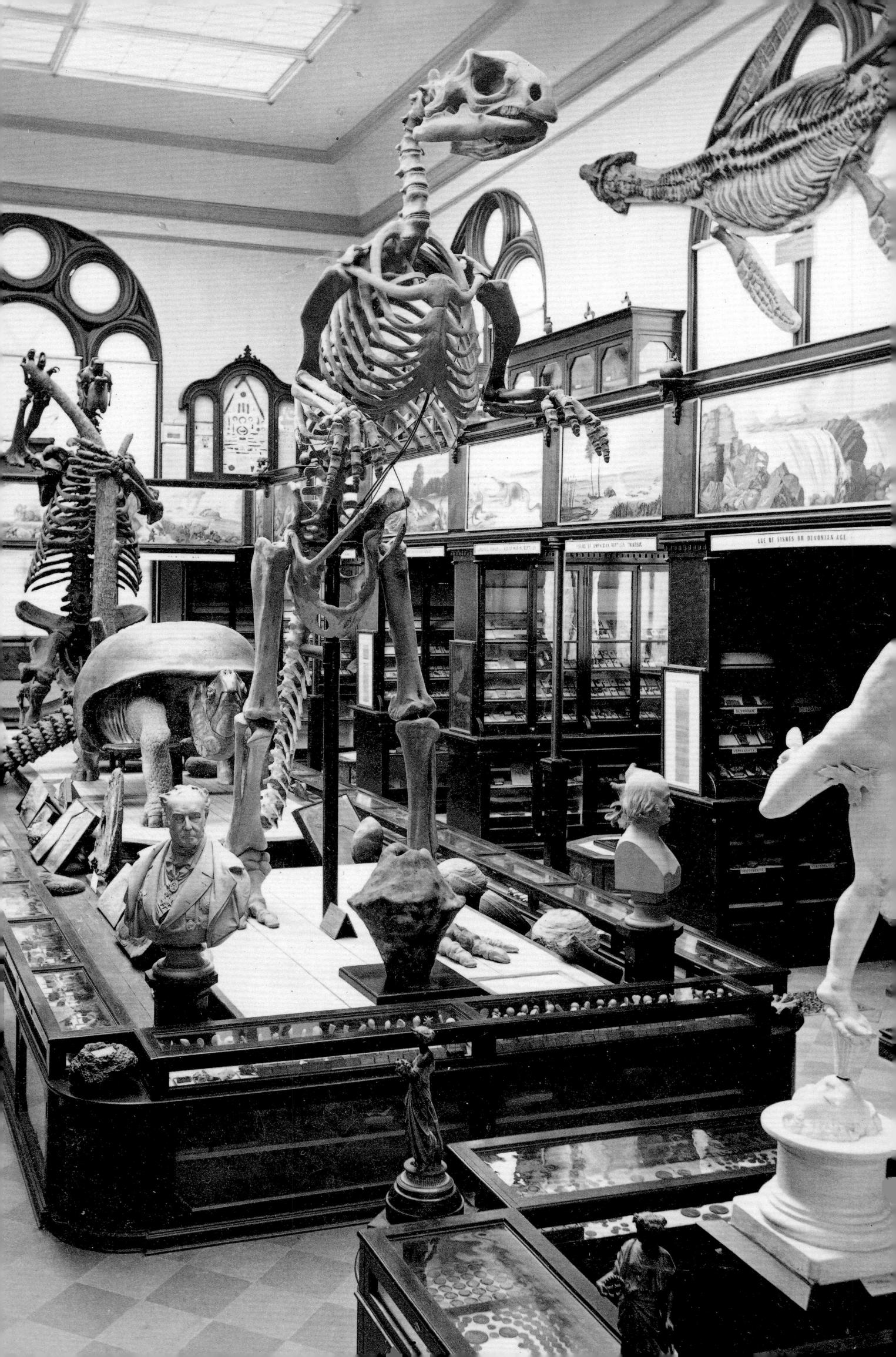

Building, Rebuilding, and Renewing a Museum for Princeton: A New Episodic History

JAMES CHRISTEN STEWARD

The concept of a "university museum" can be traced back to Europe's medieval universities, where collections of objects served as learning aids, particularly anatomical specimens used in the teaching of medicine. The first botanical garden (*hortus botanicus*) and anatomical theater (*theatrum anatomicum*) were established at universities in Italy during the sixteenth century. The first modern university museum is generally understood, however, to have been the Ashmolean Museum at the University of Oxford, founded by Elias Ashmole and opened in 1683, marking the beginning of the widespread development of university museums across Europe and North America, which continued quietly but steadfastly in the eighteenth century and gained momentum in the nineteenth century. This phenomenon was distinguished by three key characteristics. The first was the rise of specialized disciplines in the formation of such museums and collections, including art, archaeology, natural history, and ethnography. The second was the understanding that such collections should play an important role in both research and teaching, affording scholars and students the opportunity to study artifacts and specimens firsthand, rather than from reproductions or illustrations. The third was the precedent set by the Ashmolean of inviting public access to its collections.

All three characteristics inform the advent and history of collecting and of museum making at what is now Princeton University. Chartered in 1746 as the College of New Jersey, the school moved into handsome new stone-built quarters in Princeton in 1756, but even before doing so, the College had begun to acquire its first works of art. New Jersey's colonial governor Jonathan Belcher made a gift of what he termed "my own Picture at full length in a gilt Frame" in 1755, which can thus be cited as the dawn of art collecting at Princeton. Belcher's portrait was duly installed by the College's grateful trustees in the central prayer hall in Nassau Hall, where it was soon joined by a portrait of England's King George II, who served as monarch at the time of the College's founding. These two works were in turn joined by ancient architectural fragments, natural history specimens, and other objects to form a kind of "museum" of the Enlightenment, building on the model established at Oxford. Such a collection was understood as a way of both organizing knowledge and reinforcing the legitimacy of the collecting institution, in the spirit of the cabinets of curiosity that had preceded the academic museum as a collecting typology starting in the fifteenth and sixteenth centuries.

If Princeton aspired from its beginnings to be seen as an Enlightenment enterprise and regarded the collecting of objects as part of such an act of identity building, its efforts to do so proved to be uneven for a very long time, a history reflected in both its collections and its trajectory of building, demolishing, and rebuilding homes for such collections. It lost its first home during the Battle of Princeton on January 3, 1777, when a conflagration sparked by cannon fire gutted Nassau Hall and most of the works in it, including the portraits of the previous king and his colonial governor. With the cessation of conflict in 1783 and the advent of the American republic, the trustees of the College determined that collecting should begin again. They inaugurated their efforts with panache, commissioning a full-length portrait of the hero of both the Battle of Princeton and the Revolutionary War, George Washington (fig. 1), then resident in Princeton during the months when the Continental Congress had evacuated there from Philadelphia. Philadelphia's Charles Willson Peale, probably the early nation's most distinguished portraitist, was given the job and received an unsurpassed seven sittings with the great general and future president. By 1787, according to an eyewitness, the prayer hall was ornamented by several paintings, "particularly [of] the famous battle in the town."[1] It is sadly impossible to know what they were, for disaster struck again with another fire on March 6, 1802, which once again destroyed the College's early collections, although this time at least one of the key works, Peale's portrait of Washington, was rescued by students and staff of the College and happily endures to this day.

Despite a period of institutional decline and decay in the early years of the nineteenth century, efforts were made to bolster the College's art collections, particularly by the young professor John Maclean, Class of 1816, who carried out a lifelong effort to secure for the College a collection of portraits of its presidents and other notables. As Karl Kusserow, the Museum's John Wilmerding Senior Curator of American Art, has argued, Maclean understood the value of history and of historical portraiture to the strengthening and durability of an institution.[2] That the same John Maclean should go on to found the Alumni Association in 1826 as a mechanism for raising funds and strengthening ties to the young college—ultimately an enormously successful effort that had profound consequences for the College's later collections building—suggests the degree to which a single academic can shape an institution's course.

Fig. 1   Charles Willson Peale (1741–1827; born Chester, MD; died Philadelphia, PA), *George Washington at the Battle of Princeton*, 1783–84. Oil on canvas, 237 × 145 cm. Princeton University, commissioned by the Trustees (PP222)

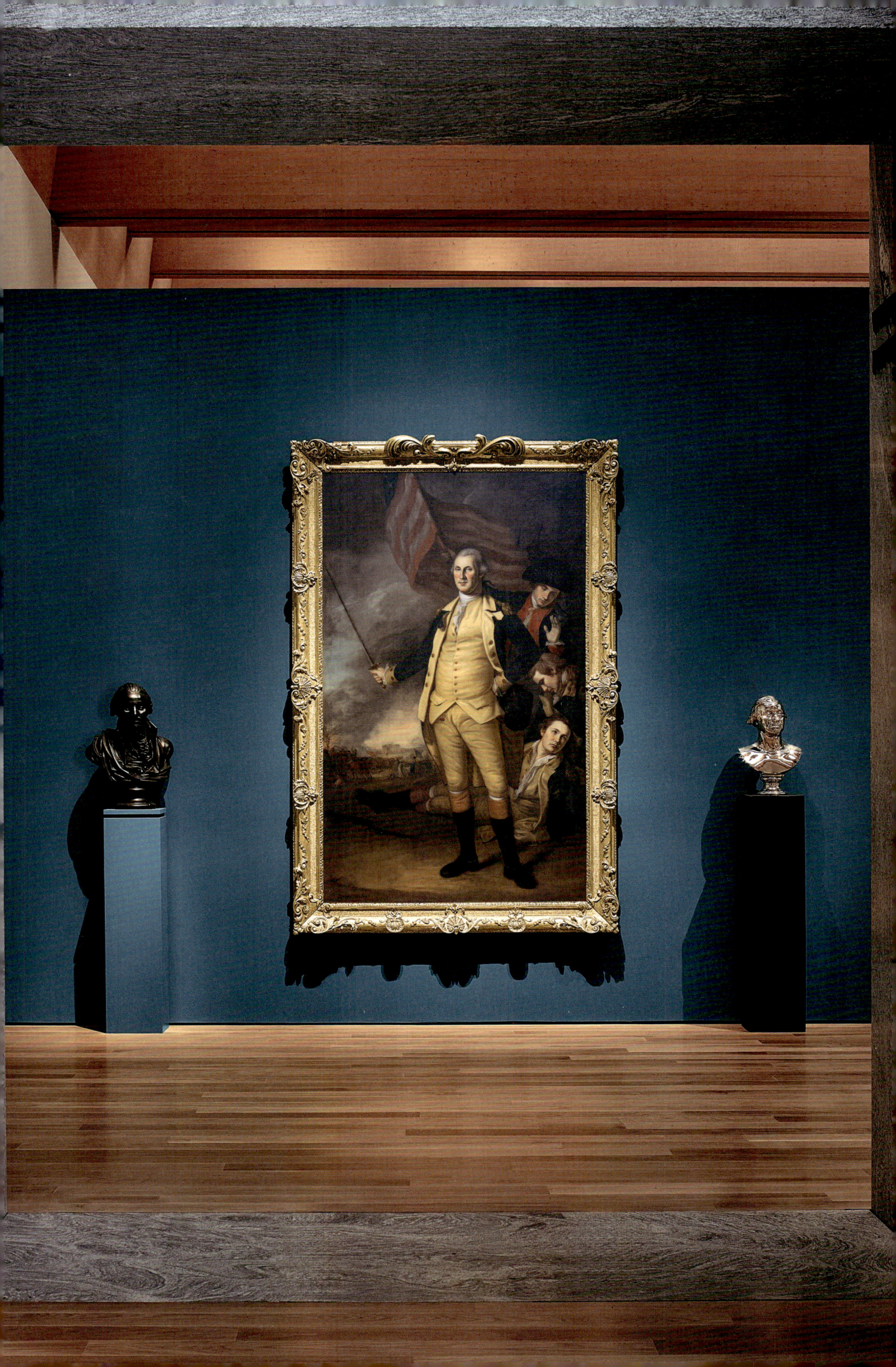

These initial efforts set the tone for Princeton's collecting over the next century and suggest an early commitment to teaching from original objects and using them as tools for accessing and understanding the wider world. By the middle years of the nineteenth century, the College was deeply involved in the development of systems of classification, including the need to develop more complex historical narratives, which gave rise elsewhere to the founding of encyclopedic museums of science and art in Boston in 1870 and in New York in 1869 and 1872.[3] No images of this period of collecting at Princeton survive, for fire struck yet again on March 12, 1855, although this time much of the collection was rescued "without injury to a place of safety" by students and residents of the town, who rallied to save it.[4] Upon the subsequent rebuilding of the space to designs by John Notman, the room that had once been the College's prayer hall evolved yet again, initially from library to museum, befitting the increasing importance of a collection that had been "rather wandering in its character...hustled from one room to another," in the words of the *Nassau Literary Magazine*.[5] To support such use, a raised second-floor gallery was built around the room's perimeter, and large skylights were installed.

Princeton's first proper museum was shaped by the geography professor Arnold Guyot and named the E. M. Museum, for an anonymous benefactor. Opened in 1874, the new museum dedicated its first zone to the College's historic portraits, followed by diverse archaeological, paleontological, and geological materials, in an array that to today's eyes can only be described as chaotic (fig. 2). Underpinning that chaos, however, was the age's commitment to epistemological and museological evolution, an effort not incidentally propelled by Princeton in the development of its first properly understood museum. Guyot's achievement, building on what Maclean had begun, was said at the time to rival the collections of the Smithsonian Institution in Washington, DC.[6]

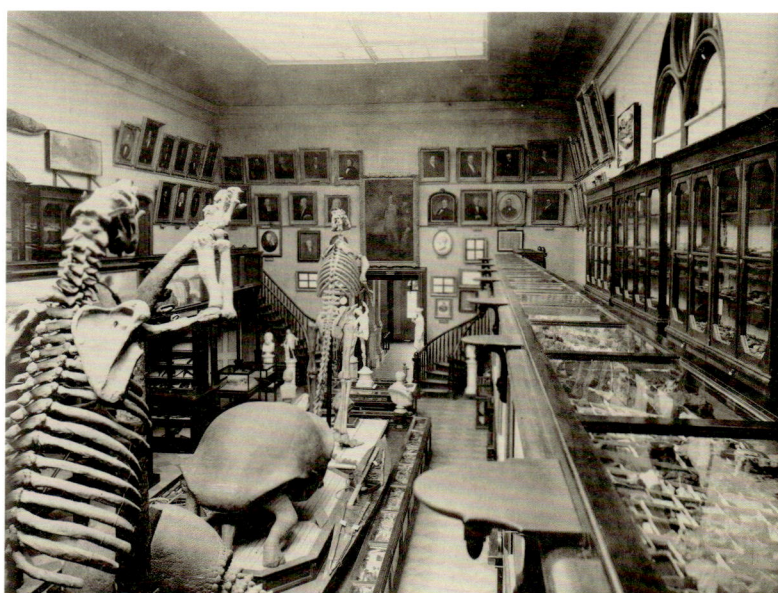

Fig. 2   E. M. Museum of Geology and Archaeology, Nassau Hall, Princeton University, ca. 1870s–1890s. Princeton University Library. Department of Special Collections

Fig. 3 E. M. Museum of
Geology and Archaeology,
Nassau Hall, Princeton University,
ca. 1886. Princeton University
Library. Department of Special
Collections

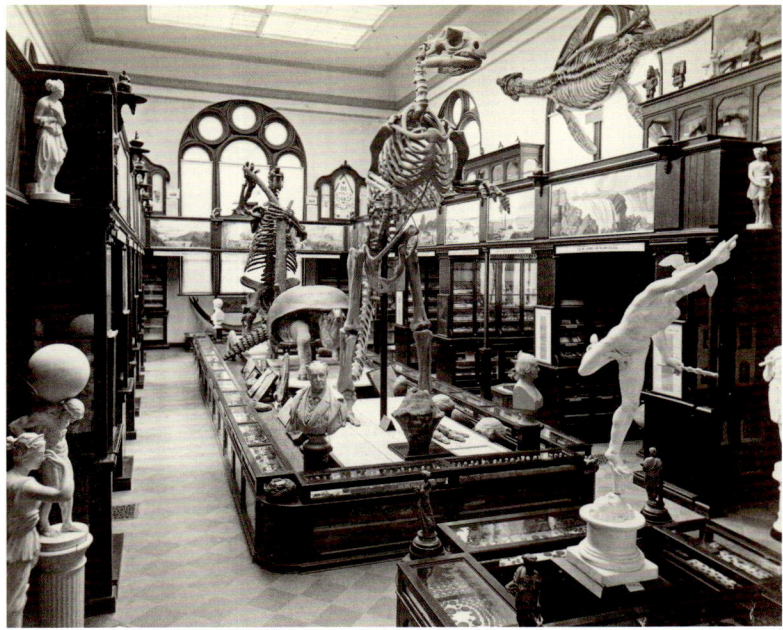

Guyot referred to the gallery as his "Synoptic Room," where "the leading idea in the arrangement…is that [the displays] should strike the eye as an open book in which the student can read, at a glance, the history of the creation from the dawn of life to the appearance of man."[7] Essential to such an idea was the addition of a suite of seventeen newly commissioned paintings by the British natural history artist Benjamin Waterhouse Hawkins depicting prehistoric life as it was understood at the time. Commissioned by Guyot in 1875, the paintings suggest a linear, progressive account of life on earth from its imagined beginnings to the development of mammals, urged on, seemingly, by a stone statue of the flying figure of Mercury, who in turn points upward to the gallery of portraits of the College's historical luminaries (fig. 3).[8]

The E. M. Museum, as curated by Guyot, exemplified the university museum's growing role in research and teaching, allowing scholars and students to study objects and artifacts firsthand, just as it advanced the precedent set by Ashmole in the seventeenth century of affording the public access to expanding collections in the fields of fine art, archaeology, natural history, and ethnography. But apart from collections of historic portraits, plaster casts after works of antiquity acquired for teaching, and occasional paintings such as the series by Hawkins, the E. M. Museum's art collections were modest.[9] This began to change due to dramatic curricular revisions that swept the College under the presidency of James McCosh (fig. 4), who was himself a collector who donated works of Chinese and Japanese art to the College in the early years of his presidency.[10] Scottish by birth and training, McCosh brought with him progressive European ideas about education, including the then-new field of art history, first developed in Germany. Guided by the concept of a coherent and holistic integration of disciplines, he built on the College's traditions and strengths, including the classics and an understanding of Greek and Latin as the

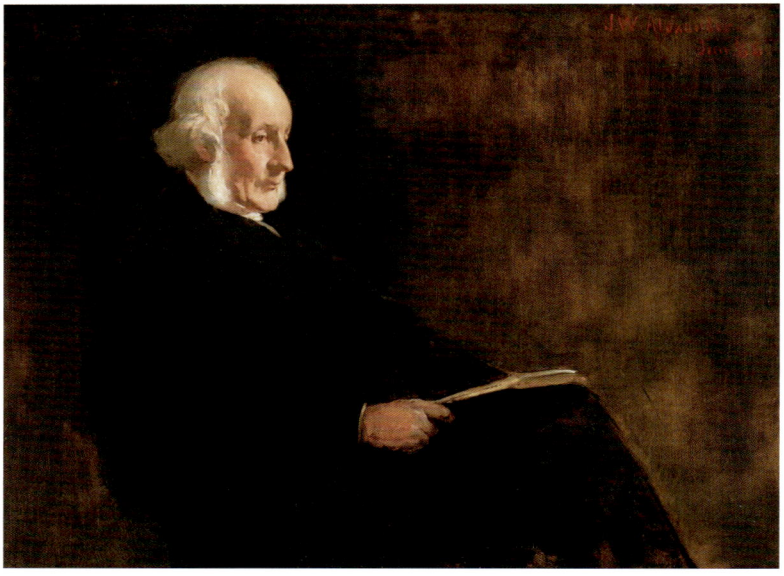

Fig. 4   John White Alexander
(1856–1915; born Allegheny, PA;
died New York, NY), *James
McCosh (1811–1894), President
(1868–88)*, 1886. Oil on canvas,
89.2 × 123 cm. Princeton
University, gift of alumni (PP37)

essential instruments for conveying to the modern man a knowledge
of the ancient world. It was McCosh's desire that the modest art holdings of the E. M. Museum should become the nucleus of something
grander, which, beginning as early as the 1870s, he termed a "Museum
of Historic Art."[11]

The project of making such a museum both administratively and
architecturally preoccupied McCosh through much of his tenure. By
1882 he was building a team that he charged with bringing his vision
to life, including William Cowper Prime (fig. 5), a Princeton alumnus
and a founding trustee of the Metropolitan Museum of Art in 1870, and
George McClellan, the Civil War general and hero who was by then
the governor of New Jersey. Prime was, like McCosh, a collector of art,
one of arguably only a handful of American collector-connoisseurs at
the time, who committed his holdings of decorative art to the nascent
museum, which he and McClellan argued had to be at the center of a
new curriculum. Forging their ideas at a series of intellectual discussions called Library Meetings, held at the president's home in Prospect
House, they argued that "the foundation of any system of education in
Historic Art must obviously be in object study"—a term that remains
at the heart of today's Museum—and that such object study should
go well beyond the fields of art and the classics to include "many other
branches of the collegiate course."[12]

The first steps in the implementation of their proposed curriculum included the appointment of Allan Marquand, Class of 1874
(fig. 6), as director of a newly created administrative unit and as chair of
what is now the Department of Art & Archaeology, as well as the commissioning of A. Page Brown in 1882 to design a building that would
house the art museum. Like Prime, Marquand—the son of Elizabeth
Love Allen and Henry Marquand, who served as the second president of the Metropolitan Museum of Art—came with credentials.
But his appointment was also a bold one. Trained as a theologian and
a philosopher, Marquand in his first year on the faculty at Princeton

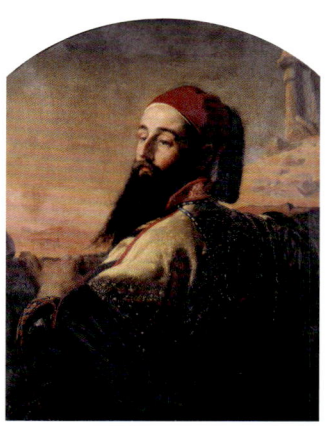

Fig. 5   Fridolin Schlegel (born
ca. 1820, Germany; died after
1874; active United States),
William C. Prime, 1825–1905, 1857.
Oil on canvas, 91.4 × 74 cm.
The New York Historical. Gift of
Benjamin L. Prime (1953.188)

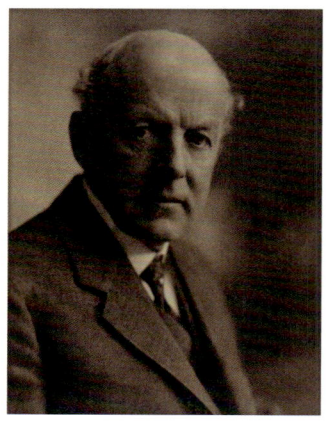

Fig. 6   Orren Jack Turner Sr.
(ca. 1889–1968; active Princeton,
NJ), *Allan Marquand*, 1922–25.
Photoengraving, 22.7 × 18 cm.
Princeton University Art
Museum. Most likely a gift of
the sitter (x1983-217)

devised a mechanical logical machine that was a precursor to modern computing. McCosh found Marquand's approach to teaching logic "unorthodox and uncalvinistic";[13] coupled with his inventions, this must have recommended him to McCosh as the person to take on something so novel as the making of a new museum.

Marquand set a laudable example by serving as the inaugural director of the museum for forty years, retiring in 1922, and bringing with him the financial capacity not only to be a noteworthy collector in his own right but also to buy works of art for the Museum and essentially fund it and the department's operating expenses out of his own pocket. His early efforts were abetted by student activists. In addition to crying out for courses on art, the students called for the College to build on its then-meager holdings of art, so that there could be "something more than the engravings in the Library and the portraits in North to interest and instruct the sketcher, to cultivate the taste of the general student, and to add to the reputation and real value of the College equipment."[14] In fact, the collections were growing and taking on an increasingly international character in these years, which saw a large collection of pre-Columbian objects gifted in the 1870s, followed by documentary photography in 1876–77 and an important corpus of Native American material in 1877–78.

The College agreed that monies should be raised to create a purpose-built—and fireproof—building to house McCosh's new Museum of Historic Art. University trustee and patron Moses Taylor Pyne, Class of 1877—arguably still Princeton's greatest historical benefactor—summarized the situation in a letter to a Mr. Murray, dated November 12, 1886:

> Now we have a large number of valuable Art Books, engravings, etchings, etc., Collections of Assyrian, Greek and Cypriot remains, a number of valuable gems etc. etc. which need someplace where they can be displayed. At present most of them are kept in drawers and closets in Dr. Marquand's house, the College affording no room for them.... With these collections & with other valuable Art Works, already promised in case the building be created and with a few plaster casts of the more celebrated sculptures of Europe we should at once have a very good Museum of Art. We can create a wing of a building to be hereafter completed, for the sum of say $40,000 [$1.3 million today]. Of this we have already raised $18,000. Here is the subscription list.
>
> Henry G. Marquand $10,000 [$334,000 today]
> Mr. Robert L. Stuart 5,000
> Allan Marquand 2,000
> M. Taylor Pyne 1,000
>
> We cannot afford to wait much longer.[15]

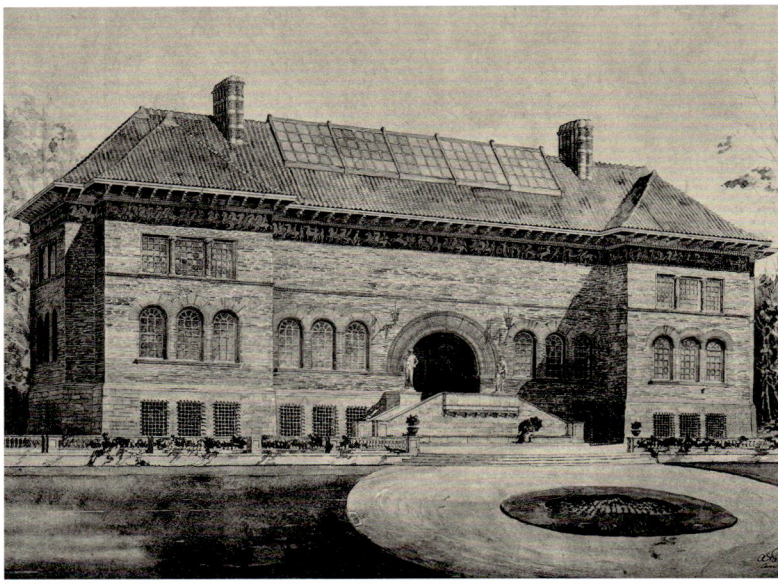

Fig. 7   Arthur Page Brown
(1859–1896; born Ellisburg, NY;
died San Francisco, CA),
Accepted proposal for the Art
Museum, Princeton University,
1887. Princeton University
Library. Department of Special
Collections

A Mr. Robert Garrett (possibly the father of Robert Garrett, Class of
1897) subsequently subscribed $7,000, leaving only $15,000 to be raised,
as of November 17, 1886. Six months later, on May 13, 1887, the goal of
$40,000 had been met.[16]

In a story that seems all too familiar today, the process of con-
structing what became known as the Page Brown building, after the
New York architectural firm that designed it, did not prove straight-
forward. The initial designs, largely the work of a junior member of
the team in Brown's firm, were rejected. The funds raised proved in-
adequate to achieve the accepted full design (fig. 7), which had been
shaped in large part by Stanford White, whose offices were in the
same building as Brown's; flanking wings to the Richardsonian Romanesque Revival core were removed from the plan and never built
(fig. 8). The site selected was personal for McCosh: he chose it himself for its adjacency to his home in Prospect House, on a gentle rise
known as the Acropolis, suitable to his ambitions for a new cultural
center (fig. 9). Even after sustaining substantial cuts—what today
would be termed value engineering—the design retained a commitment to the use of noble materials. Newark brownstone with broken
ashlar was chosen for the exterior walls, with North River bluestone
to be used at the ground plane and a frieze in terracotta, a gift of the
Perth Amboy Terra Cotta Company, below the roofline, while the
floors were six-inch-thick concrete, a material that came into widespread use in building construction in the mid-nineteenth century.[17]
Ground breaking took place during commencement week, on June 21,
1887, on which occasion students wrote, "Our Museum of Art will not
only provide for better storage and exhibition of the fine collections
already gathered, but will add to that fame of ennobling ideals and devoted purpose to the higher type of culture and refinement by which
Princeton has ever been characterized" (fig. 10).[18]

Completed in 1890, two years after McCosh's retirement, the new Museum was not without its critics, some of whom felt that he had lavished too much money on new buildings, but it certainly served as the catalyst for collecting that students and others had anticipated.[19] The Trumbull-Prime collection of pottery, assembled by William Prime and his wife, came upon the Museum's completion as promised, followed that same year by the purchase of a large corpus of Cypriot pots being deaccessioned by the Metropolitan Museum of Art and purchases of Etruscan, Roman, and South Italian pottery. Located in what is now Princeton's Marquand Park, Allan Marquand's home, which he had named Guernsey Hall, became a locus of bachelor communal living in the years prior to his marriage to Eleanor Cross in 1896. It acted both as an incubator of ideas for the Museum and ultimately as

Fig. 8   Arthur Page Brown, *Art Museum, Princeton College: Front Elevation*, 1886. Pen, black ink, and watercolor, 68.4 × 80 cm. Princeton University Art Museum. Gift of A. Page Brown (x1963-33)

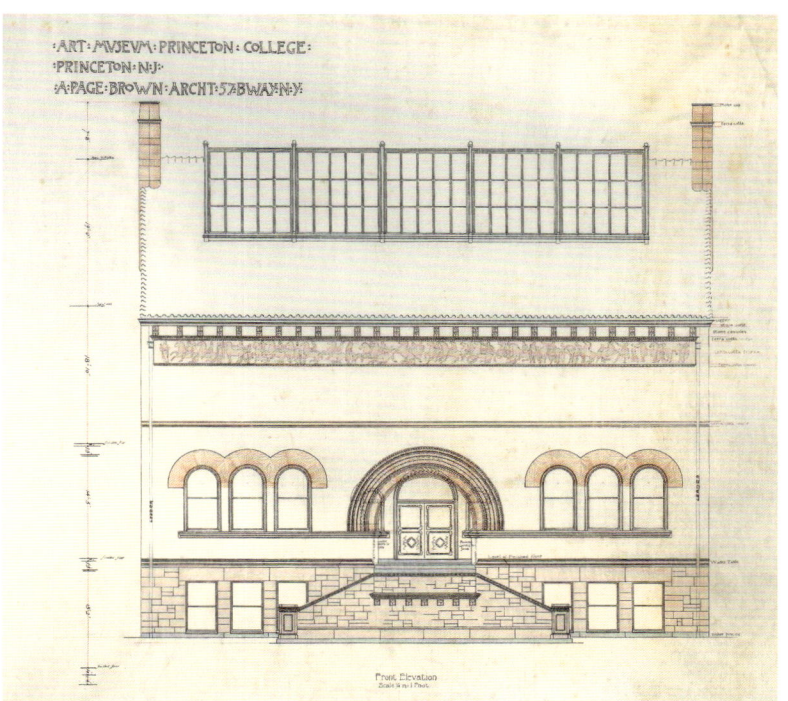

Fig. 9   Museum of Historic Art, Princeton University, mid- to late 1890s. Arthur Page Brown, architect; completed 1890. Princeton University Library. Department of Special Collections

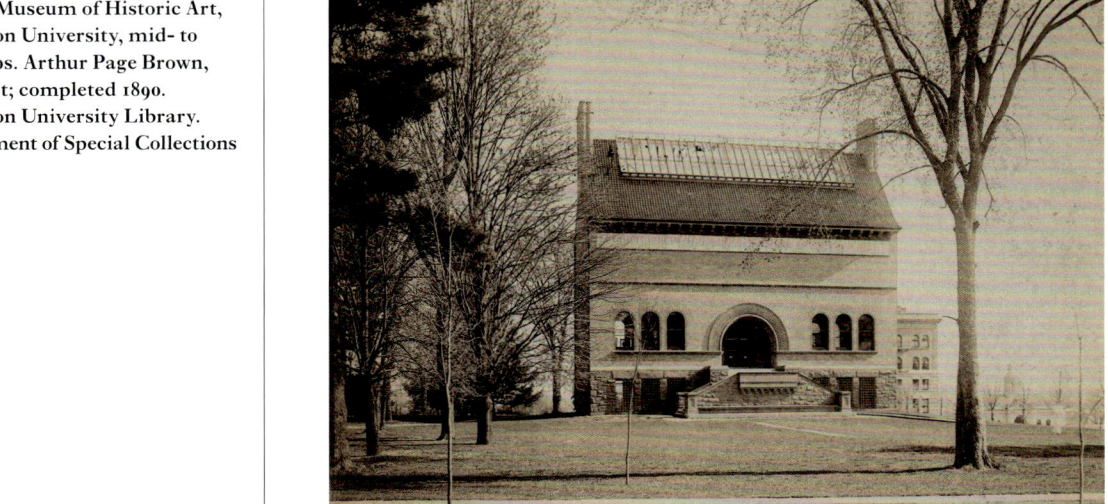

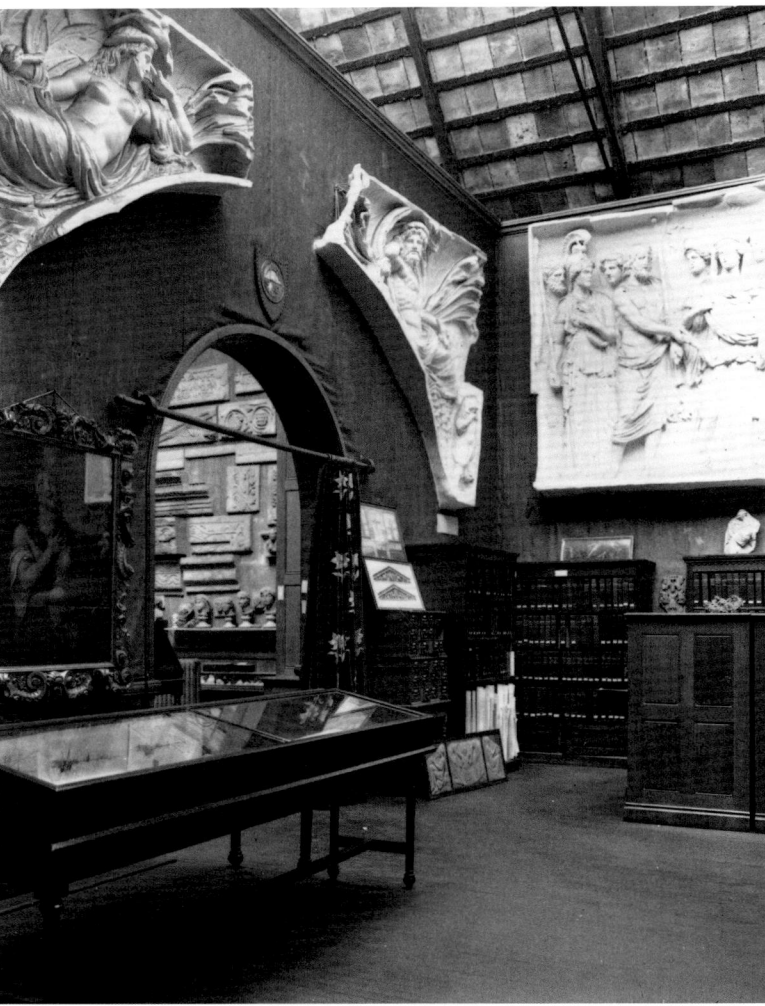

Fig. 10   The Museum's Upper
Hall, early 20th century.
Collection of the Historical
Society of Princeton

a feeder of objects to the Museum's collections. By the time of Marquand's death in 1924, *Christ Before Pilate*, attributed to Hieronymus
Bosch, had entered the Museum's holdings; other works collected by
the Marquands, such as the monumental Venetian doorway acquired
in 1892–93, came after their deaths in 1924 and 1970, respectively.

Marquand's tenure was characterized by a pattern of building,
repairing, demolishing, and rebuilding that would be repeated throughout the Museum's subsequent history. By 1895—a mere five years after
its opening—the collections and classrooms were already competing
for space, and a plea went out to alumni for the money with which to
construct the originally proposed side wings. As director, Marquand
was thwarted in this by the university architect, Ralph Adams Cram,
who had other ideas, aligned with his insistence on the Collegiate
Gothic as the style for all new construction at Princeton. Indeed, Cram
fought Marquand by arguing that the Page Brown building should
be wrapped in a curtain wall of Gothic Revival, to which Marquand
adamantly objected. Cram ultimately won out when the creation of a
School of Architecture at Princeton—initially housed alongside the
Museum of Historic Art and the Department of Art & Archaeology in
the Page Brown building—gave rise to the need for expansion.

Delayed by World War I, this expansion was designed by Cram himself, who already had the challenge of grappling with the diversity of architectural styles in the immediate campus neighborhood, from Italianate Brown Hall to Romanesque Dod Hall to the classical temples of Whig and Clio Halls, so Cram chose something "neutral," derived from northern Italy. This addition was given the green light in March 1921, thanks to a generous commitment from Mrs. Cyrus Hall McCormick Sr., widow of the Class of 1879, for whose family the new construction was named. Of an estimated project cost of $125,000, the vast majority ($100,000) came from the McCormick family, who would go on to be among the most important philanthropists in the Museum's history.[20] In a precedent relevant to our own time, when the University has once again made an essential financial commitment to the creation of a new building, an additional $35,000 came from the University's Finance Committee.

By the time the new wing was completed and dedicated on June 16, 1923 (fig. 11), the scholar and collector of medieval and Renaissance art Frank Jewett Mather Jr. had succeeded Marquand as director, going on to serve until 1946. Mather described the Museum he took on in 1922 as "the oddest kingdom of shreds and patches imaginable."[21] The same two priorities that had preoccupied Marquand—building and making sense of the collections as well as grappling with space problems—quickly came to absorb Mather too. Like Marquand, he used his substantial personal fortune to acquire works of art for the Museum, including classical and pre-Columbian antiquities, not the least of which were Princeton's share of the results of the partage excavations at ancient Antioch-on-the-Orontes, in what was then Syria. Mather also acquired one of the finest collections of American drawings in the country, an endeavor that was pioneering at a time when few museums accorded significance to American art and that enabled Princeton over time to acquire a collection in this area that is among the best of any academic museum, particularly in the field of nineteenth-century landscape painting. Mather recalled his acquisition of the Museum's *Martyrdom of Saint George* window when "in September of 1923 I found myself at Lausanne to put my children in school."[22] The *Martyrdom* was described by the dealer as an authentic, intact stained-glass window from Chartres Cathedral, supposedly from the collection assembled by the French architect-critic Eugène Viollet-le-Duc. It is in fact a composite of both medieval and modern glass, assembled in the early twentieth century, after Viollet-le-Duc's death in 1879.

From others, Mather was able to secure major gifts of works of art, including a significant collection of Italian paintings assembled by Henry White Cannon Jr., Class of 1910; a collection of more than five hundred snuff bottles (primarily Chinese) assembled by Colonel James Blair, Class of 1903; a collection of several thousand paintings and prints by bequest in 1933 from Junius Spencer Morgan II, Class of 1888, nephew of the industrialist J. P. Morgan; and also by bequest, in

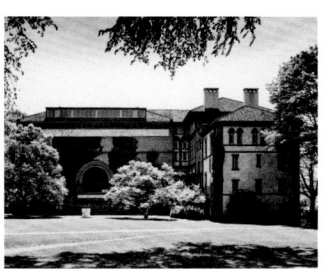

Fig. 11   Museum of Historic Art, after McCormick Hall addition, ca. 1925–30. Princeton University Library. Department of Special Collections

1938, a gift of Italian drawings from Dan Fellows Platt, Class of 1895, that laid the foundation for the Museum's drawings collection. Another key benefactor and Museum champion of the time was Baron Carl Otto von Kienbusch, Class of 1906, a tobacco merchant who, his rather grand name notwithstanding, lived out the whole of his ninety-one years on New York's East Seventy-Fourth Street. Kienbusch was a donor from the 1930s to the 1970s of both art and funds that supported the acquisition of works as varied as ancient bronzes, medieval stained glass, and a print by Josef Albers.

Even so, achieving the quality of what he intended for Princeton was, for Mather, a perpetual struggle. His goal was to create "not a place that will be occasionally visited, but one that will be used by Princeton men and their friends all the time." But against this goal, he observed: "I have found that there is an impression that what encumbers a home may adorn a museum. The Princeton Museum is not going to be adorned that way, even at the risk of occasionally disappointing an eager donor. Our space is small and precious. We have tried being a kind of storage warehouse and have found it unsatisfactory. We want the things that a trained collector hates to let go, and we shall get them when our collecting friends and alumni realize that to give Princeton a fine work of art is to assure it worthy and permanent exhibition in best company."[23]

Early in his tenure, Mather was again confronting the second priority—space, not least having inherited from Marquand a marriage of buildings rife with inadequacies that had been noted practically from the opening of the Cram wing. At one point, leaks from the primary skylight in the Page Brown building led to a proposal to remove the skylight, replace it with a solid roof, and make windows to bring daylighting in, in lieu of the terracotta frieze adorning the exterior of its upper level. Alumnus Cyrus McCormick, who had been one of the building's original donors, was asked to pay for half the cost, in order to avoid having to close the Museum indefinitely.[24] A debate about whether to go from depending entirely on natural light to a system using only artificial light ensued, thus ensuring that the necessary fix was not undertaken and ultimately leaving Mather with a larger problem to solve—one that had already been on his mind for some time. In a letter of January 30, 1925, Mather wrote, "I have talked the matter over with [University] President Hibben and he agrees with me that in a not very remote future the Museum to survive and grow must have its own building." He then went on to request a variety of potential campus sites in ranked order, before concluding, "Accessibility should be considered for in a few years I shall make the Museum a place of resort second only to Old Nassau," by which he meant the oft-burned Nassau Hall.[25]

Citing various spatial, design, and lighting problems, including the challenge of sharing space with not one but two academic departments, Mather continued his lobbying campaign through 1926, arguing that the kind of small interventions that were being considered were short-term fixes at best and that what was needed was a free-standing museum, divorced from the competing needs of the School of Architecture and the Department of Art & Archaeology. His requested location offered proximity to the latter, and he argued in a letter of November 10, 1926, that this would make it likely that a donor would support the project.[26] That location, perhaps ironically, is approximately where the present Museum has been constructed.

Just as Marquand fell short of his ambitions, losing the two wings from the original Page Brown design, Mather, too, did not achieve his goal and instead had to be satisfied with another in a series of additions. What became the 1927 addition was the subject of much debate architecturally, with Mather again arguing that it should hew to the Collegiate Gothic. Ultimately, the design was made by three professors in the School of Architecture whose primary focus was on creating monumental studio space. Completed in 1928, the result was a little-remembered addition that moved the entrance to the complex to the south, under a tower intended to announce it (figs. 12, 13), and included a courtyard in which some of the Museum's Antioch mosaics were later displayed outdoors and a large atelier with north- and east-facing light, which marked a new Beaux-Arts model of architectural instruction for Princeton.

By 1935 advocacy had emerged for yet further additions or renovations, intended at least in part to "counteract the drift away from the

Fig. 12 Drawing of proposed addition to McCormick Hall, 1927. Princeton University Library. Department of Special Collections

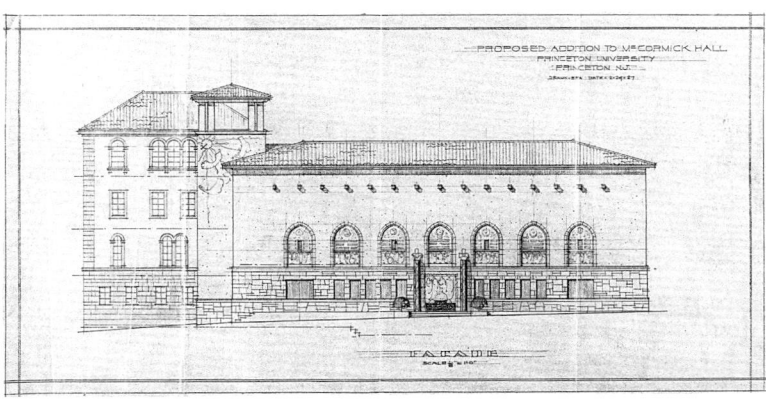

Fig. 13 McCormick Hall with the addition to the south side, 1928. Princeton University Library. Department of Special Collections

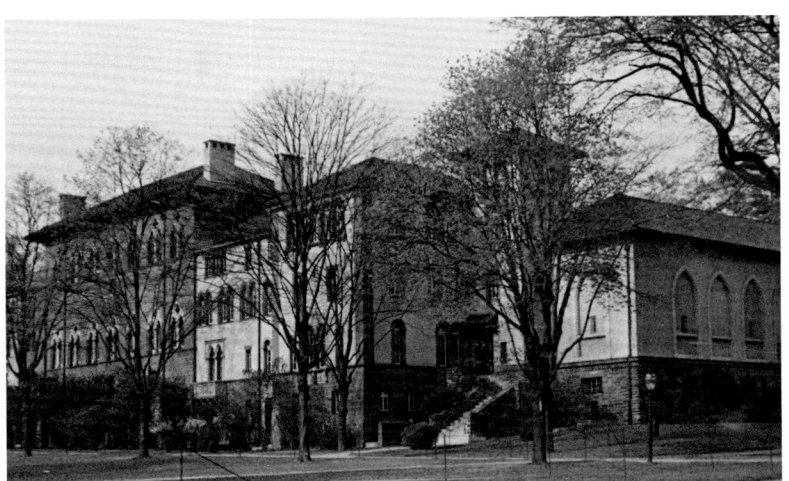

Humanities to the Social Sciences."[27] Perhaps most importantly, the Museum already seemed to be shrinking relative to its cohabitants: at this time, the whole of the Museum constituted a space of about 5,000 square feet, of which 4,490 were for exhibitions, 182 for offices, and 336 for art storage. A writer described the dilemma in the *Bulletin of the Department of Art & Archaeology* in June 1939:

> This institution [the Museum of Historic Art], if exception is made of the support of a very small group of generous and discerning alumni, has shared the incredible neglect experienced by the University Library during the past twenty-five years, and deserves it no more than that other step-child of Princeton. The Museum may be a vague term to some Princetonians, but it is well-known to art-lovers and scholars of this country and abroad as one of the best small collections in America. The Chartres Window, the Princeton Saint, the Bosch Christ before Pilate [fig. 14], the Antioch mosaics, the Cannon paintings[28] (and several other items of first rank), are names found frequently enough in the literature of art to lift the Princeton Museum out of the common run of American collections and make it a place that foreign connoisseurs feel that they must not omit from their itineraries in the United States.

But, the article continues, "This excellent collection is crowded into the old museum building with no chance of the effective display with which museums of less importance attract greater interest than does ours." Yet another proposed addition to McCormick Hall "would solve a crucial problem of the present, viz. how to secure for the University the fine collections that are ready to come to it when assured of proper housing.... The proffer of such contingent gifts is becoming more and more frequent: the impossibility of accepting them for lack of space all the more distressing."[29]

By the time Ernest DeWald became director of the Museum in 1946, storage was bursting at the seams; even the basement of Nassau Hall had been called into action for art storage. DeWald, who became director in the same year he completed his graduate training at Princeton, had been one of the so-called Monuments Men charged with protecting and returning the cultural heritage of Europe during World War II. Because so many Princetonians, both faculty and alumni, served with the Monuments program, the Kunsthistorisches Museum in Vienna lent the landmark work *The Art of Painting* by Johannes Vermeer for what proved to be an eight-day blockbuster exhibition in Princeton in May 1950. Prior to that, for the University's bicentennial in 1946, DeWald took on the task of refurbishing the Museum's galleries, including the inaugural display of a new collection of Chinese scroll paintings donated by DuBois Schanck Morris, Class of 1893.

That bicentennial reinstallation marked a major turning point for the Museum in heightening interest and awareness, anchored by an

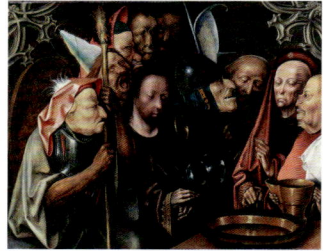

Fig. 14   Follower of Hieronymus Bosch (ca. 1450–1516; born and died 's-Hertogenbosch, Netherlands), *Christ Before Pontius Pilate*, ca. 1520. Oil and tempera on oak panel, 80 × 104 cm. Princeton University Art Museum. Gift of Allan Marquand, Class of 1874 (y711)

Fig. 15   Northern Wei dynasty
(386–535 CE), China, Tomb
retinue, early 6th century CE.
Earthenware. Gift of J. Lionberger
Davis, Class of 1900 (y1950-93,
-102, -88, -86)

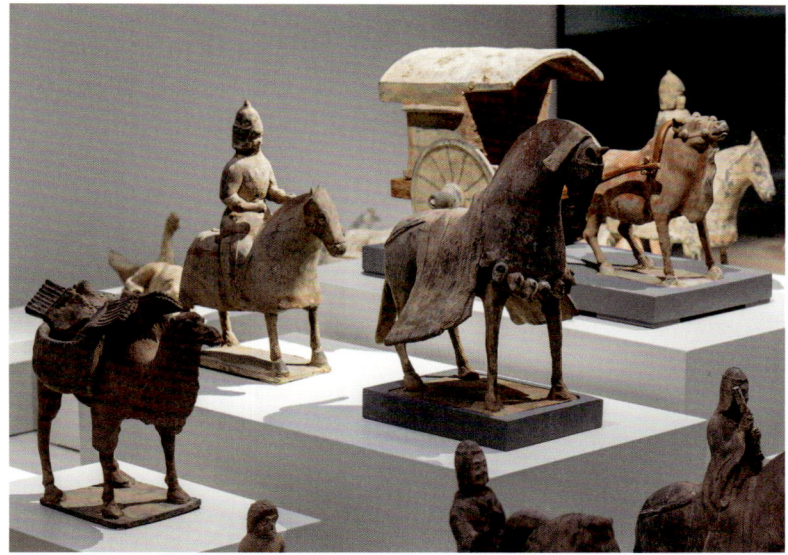

exhibition of its new Chinese paintings. Asian art proved to be one of
the most important arenas for expansion during DeWald's tenure (fig.
15). He was enormously aided by Professor Wen Fong, Class of 1951,
who would go on to become one of the world's leading authorities on
Chinese art and the founding director of the Metropolitan Museum
of Art's Asian art department. Among their many joint successes was
the gift of the Lowrie collection of Asian art in 1960 from Mrs. Walter
Lowrie, who also donated the house that later became the University
president's official residence on Princeton's Stockton Street. A gift
from Mrs. Donald Doyle in 1947 was another turning point, the first
bequest to Princeton of works of African art, in this case assembled
before 1923 in what is now the Democratic Republic of the Congo. In
1949 Alfred Stieglitz's photograph of 1907 *The Steerage* (fig. 16) became the first fine art photograph to enter what would grow into one
of the Museum's most robust collections, at a time when few museums
were ready to embrace photography as a fine art form.

Against this background of growth was the by-then-familiar re-
frain of concern about the dramatic shortcomings of the Museum's
physical plant—as well as its staffing. Early in DeWald's tenure, in
May 1949, *The Nassau Sovereign* ran an article titled "Campus Treasure House," with the lede "Once unknown, the Art Museum now
overflows with sights and sight-seers." The article went on to note that
"a great change has taken place within the collegiate mind during the
last ten years, one which has placed the Museum of Historic Art on the
Princeton map."[30] Citing attendance of one thousand visitors a month,
the writer went on to refer to the Museum's physical home as "the
phantom of the Princeton campus," arguing energetically that "a new
building or an addition to the present one is necessary if the Museum
is to reach its full efficiency and rank with Harvard and Yale in this
field."[31] The work of mounting exhibitions, caring for the collections,
and welcoming the public was carried out by a skeleton staff of four—
a director, an assistant director, a secretary, and an assistant curator of

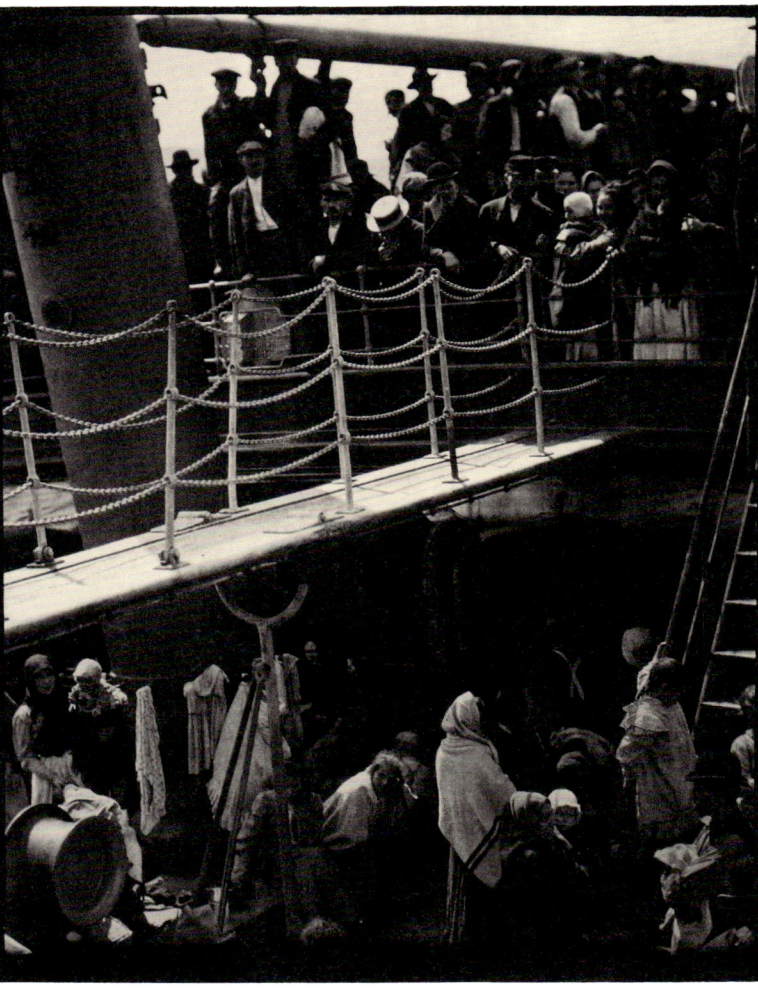

Fig. 16   Alfred Stieglitz (1864–
1946; born Hoboken, NJ; died
New York, NY; active New York),
The Steerage, 1907, printed 1911
or later. Photogravure, 33.3 × 26 4
cm. Princeton University Art
Museum. Gift of Frank Jewett
Mather Jr. (x1949-154)

classical art—two of whom were part-time, in addition to two faculty
curators of classical and "Far Eastern" art. As Sara E. Bush writes in
her architectural history of the Museum, "Princeton might have had
a collection equal to that of other university museums, but its prestige
was crippled by the physical conditions of its building, which still had
no running water, no means of controlling the heat, and no space for
art storage or supplies or for unpacking or conserving the collections."[32]

By January 19, 1953, in a report for University President Harold
Dodds, DeWald described the situation as "desperate" and lacking
in any "modern museum equipment"—with a tiny staff who were
charged with presenting, as if by magic (to paraphrase *The Princeton
Bulletin* of March 9, 1945), examples of artworks from the earliest times
to the present and with supporting the teaching of the Department of
Art & Archaeology.[33] An ardent champion of a "final" resolution to
these decades-long spatial dilemmas was Rensselaer W. Lee, Class of
1920, then chair of the Department of Art & Archaeology, who wrote
of his ambitions for the Museum in 1957:

> The new museum would be above all a teaching museum in
> which maximum use would be made by undergraduates as well

as graduate students of the museum's collections. While many of our finest objects would continue to be on permanent exhibition, a large proportion of our collection would be readily available to students in "live" or "study" storage (as opposed to dead storage as at present) from which objects could be easily moved into nearby preceptorial rooms located in the museum itself. This is the notion of the "humanistic laboratory" already made concrete in the Firestone and Marquand libraries, applied to the museum. Also changing exhibitions of works of art in the corridors...would constantly invite the attention of students on their way to and from classes.[34]

Lee's invocation of the Museum as a humanistic laboratory was an arresting resuscitation of the concept that prevailed in discussions of making a museum building for the first time in the 1870s and 1880s and that, unknowingly, I invoked again in describing a "new" yet old typology for the Museum in the 2010s.

Faced with such a divergence between reality and possibility, it is little wonder, then, that DeWald's tenure as director was shorter than that of his predecessors. Retiring in 1960, DeWald was succeeded as director by a fellow Monuments Man, Patrick Joseph Kelleher, Class of 1947. It fell to Kelleher to spearhead the fundraising for and construction of the long-awaited new home for the Museum, made possible by the University's landmark $53 million capital campaign, which set a new standard for nonprofit fundraising. The lead gift of $250,000 to the new building was made by Carl Otto von Kienbusch (fig. 17), who was described by Kelleher as "patron saint of the Art Museum for almost half a century."[35] Among other patrons, George Craig Jr., Class of 1921, of Pittsburgh, named a Gallery of Contemporary Art; James F. Lawrence, Class of 1929, endowed a gallery of pre-Columbian and other "Native Arts"; George S. Heyer Jr., Class of 1952, endowed a "Treasure Room"; and Louise La Beaume, an architect from Saint Louis, made a gift to construct a "Laboratory for Conservation and Restoration," termed "an essential for any museum." The Class of 1929 led the charge, naming galleries of ancient Near Eastern, Egyptian, and classical art; the art of the Middle Ages; Far Eastern art; and temporary exhibitions. In total, members of the Class of 1929 donated $1 million—philanthropy remarkable for its time and equal to more than $10 million today. Throughout, Kienbusch, in Kelleher's words, "with a romantic recklessness in character with his magnificent collection of armor and his penchant for the hauteur of a medieval knight, continued to pass out shekels to an impecunious, if ardent museum staff."[36]

In 1962, following years of challenge in reaching an agreement as to the scale and design of the project—a first design proposal was put forward by the New York architectural firm of Steinmann and Cain in 1960—packing and removal of the Museum's collections began, and by the summer of 1963, Marquand Library had been moved to

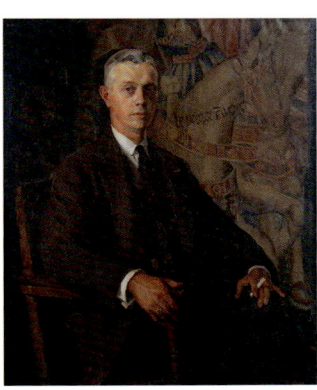

Fig. 17   Margaret Wood White (born 1893, Chicago, IL; active United States), *Carl Otto von Kienbusch*, 1927. Oil on canvas, 107 × 91.5 cm. Princeton University Art Museum. Bequest of Carl Otto von Kienbusch, Class of 1906, for the Carl Otto von Kienbusch Jr. Memorial Collection (y1977-28)

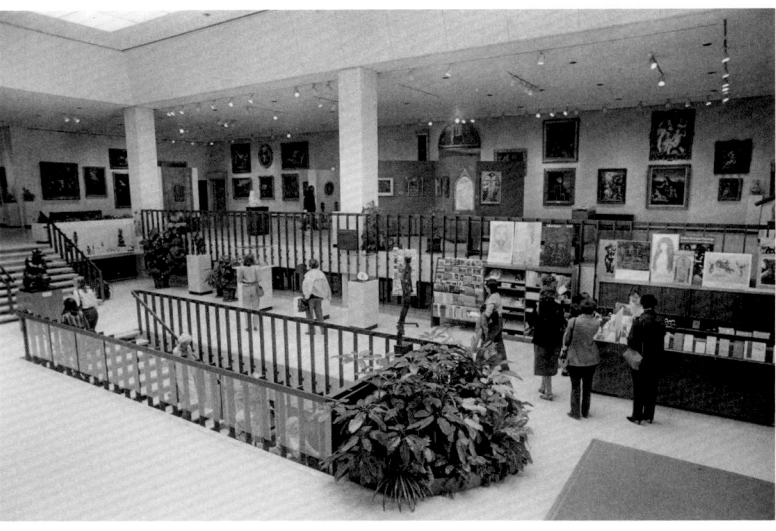

Firestone Library, while department and Museum offices moved into
Aaron Burr Hall, and many objects from the collections went on the
road to Baltimore, New York, Oberlin, and Williamsburg. Demolition of the 1890 Page Brown building and of the 1927 addition began
in 1963, and the debris was left on a site off Alexander Street between
the Stony Brook and the Delaware and Raritan Canal. A press release
dated October 26, 1966, announced an event to be held three days later
to celebrate the opening of the new Museum, some forty-one years
after such a project had first been mooted. The new building, designed by Steinmann and Cain, was greeted with widespread acclaim
and more than a little surprise that a campus museum should see itself as a lively, and public, destination (fig. 18). The *Princeton Alumni
Weekly* noted, a bit gruffly: "The old Art Museum hid away in a loft;
the new spacious one, oddly enough, is one of the liveliest places on
campus. Several thousand visitors stroll through every year, hundreds
of undergraduates in precepts."[37] *Antiques Magazine* wrote that the
Museum "welcomes the serious student, the interested collector, the
browsing Sunday public, as each gives the lie to Edith Wharton who
complained that Americans tolerated art only so lofty and remote 'that
it bored people to death, and they locked it up in Museums to get rid
of it.'"[38] The new Museum complex was deemed to be so large that
undergraduates dubbed it the "Massif Central," after the highland
region of France (fig. 19).[39]

    Like his predecessors, Kelleher excelled at collections building
even as he pushed boulders up hills to solve spatial problems successfully. Among the highlights of his tenure was the acquisition in
1965 of the Chester Dale Carter collection of eighty-three ancient
Chinese bronzes as a donative sale, funded by William McAlpin,
Class of 1926; David Hunter McAlpin, Class of 1920; and Hugh T.
Adams, Class of 1935, all of them members of the Museum's Advi-
sory Council, formed to guide the director and secure needed funds
for both capital projects and operations. Another highlight was the
acquisition of the Sackler collections in 1968, from Arthur Sackler

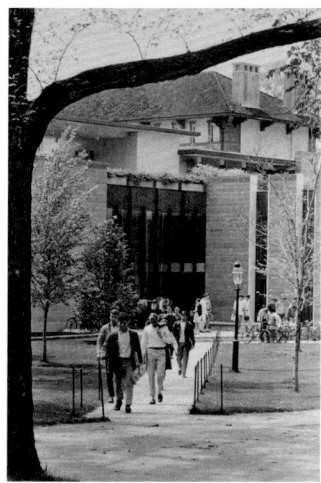

and the Sackler Foundation, including the most important body of work by Tao-Chi (born 1641). Kelleher's directorship also saw dramatic strides in Princeton's standing in the field of photography. David Hunter McAlpin donated a collection of nearly five hundred photographs to the Museum in 1971, as well as endowing a fund for further purchases and the nation's first professorship in the history of photography, a position first occupied by Peter Bunnell in 1972. Key additions to the Museum's curatorial staff such as Bunnell may have been Kelleher's most lasting legacy: he also appointed Gillett G. Griffin as curator of pre-Columbian art in 1967, a position he held until 2004, shaping for Princeton what is probably the finest collection of Mesoamerican art in any museum in the United States.

Perhaps the most visible art on the Princeton campus is the Putnam Collection of Sculpture (fig. 20), whose origins also date to Kelleher's directorship, when, in 1968, Princeton received an anonymous gift of $1 million in honor of Lieutenant John B. Putnam Jr., Class of 1945, who had been killed in a plane crash during World War II. Begun in 1969 and 1970 under the leadership of a committee led by Kelleher that also included Alfred H. Barr Jr., Class of 1922, the

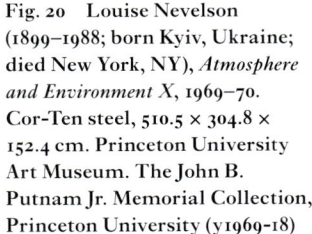

Fig. 20   Louise Nevelson (1899–1988; born Kyiv, Ukraine; died New York, NY), *Atmosphere and Environment X*, 1969–70. Cor-Ten steel, 510.5 × 304.8 × 152.4 cm. Princeton University Art Museum. The John B. Putnam Jr. Memorial Collection, Princeton University (y1969-18)

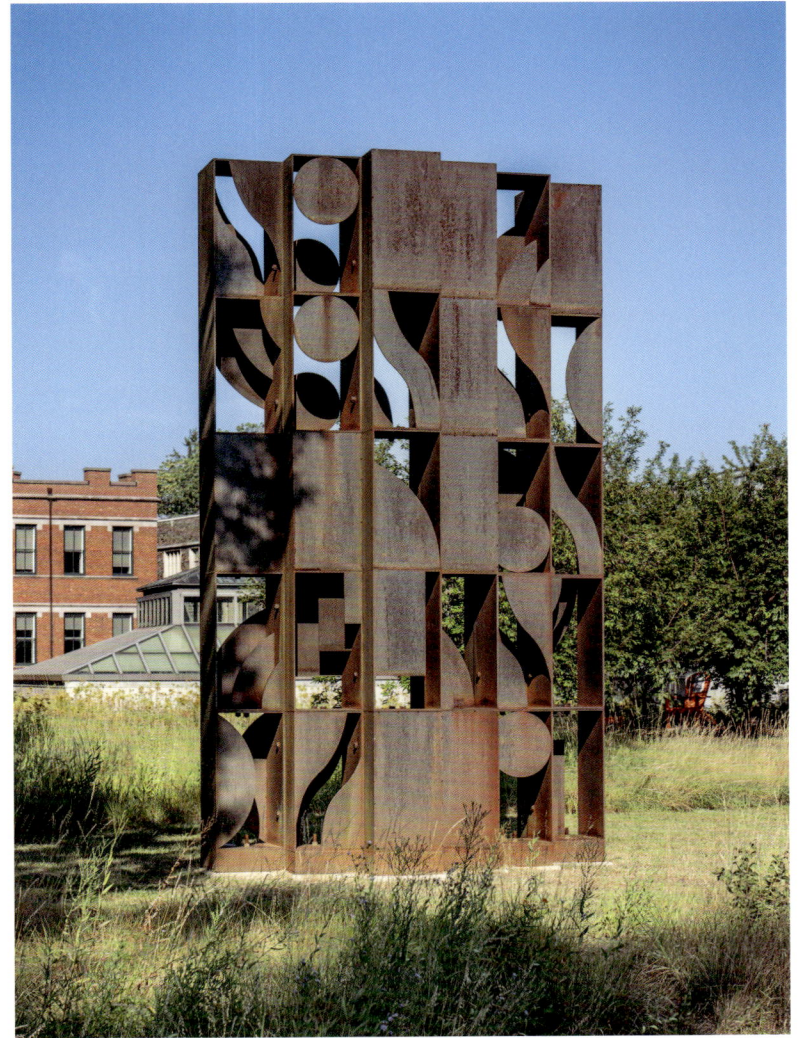

founding director of the Museum of Modern Art, and Thomas Hoving, Class of 1953, then the director of the Metropolitan Museum of Art, the early years of this effort led to commissions by major artists of the time, including Alexander Calder, Henry Moore, Louise Nevelson (see fig. 20), David Smith, Tony Smith, and many others. Two other initiatives launched during these years continue to be hallmarks of the Museum's work: the precursor to the docent program launched in 1967, one year after the opening of the then-new Museum, with teacher engagement and outreach efforts beginning in earnest the following year, and the Museum Travel Program, inaugurated in 1969 with a tour to the lands of the ancient Maya (Guatemala, Honduras, Mexico) led by Griffin.

Like other museum directors of his time, Kelleher understood the importance of temporary exhibitions as drivers of both original research and attendance. Building on DeWald's innovations in previous decades—including his presentation in 1948 devoted to the art of Pablo Picasso (fig. 21), deemed a blockbuster before the term had been applied to exhibitions—Kelleher championed exhibitions that not only utilized the spaces newly available to mount them but also would have an outsize legacy, even into our own times. *The Arts and Crafts Movement in America from 1876 to 1916*, presented in 1972 and curated by faculty member Robert Judson Clark, was heralded at the time as "the most comprehensive exhibition of its kind ever mounted."[40] It led to a wholesale reconsideration of the Arts and Crafts movement in the United States as one of singular craftsmanship as well as to a renewed appreciation for now-canonical makers such as Charles Rohlfs and Frank Lloyd Wright (as furniture designer and metalworker).

Only a few years later, Peter Bunnell (fig. 22) added the Museum's directorship to his portfolio of responsibilities, succeeding Kelleher in 1973 as the first non-Princeton-educated individual to hold the position. In a press statement of May 14, 1973, announcing his appointment as director, Bunnell is quoted as saying, in words I might have used at my own appointment in 2009: "I want, for example, to make the Museum a focal point for the student body in general, not only the art history majors. The Museum should become more a part of every student's experience."[41] In addition to training a generation of leading scholars and curators in the history of photography, Bunnell built on the platform established in the late 1960s to shape one of the great institutional collections of photography anywhere, now numbering more than twenty-seven thousand works, as well as holding the archives of the artists Clarence H. White, Minor White, and Ruth Bernhard. (To these were added, in 2023, the photographic archive of Emmet Gowin, whom Bunnell hired to teach photographic practice in 1973, the year after he joined the faculty.)

Bunnell's tenure as director lasted only five years, before he returned to full-time teaching and research and passed the baton to Allen Rosenbaum, who became director in March 1980. Like so many before him, Rosenbaum faced the dilemma of once again needing to grapple

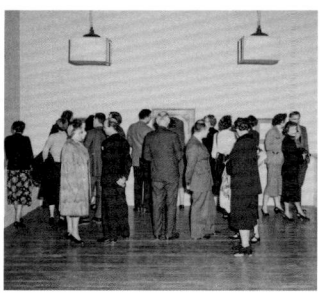

Fig. 21   Visitors to *Picasso Drawing*, Princeton University Art Museum, 1948. Princeton University Library. Department of Special Collections

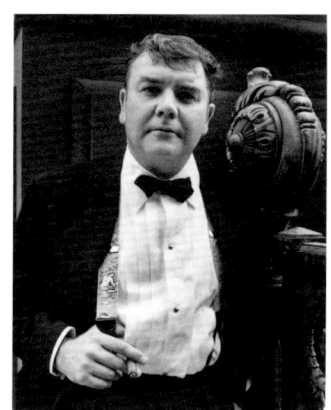

Fig. 22   Judy Dater (born 1941, Los Angeles, CA), *Peter Bunnell*, 1977. Gelatin silver print, 34.1 × 26.7 cm. Princeton University Art Museum. The Peter C. Bunnell Collection, gift of the artist (2002-138)

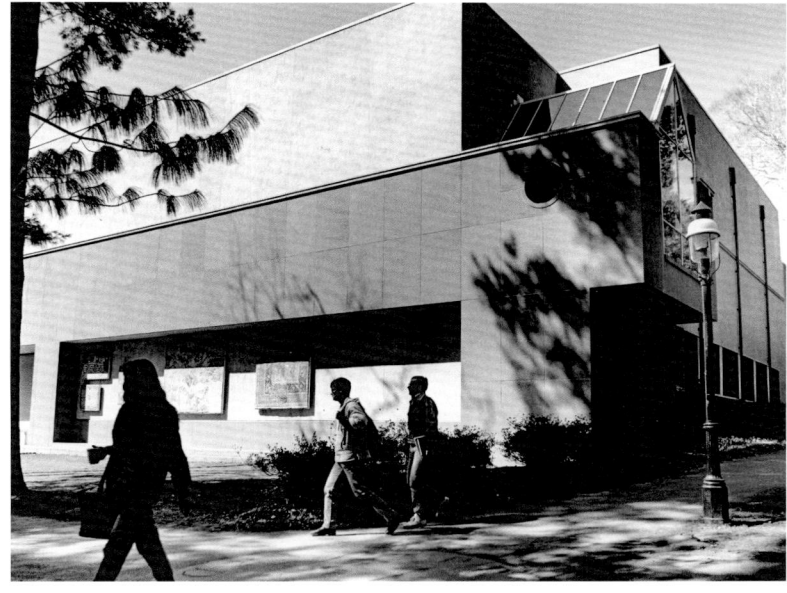

Fig. 23 The Mitchell Wolfson Jr., Class of 1963, Wing, Princeton University Art Museum. Mitchell Giurgola, architects; dedicated 1989. Princeton University Library. Department of Special Collections

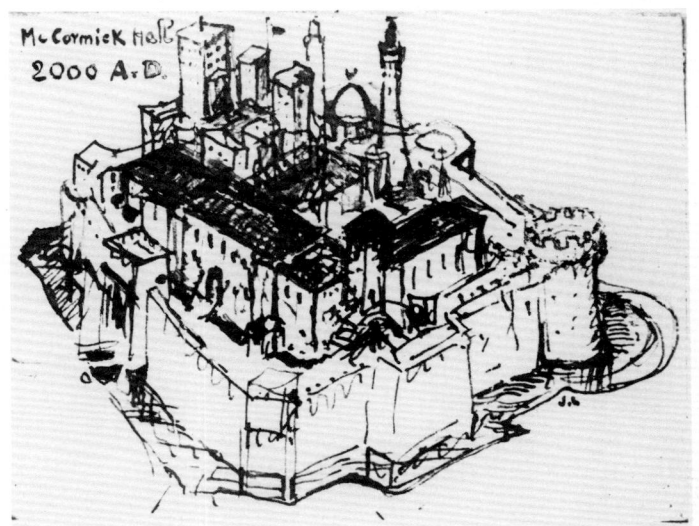
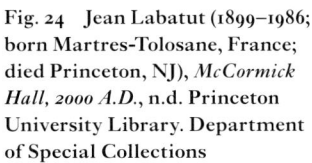

Fig. 24 Jean Labatut (1899–1986; born Martres-Tolosane, France; died Princeton, NJ), *McCormick Hall, 2000 A.D.*, n.d. Princeton University Library. Department of Special Collections

with the inadequacies of space even as he continued to build the collections, making particularly noteworthy acquisitions from Renaissance and Baroque Europe, including what may be the most important collection of northern Mannerist paintings in the United States. In 1989 he initiated yet another series of improvements to the Museum's physical plant, including renovations to the 1966 building as well as the addition of a 27,000-square-foot wing designed by the New York firm Mitchell Giurgola in a loosely postmodern style (fig. 23).

By this point the Museum had indeed begun to resemble the village that had been sarcastically predicted as early as the 1930s by Professor Jean Labatut, who imagined a future museum that was by the year 2000 a random and chaotic assemblage of additions in a host of disparate and even jarring historicizing styles (fig. 24). My immediate predecessor, Susan Taylor, imagined that the only way forward with an essentially landlocked facility was to build a series of satellite facilities in disparate campus locations, a scheme that imagined relocating the bulk of the Museum's collections and its conservation program to an area a few miles distant and creating a new venue for contemporary art and temporary exhibitions elsewhere on the main Princeton campus. This concept might well have gone forward but for the Great Recession of 2008–9, which put a pause on most of the University's anticipated capital projects. Even so, Taylor's leadership continued the process of growth and professionalization that had in many ways been inaugurated by Bunnell and Rosenbaum, stabilizing the Museum's operating resources and raising funds for endowed curatorships. Taylor was instrumental in assuring a sustained, dedicated focus on the art of our own times, modern art having been broadly marginalized in the Museum's collecting activities through much of the twentieth century.

With ambitions for a long-awaited solution to facilities shortcomings on hold when I became director in April 2009, our focus instead turned to deepening the Museum's reach across both the Princeton campus and the wider communities around us. A renewed emphasis on what Bunnell had termed a commitment to making the Museum matter to every Princeton student, along with a parallel investment

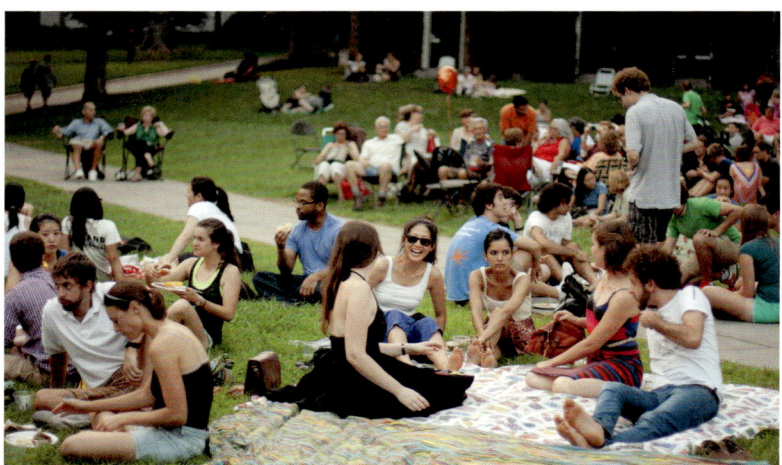

Fig. 25   The Museum's annual Picnic on the Lawn, 2012

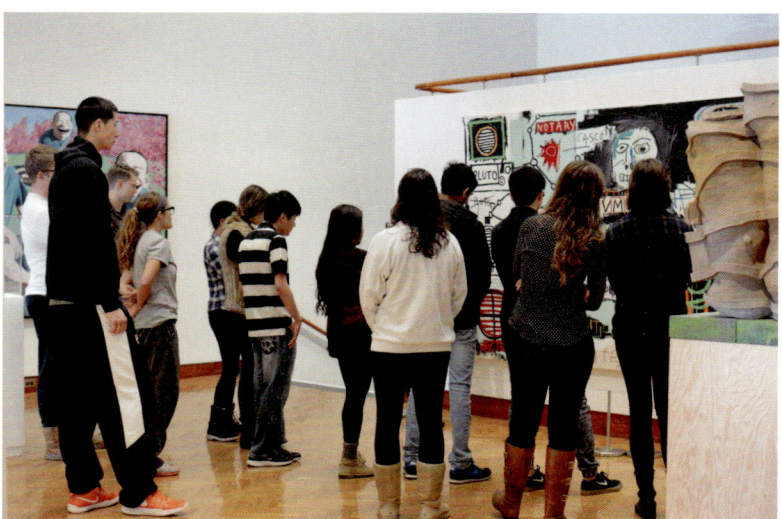

Fig. 26   Students visiting the Museum, 2015

in opening it out more successfully to the non-University communities around it, led attendance to double to more than 200,000 visitors a year, while use of the Museum's collection-specific object study rooms by University students rose by as much as 700 percent (figs. 25, 26). At the time of the publication of the most recent handbook of the collections in 2013, the Museum's holdings were thought to comprise 80,000 works of art; they now number more than 117,000 objects.[42]

The result was that the dilemma of space had to be addressed, not least because the Museum had outgrown its physical plant. By my estimate, no more than 2 percent of the collections were ever on view at one time (a far cry from Mather's museum), and the galleries simply could not contend with the scale and physical and technical requirements of contemporary art. It was also becoming clear that significant interventions of one kind or another were inevitable, as the systems of the 1966 building and even of the 1989 wing were beginning to fail, and it was unclear how, among other things, new state-of-the-art climate systems could be installed in a building that by then contained no fewer than eighteen floor plates—eighteen moments where visitors, artworks, and even ductwork had to negotiate changes in elevation. Charged with truly understanding the Museum's needs then and for the next generation (the planning horizon was determined to be thirty years), we elected to hire an architect who plans, rather than a planner who designs, to partner with us in undertaking a deep feasibility study.

Fig. 27　Architect and planner Frederick Fisher described the McCormick Hall complex as a Rubik's Cube of tangled connections. Drawing by Frederick Fisher and Partners, 2012

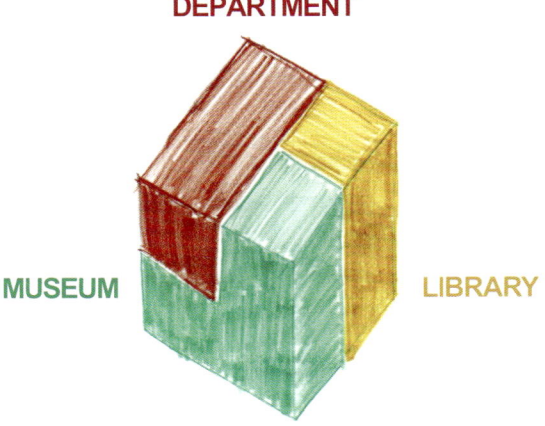

DEPARTMENT

MUSEUM

LIBRARY

The effort was led by Fred Fisher of Frederick Fisher and Partners in Los Angeles, who happily for us came with a thorough knowledge of the Princeton campus, having designed both Sherrerd Hall and the interiors of the refurbished Firestone Library. The most important questions asked and answered were (1) how large a new museum would need to be to meet the needs of at least the next thirty years, (2) what its building program would need to be, and (3) whether a museum of sufficient scale could be built or expanded on the site of the already much-expanded complex then known as McCormick Hall (fig. 27). The answers to these questions ultimately led to the realization that what was needed was a building approximately double the size of the 77,000-square-foot structure that housed the Museum at that time and that indeed such a facility could be constructed at the present location—but only by demolishing much if not all of the complex that had arisen between the years 1922 and 1989.

From the outset, it was understood that a new Museum could come about only if an adequate degree of philanthropic support would be available to fund such a project—one whose costs at that stage could only be estimated roughly on the basis of the Fisher study's recommendations. What emerged over a few years of critical conversations was a philanthropic and University partnership, with a handful of enormously generous benefactors stepping forward even prior to the selection of an architect or the schematic design of a new facility. In contrast to previous building campaigns, there was no single lead benefactor; instead a consortium of donors emerged, assuring that the result could continue to be known simply as the Princeton University Art Museum. Such philanthropic success, coupled with a major investment of University assets in the project under the leadership of President Christopher L. Eisgruber and provosts Deborah Prentice and now Jennifer Rexford, enabled the project to go forward.

Our mandates to an architect were complex. We wanted a facility that would declare itself as a center of University life and in particular as a hub for the humanities and an entry point for wider publics, building on decades of experience in the public humanities and in cross-curricular engagement. We wanted a facility that would nestle within the complex planning environment of its neighborhood on campus, large but hopefully without overwhelming its rather discrete neighbors already built in an abundance of architectural styles. We wanted a building that would overcome the challenge of "threshold resistance" and instead shape a sense of invitation and welcome, and in which visitors, having entered, would regularly be reminded where they were in the world, with substantial views onto the Princeton campus. Perhaps most importantly, we wanted a building that would overcome the upstairs-downstairs problem of the existing museum, built in 1966, in which European, American, and contemporary art dominated the more commodious upstairs galleries, while non-Western cultures and ancient art were consigned to the downstairs galleries, where data suggested that as many as 40 percent of Museum visitors never ventured.

Building on these and other elements of a complex value proposition, University Architect Ron McCoy and I led a process of identifying a host of architects who might have the talent and experience to meet the complex goals identified by the Fisher report. The result, ultimately determined by President Eisgruber, was that in 2020 the Ghanaian British architect David Adjaye, his firm Adjaye Associates, and executive architects Cooper Robertson were selected to design a facility of 146,000 square feet that would effectively double the Museum's size. Then best known for his design of the National Museum of

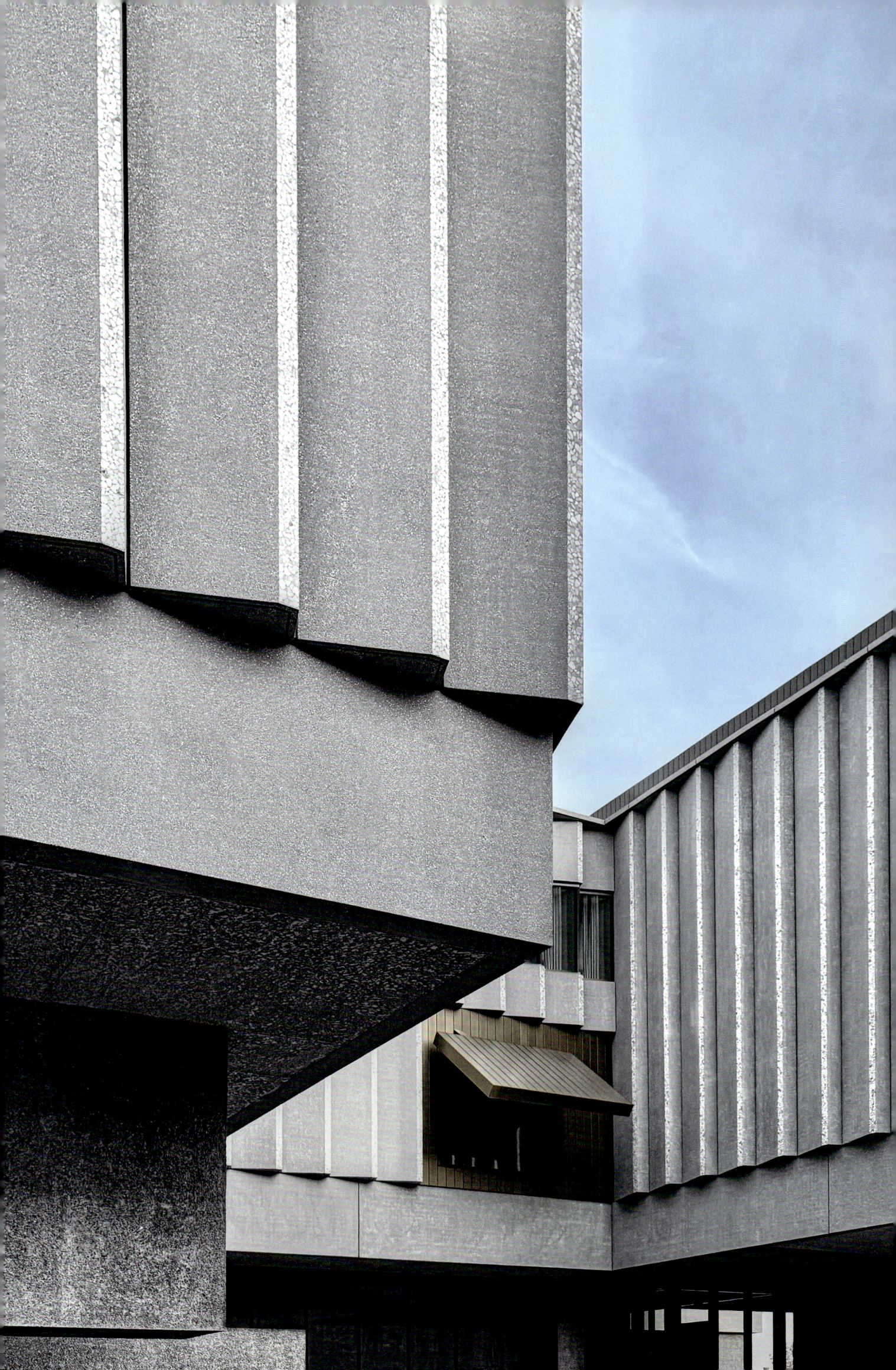

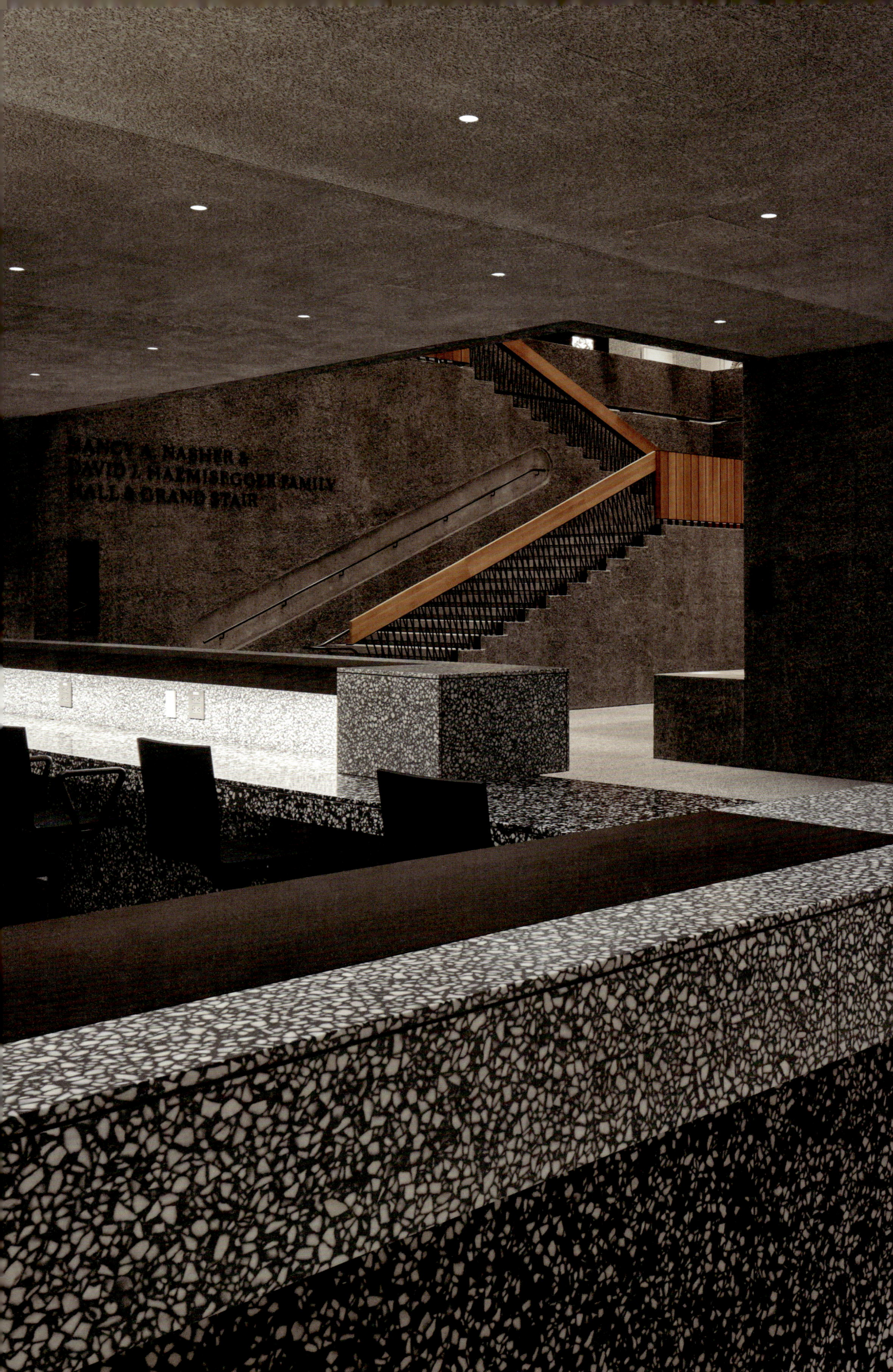

Fig. 28 The National Museum of African American History and Culture, Washington, DC. Philip Freelon, David Adjaye, and J. Max Bond Jr., architects; completed 2016

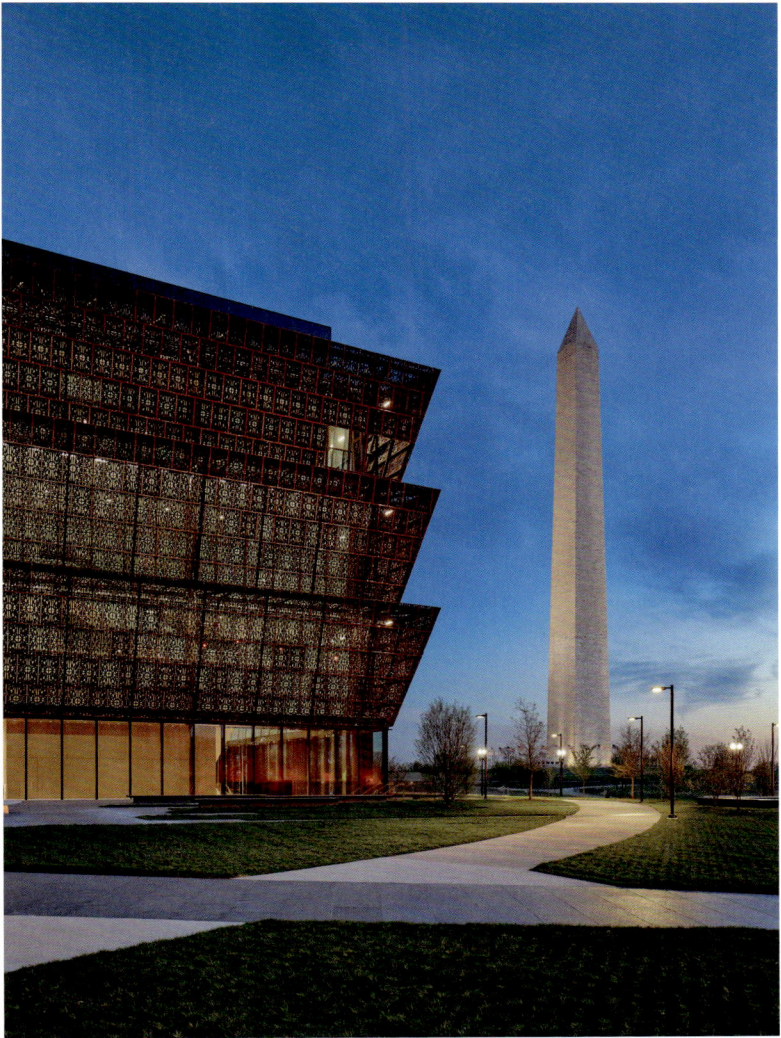

African American History and Culture, which responded to its context on the National Mall in Washington, DC (fig. 28), in richly complicated ways, Adjaye adopted an approach to the project that stood out for its understanding of the history and circulatory pathways of the campus and for its commitment to an ethical architecture. The resultant design springs from the decision to retain the footprint of Marquand Library—the University's remarkable fine arts library, which had its origins in the private library of Allan Marquand—and results in a network of nine interlocking "pavilions" (of which Marquand Library is one) (fig. 29). Built across three levels, the design shapes both a public zone and a gallery zone to facilitate operations and dramatically expand hours and accessibility, while forming gallery volumes of constant variation both to suit the needs of the Museum's varied collections and to help overcome the phenomenon known as museum fatigue. To my surprise, the design team was able to manifest our desire to overcome the prevailing hierarchy across the collections quite literally, by designing a building in which 95 percent of the galleries would occupy a single level.

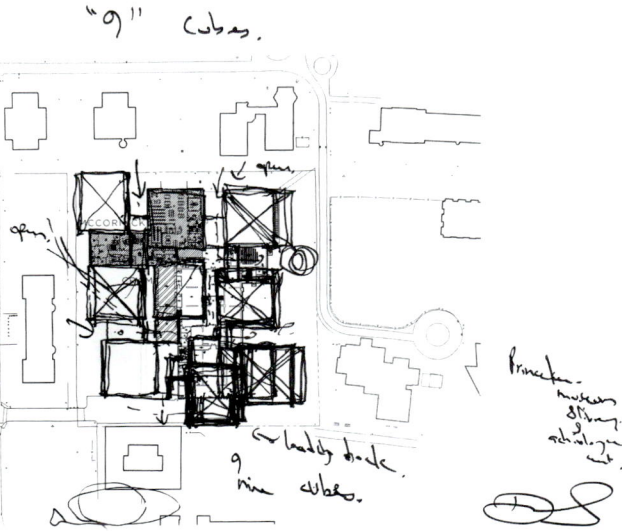

Fig. 29   David Adjaye (born
1966, Dar es Salaam, Tanzania).
Floor plan sketch for the
new Princeton University Art
Museum, 2018/19

The new Museum will, I hope, spare my successors from having to grapple with the spatial conundrums that have preoccupied my predecessors (and me) since the 1880s. Designed along principles of flexibility, its cubic "pavilions" and other gallery, teaching, and social spaces are intended to allow future generations to reassign functions should the needs of the collections and our evolving publics continue to shift as dramatically as they have in the past sixty years, since the construction of the 1966 building. These aspects of the design should afford those who come after us the ability to make changes if certain areas of the collections grow in quality or quantity more than others, or if the needs of contemporary art—including time-based media and specifically works of a scale that would have been unimaginable in the 1960s—continue to evolve or if needs we cannot even contemplate today arise over the decades to come.

The final design and the building that has now been created from that design contain a number of signature elements whose success will ultimately be determined by the nature of the visitor experience. Spatially, the building nestles into the landscape as a series of nine cubes or "pavilions" that respond to the scale of the historic buildings around them, from the brownstone of Murray Dodge Hall to the white marble of Whig and Clio Halls. The use of both elegant and basic building materials—from cast-in-place concrete to monumental honed precast panels to bronze and glass—in a variety of restrained colors seeks to respond to the tapestry of materials in those nearby buildings. The exterior element over which we may have obsessed more than any other was the color and blend of the stone aggregate, so that, when cut and faceted, the materials revealed would resonate subtly—almost subliminally—with the building's neighbors (fig. 30). Gentle uplighting designed by the project lighting designer, Tilletson Associates, picks out the ziggurat of the precast panels installed on the bias, just

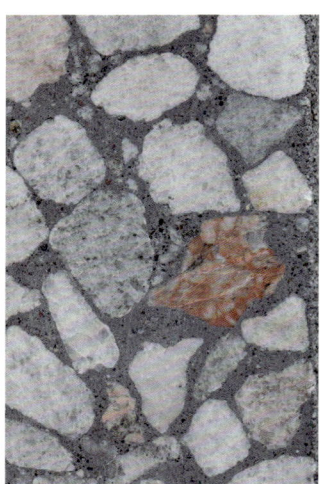

Fig. 30   The blend of the stone aggregate in the exterior curtain wall "fins" reflects the color palette of the nearby historic buildings

as sunlight radiates from above during daylight hours. Landscaping privileging native plant materials selected to withstand climate change and provide interest in all seasons was shaped by Field Operations, the New York–based landscape firm, which also sought to create compelling site opportunities for public art outside the Museum. Entrances on all four sides give the building its core organizational premise while continuing the pedestrian pathways of the campus through the structure. A similar circulatory device was deployed at the University of Michigan Museum of Art under my directorship, as part of the expansion and refurbishment designed by Allied Works Architecture and completed in 2009.

Once inside Princeton's new Museum, the visitor discovers a building in which form has largely followed function, the need for amply proportioned gallery spaces having dictated the form and volume of the pavilions. Interstitial spaces linking the pavilions afford ample opportunities for bringing daylighting into the building, while shaping vistas onto the campus in every direction that allow visitors to orient themselves and remind them of the University that has shaped the collections they now enjoy. On the second floor these areas function as both circulatory spaces and as galleries proportioned to the collections destined for them, allowing most of the building's 80,000 square feet of galleries to be gathered together on this floor—a footprint that is the second largest in the historic core campus (second only to Level A of Firestone Library). The interiors bring together a rich assortment of materials only hinted at by the more restrained exteriors, including Vermont white oak (fig. 31), Canadian blue spruce, terrazzo in two colorways that occasionally extends from the floors to the walls and casework, and Vermont granite that surrounds most of the gallery portals and is first discovered on the stair treads and risers of the Grand Stair. From the extraordinary "flying buttresses" of cast-in-place stone aggregate in the Grand Hall to the more intimate wood-lined spaces of three "viewing rooms"—moments of respite from the densely installed gallery spaces—the building is a symphony of themes and variations designed to keep visitors fresh and focused and to overcome "museum fatigue."

This idea of themes and variations emerges not only in the design of the building as it moves from grand to intimate and back but also in its curation. Rather than shaping a monochromatic or even insistent curatorial viewpoint across the whole of the institution, I have sought to foster approaches to display and interpretation as varied as the voices and perspectives of our fifteen curators and of the many educators and outside experts who have joined us in shaping the new installations. Our hope is that, as with the musical concept from which I have borrowed this language, the whole will operate cohesively while allowing for a diversity of curatorial approaches and encouraging visitors to participate in their own meaning making, no matter the nature of their previous museum experience.

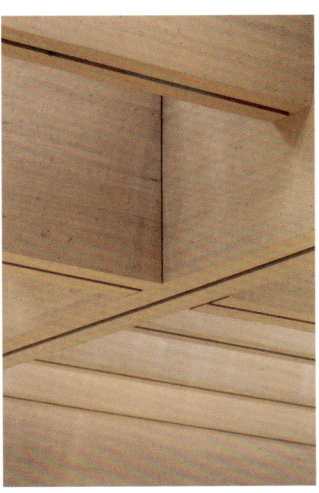

Fig. 31   Heavy timber, used in the ceiling system to carry many of the building's mechanical elements, creates the Museum's strongest aesthetic feature

The Museum we open today would have been hard to predict from its humble origins in the 1750s. The museum field has undergone a steady process of professionalization since the middle decades of the twentieth century, and by the time we open our doors in October 2025, we will be a staff of about 180 caring for collections of a size and complexity that would be unimaginable to our predecessors and responding to and anticipating the needs of audiences of a parallel complexity. The Museum we celebrate is one that builds on the past to welcome novice and expert alike; to allow every visitor to find points of resonance with their own lived experience; and to bring students, faculty, and community members together in pursuit of a shared journey of discovery, learning, and even sometimes delight.

1   Reverend Manassah Cutler of Connecticut, quoted in Donald Drew Egbert, *Princeton Portraits* (Princeton University Press, 1947), 4.

2   Karl Kusserow, "Memory and Meaning in the Faculty Room," in Kusserow, *Inner Sanctum: Memory and Meaning in Princeton's Faculty Room at Nassau Hall* (Princeton University Press, 2010), 67.

3   See Joel J. Orosz, *Curators and Culture: The Museum Movement in America, 1740–1870* (University of Alabama Press, 1990).

4   See "Nassau Hall in Ruins," *New-York Daily Times*, March 14, 1855.

5   *Nassau Literary Magazine* 29, no. 4 (April 1, 1874): n.p.

6   See Harrison Blackman, "Princeton's Lost Museum: Arnold Guyot's E. M. Museum and the History of American Natural Science," lecture, May 11, 2017, First Campus Center, Princeton University, https://mediacentral.princeton .edu/media/Princeton%27s+Lost+MuseumA+Arnold+Guyot%27s+E.+M.+ Museum+and+the+history+of+American+natural+science/1_ykcgzkin.

7   Guyot, quoted in Sara E. Turner, "The E.M. Museum: Building and Breaking an Interdisciplinary Collection," *Princeton University Library Chronicle* 65, no. 2 (Winter 2004): 237.

8   See Kusserow, "Memory and Meaning," 85.

9   The collection is enumerated in *The Catalogue of the College of New Jersey for 1875–76*, quoted in Betsy Rosasco, "The Teaching of Art and the Museum Tradition: Joseph Henry to Allan Marquand," *Record of the Art Museum, Princeton University* 55, no. 1/2 (1996): 13.

10   For a far richer accounting of the early developments of art history and an art museum at Princeton, see Rosasco, "Teaching of Art," 7–52.

11   "The College Buildings," 4, Allan Marquand Papers, CO 269, box 9, folder 2, Manuscripts Division, Princeton University Library.

12   George B. McClellan and William C. Prime, "Suggestions on the Establishment of a Department of Art Instruction in the College of New Jersey," 1882, 7. The models for their proposal were once again at Oxford, where the lectures of John Ruskin were providing a foundation in the English language for the new discipline of art history, as well as at Harvard, where Charles Eliot Norton's lectures, undertaken in 1874, were doing the same.

13   McCosh, quoted in Marilyn Aronberg Lavin, *The Eye of the Tiger: The Founding and Development of the Department of Art and Archaeology, 1883–1923, Princeton University* (Dept. of Art and Archaeology and the Art Museum, Princeton University, 1983), 9–10. Lavin explains that this is an oral tradition. In his obituary for Marquand, Frank Jewett Mather Jr. remembered, "It was Dr. McCosh's suspicion of Marquand's Calvinism that shifted the brilliant young metaphysician tactfully from the more or less contentious history of philosophy to the then quite harmless history of art. It was a step in which chance and policy seemed to conspire with predestination." Frank Jewett Mather Jr., obituary for Allan Marquand, *Princeton Alumni Weekly* 25, no. 1 (October 8, 1924): 30.

14   *Princetonian* 6, no. 13 (February 3, 1882): 157.

15   Moses Taylor Pyne to M. Murray, November 12, 1886, Department of Grounds and Buildings Technical Correspondence Records, Seeley G. Mudd Manuscript Library, Princeton University.

16   For a detailed discussion of the fundraising for and development of the building project, see Sara E. Bush, "Architectural History of the Art Museum," in "An Art Museum for Princeton: The Early Years," special issue, *Record of the Art Museum, Princeton University* 55, no. 1/2 (1996): 77–85.

17   Building Specs, Grounds and Buildings, Technical Correspondence, box 17, folder 4.

18   *Princetonian* 12, no. 24 (June 21, 1887): 2.

19   At the time of his retirement, McCosh wrote: "I never looked on these new buildings as constituting our chief work. I remember that some critics found fault with me for laying out too much money on stone and lime; but I proceeded on system, and knew what I was doing. I viewed the edifices as means to an end, at best as outward expressions and symbols of an internal life." Quoted in William Milligan Sloane, ed., *The Life of James McCosh: A Record Chiefly Autobiographical* (Scribner, 1896), 196.

20   The arrival in 1973 of a major endowment from Fowler McCormick, Class of 1921, restricted to the purchase of works of art, along with several relatively more minor endowments, made possible the process of strategic collections building in subsequent decades. Fowler McCormick was heir to two of the country's most notable economic dynasties: His grandfather was Cyrus McCormick, inventor of the reaper and founder of what became International Harvester; his mother was the former Edith Rockefeller, daughter of John D. Rockefeller Sr., who founded Standard Oil.

21   Frank Jewett Mather Jr., "An Art Museum at Princeton: The University's Growing Collection," *Princeton Alumni Weekly* 25, no. 18 (February 11, 1925): 417.

22   Mather, "Art Museum at Princeton," 417. On the origins of the *Martyrdom* window, see the entry on the Museum's website, https://artmuseum.princeton .edu/collections/objects/34722.

23   Mather, "Art Museum at Princeton," 420.

24   Henry B. Thompson to Cyrus McCormick, June 19, 1928, Department of Grounds and Buildings Technical Correspondence Records.

25   Frank J. Mather to Mr. Wintringer, January 30, 1925, Department of Grounds and Buildings Technical Correspondence Records.

26   Frank J. Mather to President John Hibben, November 10, 1926, Department of Grounds and Buildings Technical Correspondence Records.

27   Charles Rufus Morey to President Dodds, September 18, 1935, Department of Grounds and Buildings Technical Correspondence Records.

28   Forty Italian paintings, gifted in 1935 by Henry White Cannon, Class of 1910.

29   [E. Baldwin Smith], "Space," *Bulletin of the Department of Art & Archaeology*, June 1939, 15–16.

30   *Nassau Sovereign*, May 1949, 20.

31   *Nassau Sovereign*, May 1949, 30.

32   Bush, "Architectural History," 97.

33   Ernest T. DeWald to Harold W. Dodds, 1953, Archives of the Princeton University Art Museum.

34   "Rensselaer W. Lee '20: The Need for a New Art Museum," *Princeton Alumni Weekly* 58, no. 9 (November 15, 1957): 9.

35   Patrick J. Kelleher, "Interim Notes for a New Art Museum," *Princeton Alumni Weekly* 63, no. 8 (November 9, 1962): 9.

36   Kelleher, "Interim Notes," 10.

37   "New Art Acquisitions," *Princeton Alumni Weekly* 69, no. 5 (October 22, 1968): 9.

38   Hedy Backlin-Landman, "The Art Museum, Princeton University," *Antiques Magazine*, November 1967, n.p.

39   "The New McCormick Hall," *Princeton Alumni Weekly* 66, no. 8 (November 9, 1965): 9.

40   David L. Shirley, "Arts and Crafts with Vibrancy," *New York Times*, October 25, 1972, https://www.nytimes.com/1972/10/25/archives/arts-and-crafts-with -vibrancy.html.

41   Department of Public Information, Princeton University, "Bunnell Appointment," press release, May 14, 1973, 2, Seeley G. Mudd Manuscript Library.

42   Such dramatic growth certainly reflects a period of ambitious collecting but is also the result of a collections-wide inventory being conducted but incomplete at the time the handbook was being compiled. The first full inventory conducted in fifty years has led to a far more detailed understanding of the Museum's holdings.

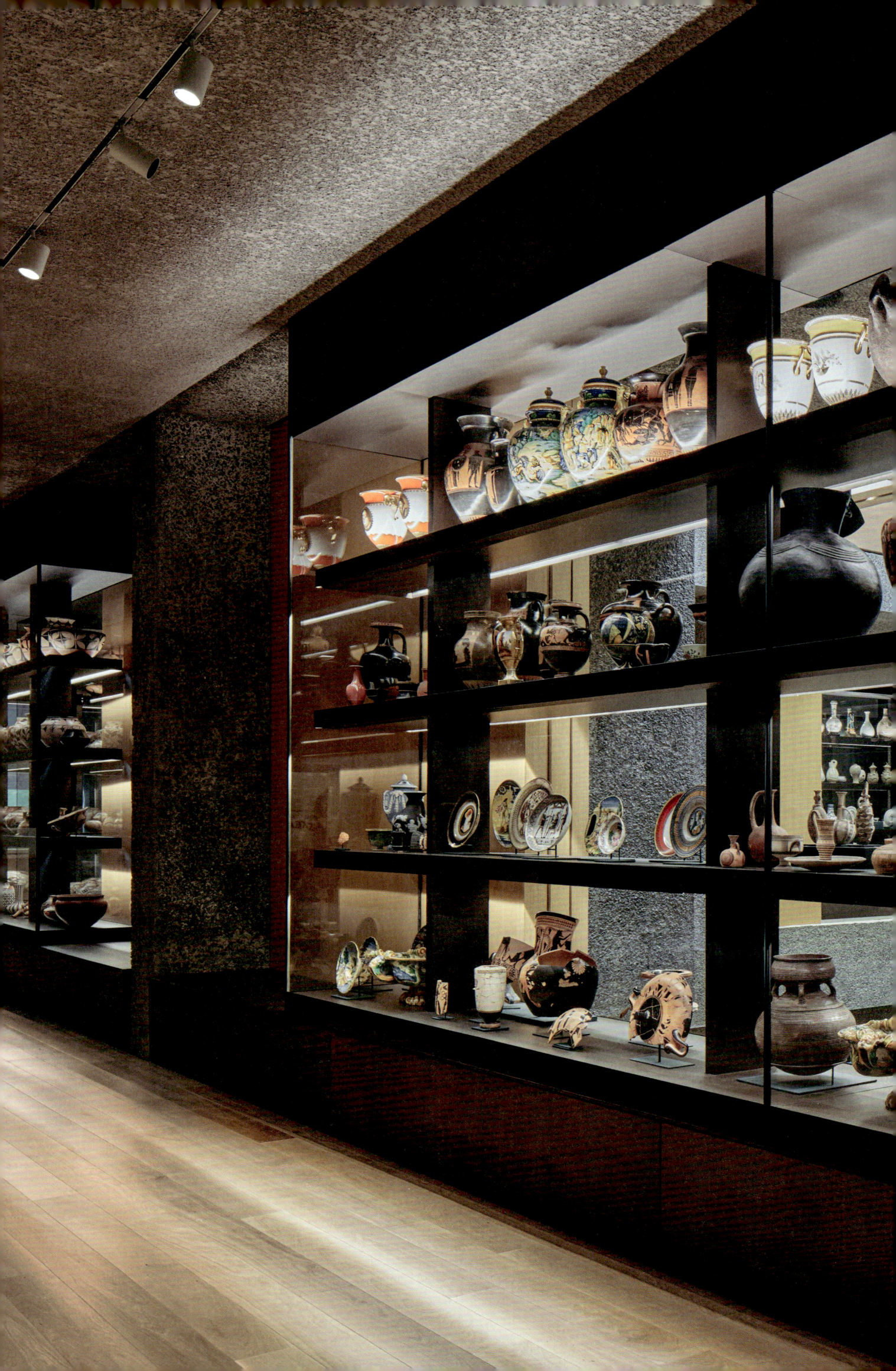

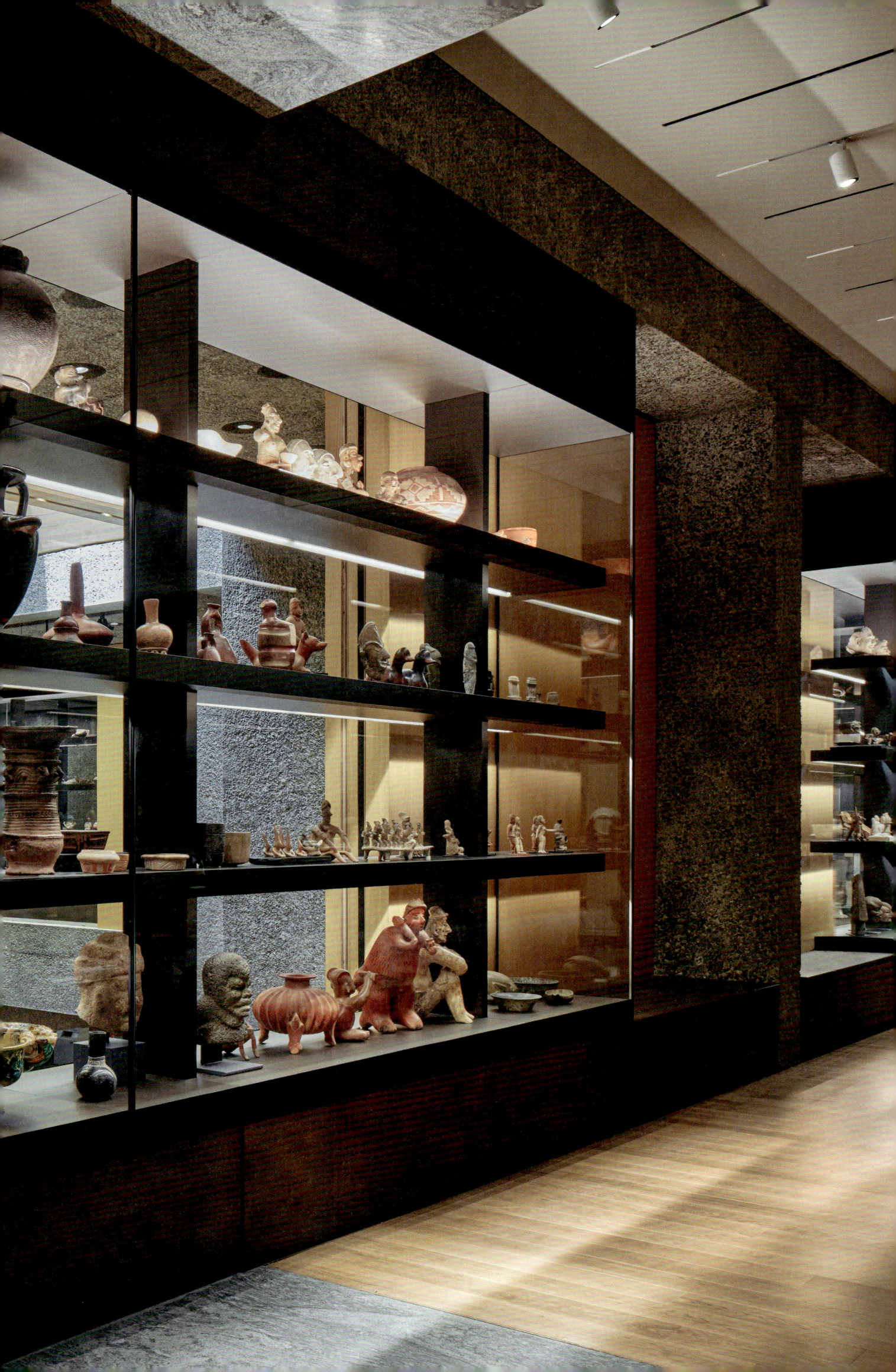

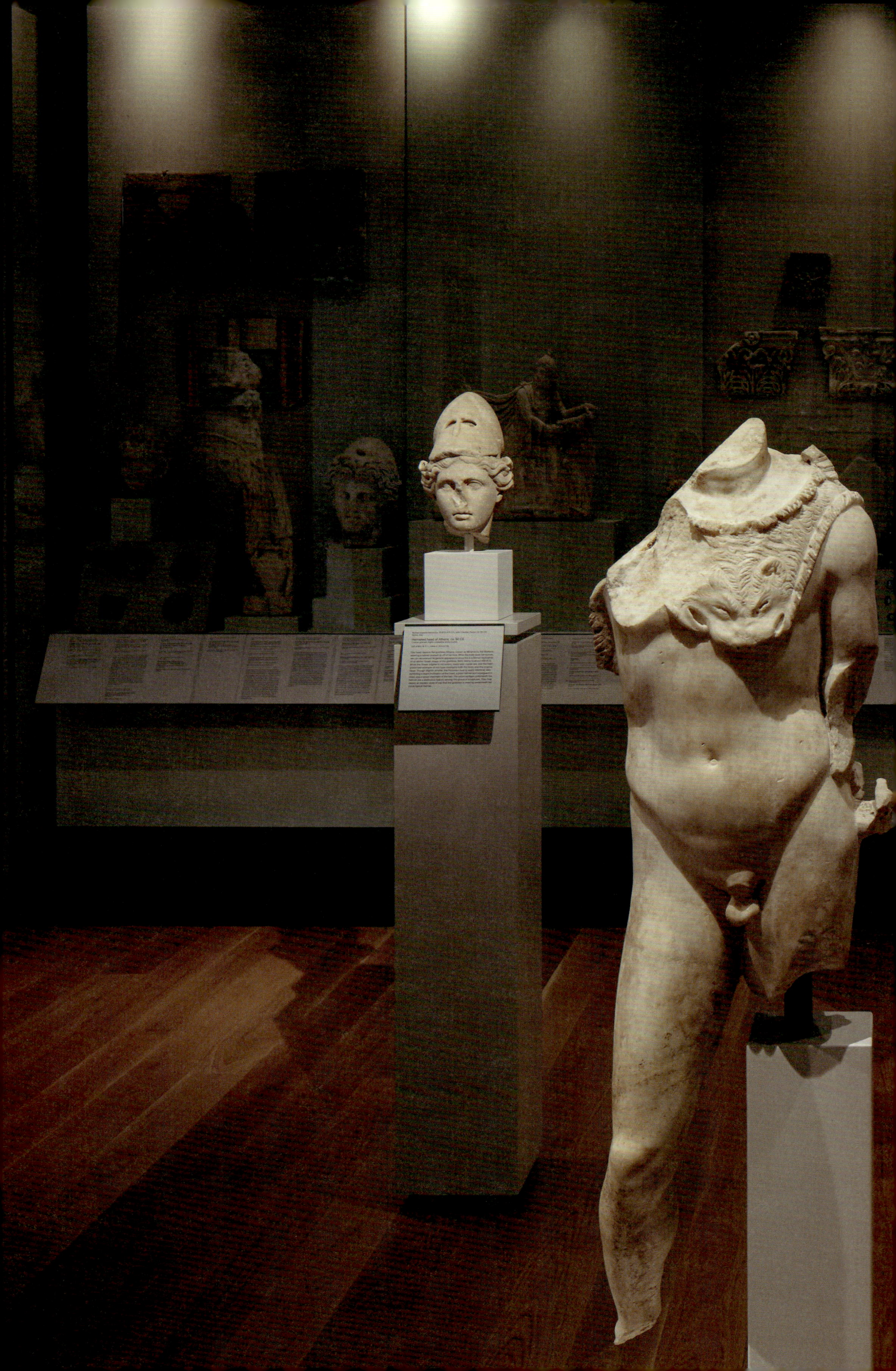

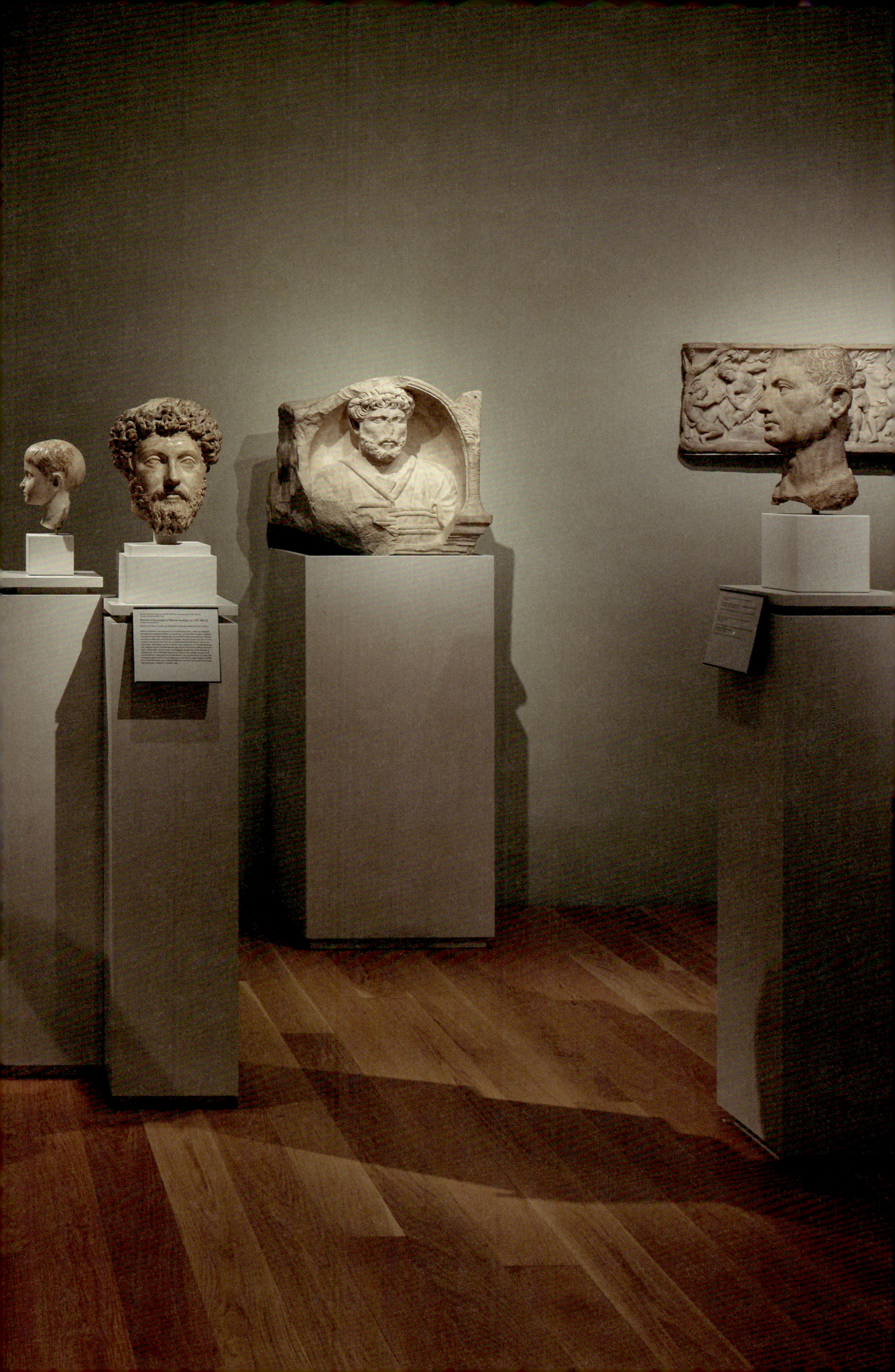

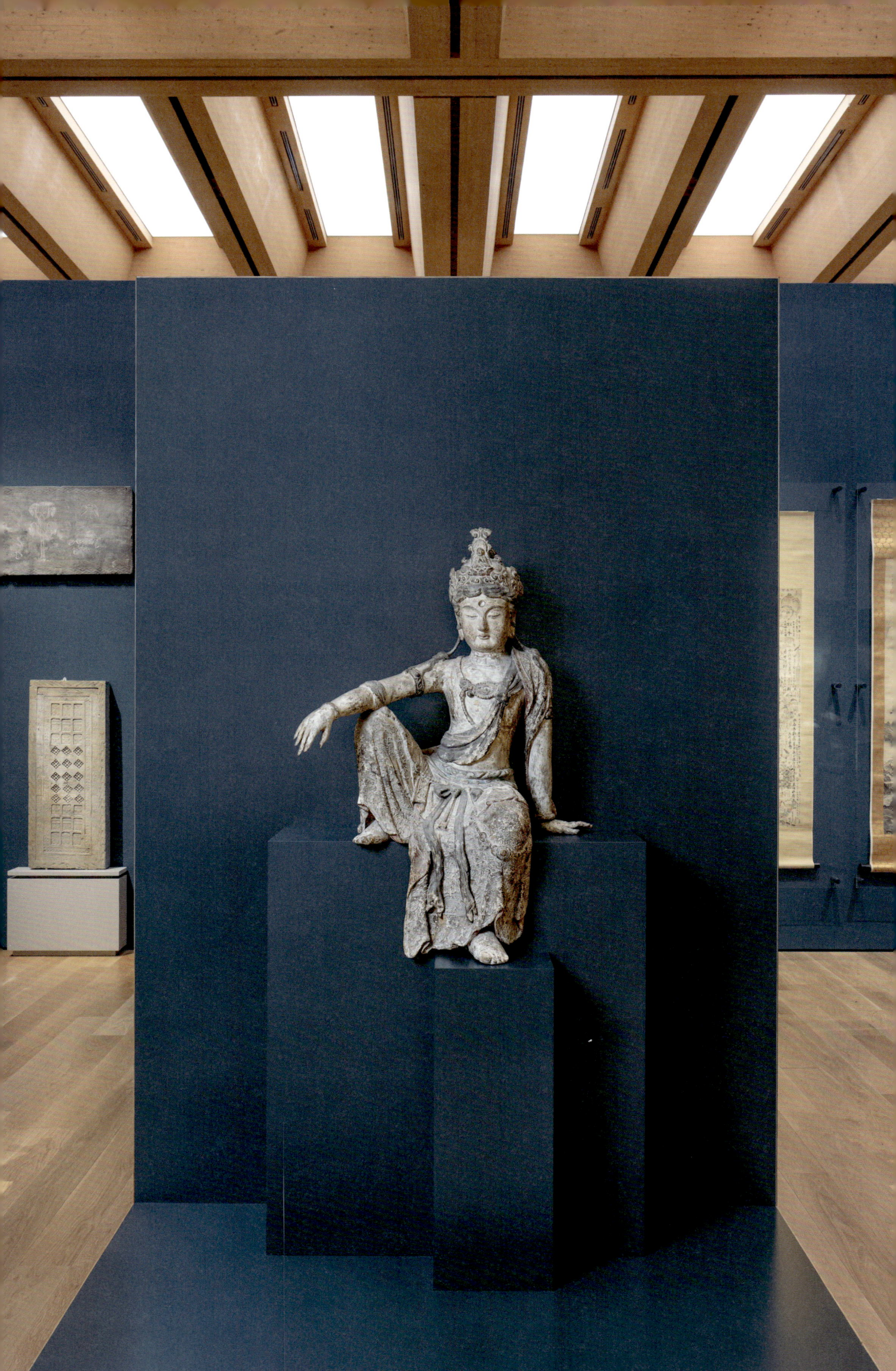

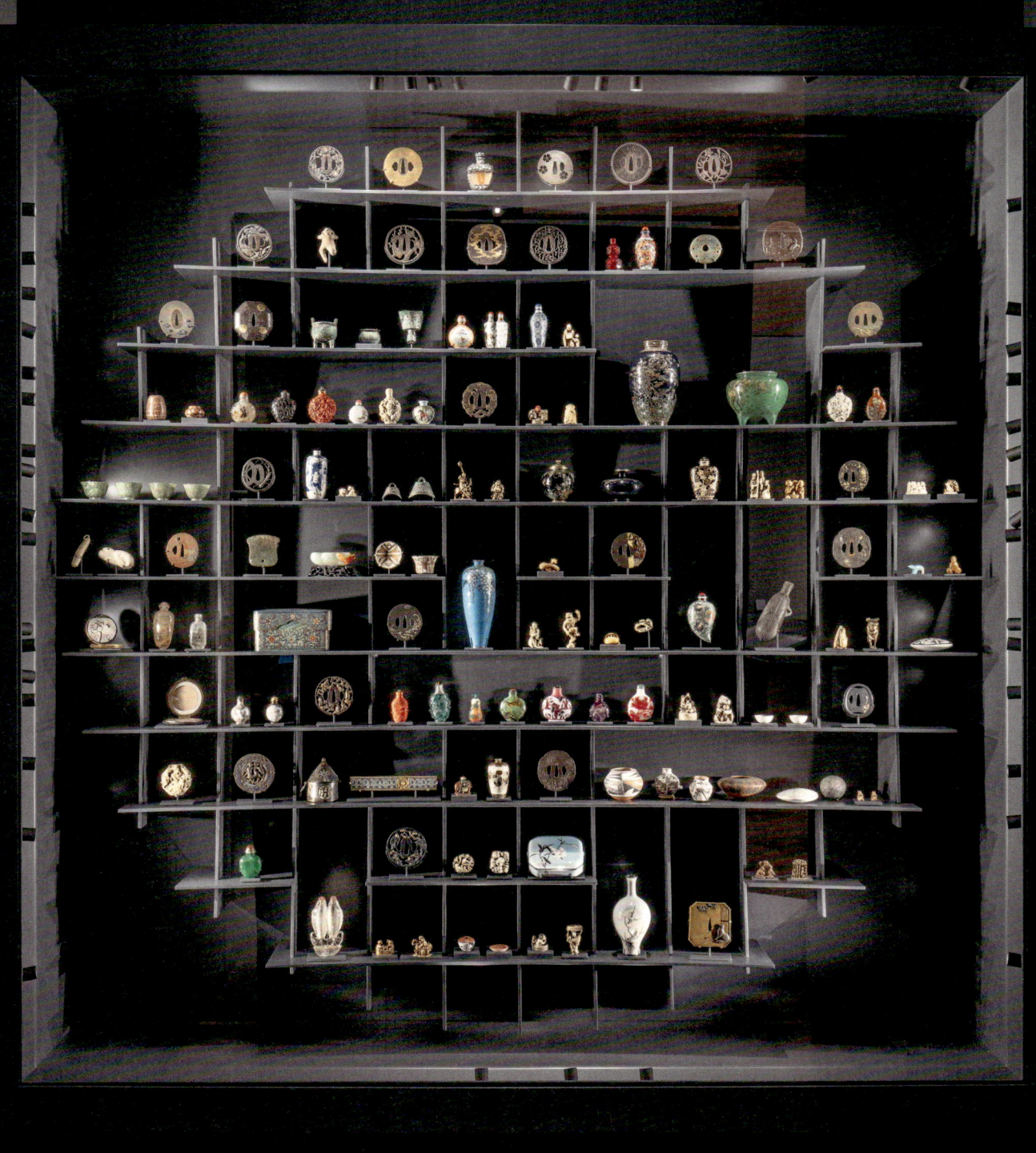

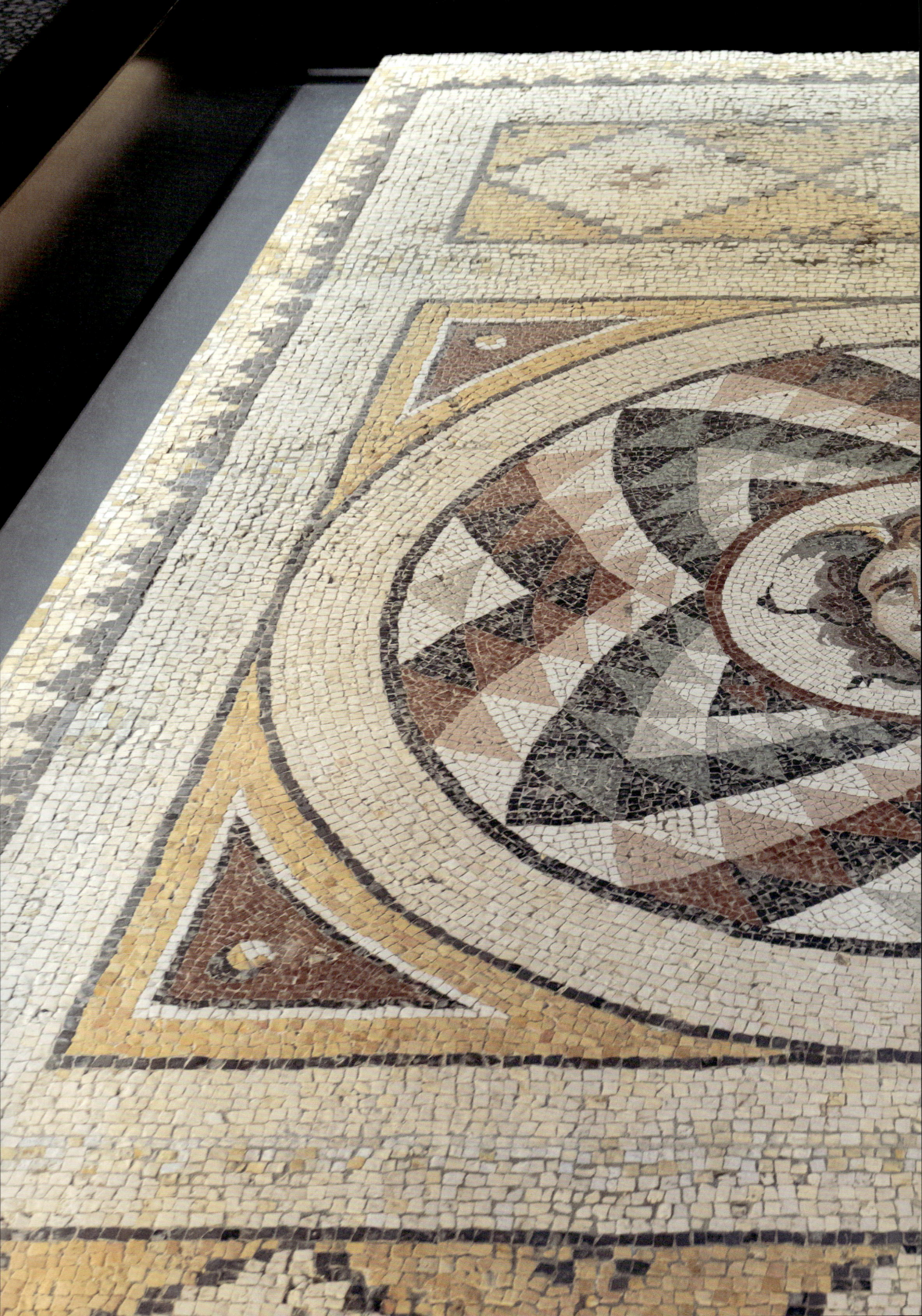

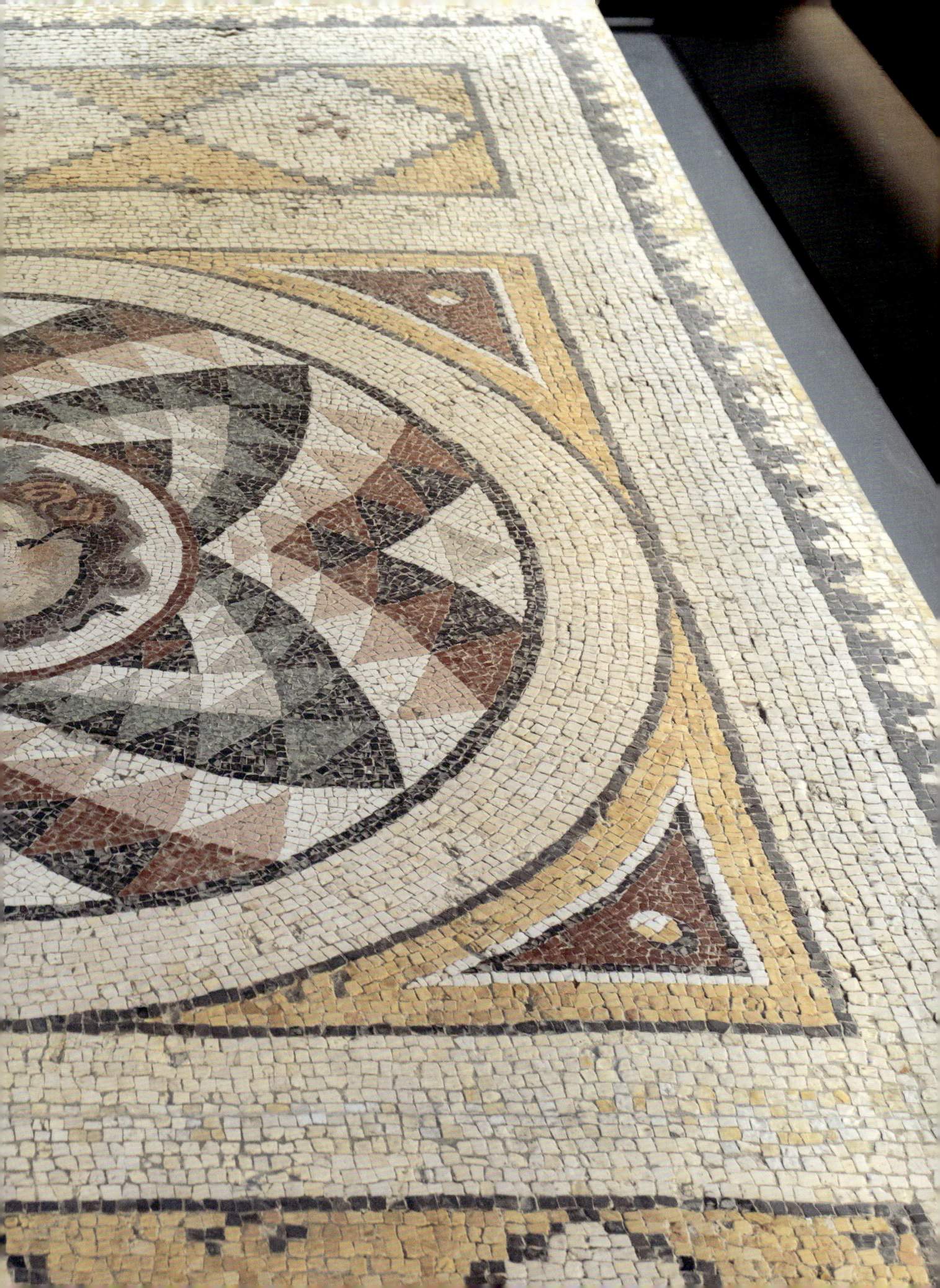

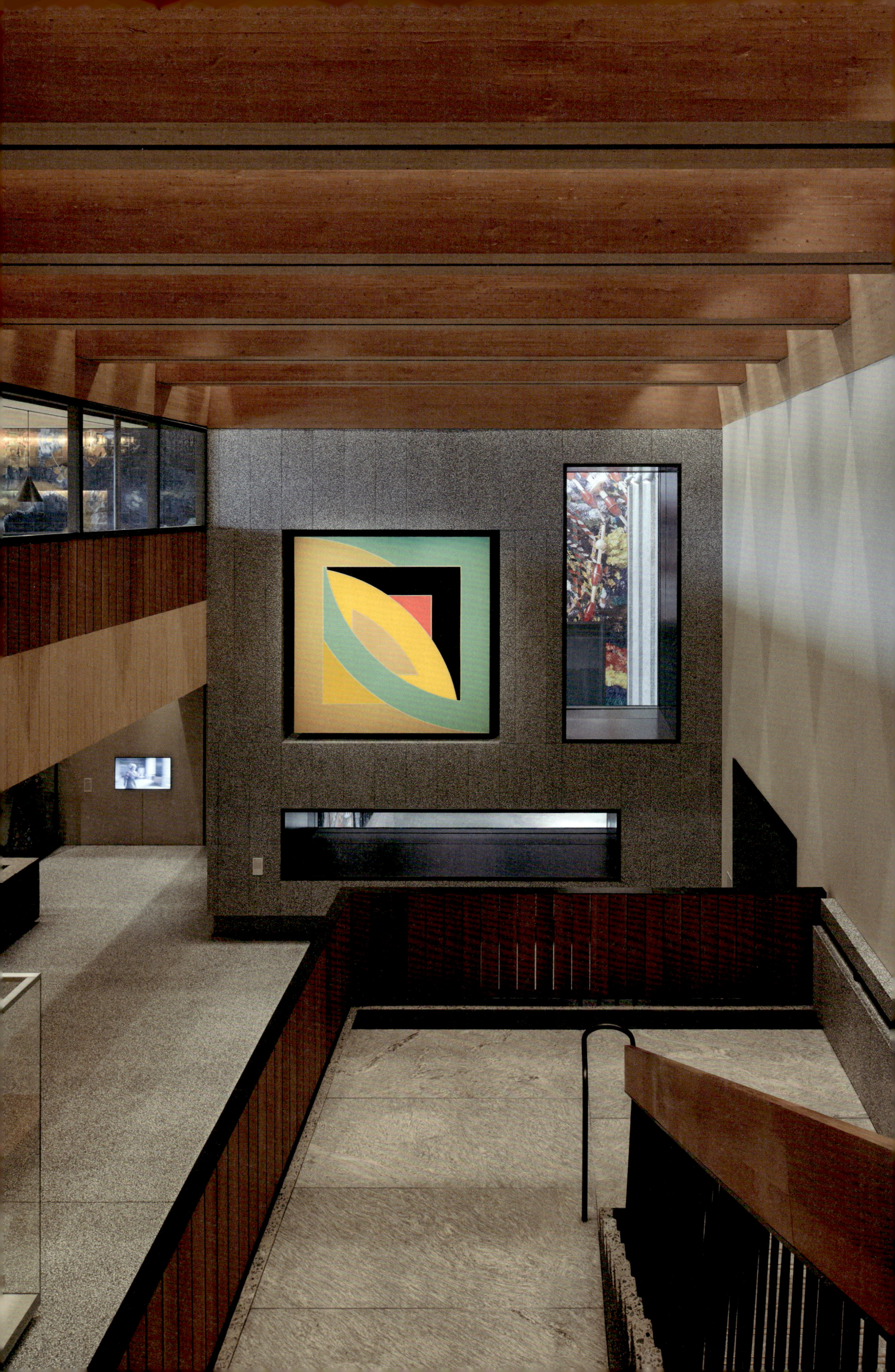

Balancing Context and Form

PAUL GOLDBERGER

With only a few exceptions, the most architecturally notable art museums of our time have been celebrated more for their qualities as formal objects than for what connections, if any, they make to their surroundings. Spiritual descendants of Frank Lloyd Wright's great Guggenheim Museum in New York, these museums are tours de force of sculptural beauty and spatial exuberance. While these qualities do not preclude an accommodating and welcoming environment in which to display works of art—it is a myth that architecturally assertive museums cannot also be sympathetic to the art they contain—deference to the art itself is only sometimes the driving factor in design. And whatever the qualities of its gallery spaces, the art museum that is designed primarily as a sculptural object is unlikely to be responsive to the physical context in which it is set. Indeed, why should it be? The art museum has always been a kind of secular cathedral, and long before the age of Louis Kahn's Kimbell Art Museum in Fort Worth (fig. 32), Frank Gehry's Guggenheim in

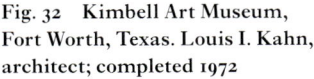

Fig. 32 Kimbell Art Museum, Fort Worth, Texas. Louis I. Kahn, architect; completed 1972

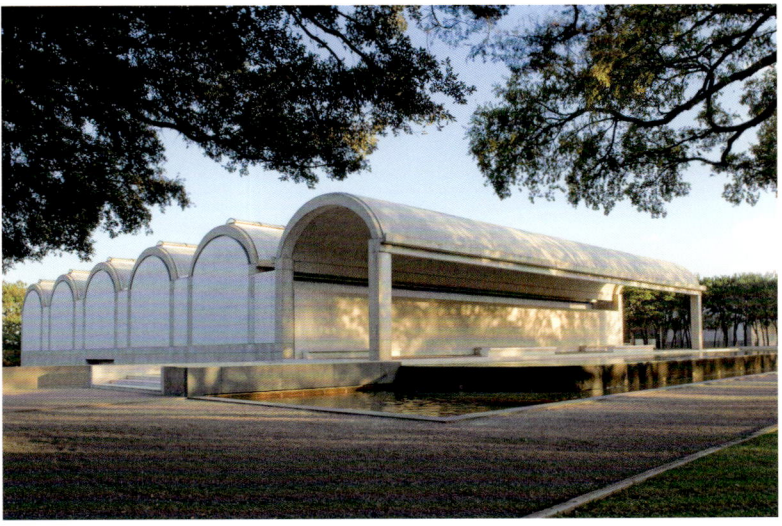

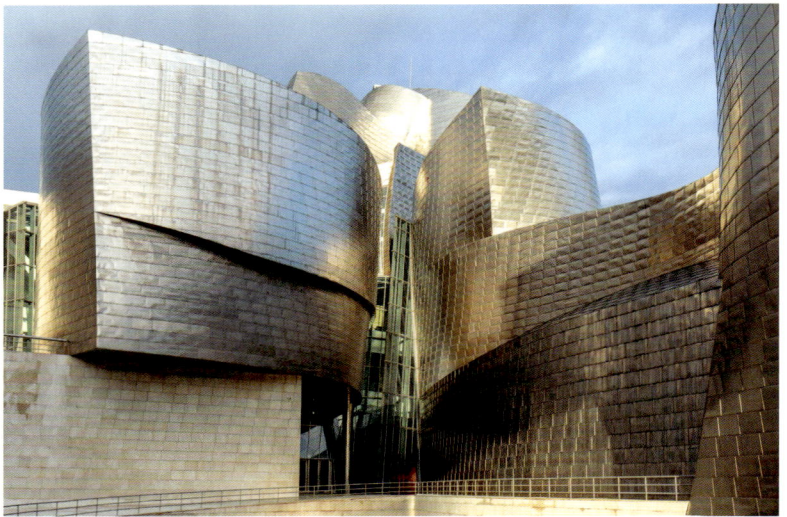

Fig. 33   Guggenheim Museum, Bilbao, Spain. Frank Gehry, architect; completed 1997

Bilbao (fig. 33), and Zaha Hadid's MAXXI in Rome (fig. 34), the museum was envisioned as something that would stand apart from the cityscape, not blend into it.

Particularly in the United States, the museum has been treated as a sanctuary for art that sought to convey both protection and uplift. It was a treasure house, a palazzo for art whose architecture was expected to communicate dignity, cultivation, power, and a certain remove from the hectic, day-to-day business of society (fig. 35). It is no accident that most art museums erected in American cities in the late nineteenth and early twentieth centuries were away from downtown centers, either in parks or adjacent to them, and generally near the quarter of town in which the rich resided. Art would be sullied, after all, by too close a connection to the commerce that enabled its purchase. Better to set it apart in a Greek temple or a Ruskinian Gothic jewel box, beauty protected by distance. The one thing the art museum did not symbolize was accessibility and openness to all.

This began, gradually, to change in the second half of the twentieth century, and it has accelerated in the twenty-first as the programs of museums have evolved toward greater openness and approachability and they have sought to shed their image as unwelcoming

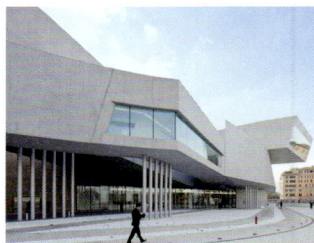

Fig. 34   MAXXI, Museo nazionale delle arti del XXI secolo, Rome. Zaha Hadid, architect; completed 2009

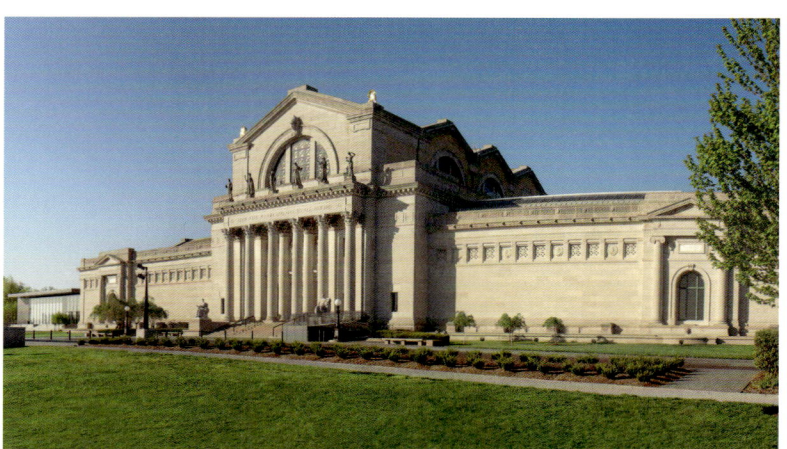

Fig. 35   Saint Louis Art Museum. Cass Gilbert, architect; completed 1904

institutions of the elite. But although no building type in our time has been more amenable to ambitious architectural expression than the art museum, a trend that has yielded no small number of buildings of serious note and even a few of genuine greatness, art museums have remained, in most cases, objects that stand apart. Neither the desire to make the art museum expressive of the most advanced thinking in architecture nor the attempt to make it more welcoming to an ever-more-diverse public has served to physically integrate the museum more fully into its surroundings.

Perhaps this should come as no surprise. After all, as the art museum plays an ever-larger role in the secular and social life of many communities, it would hardly be expected to recede physically into the background. Now, with the patrons of most contemporary museums charging their architects with the creation of buildings that assertively occupy the foreground, it has done quite the opposite. It matters little whether the architectural particulars are the powerful curves of titanium by Gehry in Bilbao (see fig. 33); the intricate, sweeping dome of Jean Nouvel in Abu Dhabi (fig. 36); or the lyrical trelliswork of Renzo Piano in Chicago (fig. 37): what they all have in common is a strong and distinctive formal presence. Now, even more than in the era in which we expected the art museum to take the form of a classical temple or an Italianate palazzo, the goal of museum design is likely to be the creation of a building that will be a striking and memorable object that can transcend its surroundings.

A college or university art museum is by nature somewhat different. However distinguished and wide-ranging its collection may be, its primary reason for being is to serve as an adjunct to an academic program, as an institution whose primary mission is to complement an education in the humanities by offering an engagement with some of the actual objects of study. In an age in which digital images prevail and so much teaching is virtual, the art museum within an educational institution is also a testament to the authentic, to the meaning and power of material objects in physical space, and as such, it has the potential to extend a halo over much of the academic program, not just the teaching of the history of art. And while the academic museum is

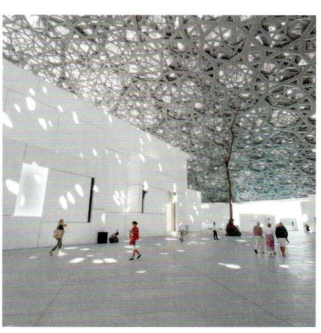

Fig. 36   Louvre, Abu Dhabi, United Arab Emirates. Jean Nouvel, architect; completed 2017

Fig. 37   The Modern Wing, The Art Institute of Chicago. Renzo Piano, architect; completed 2009

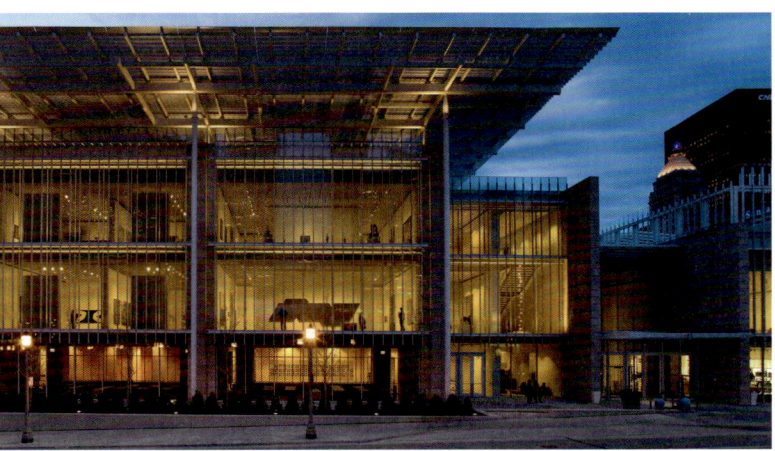

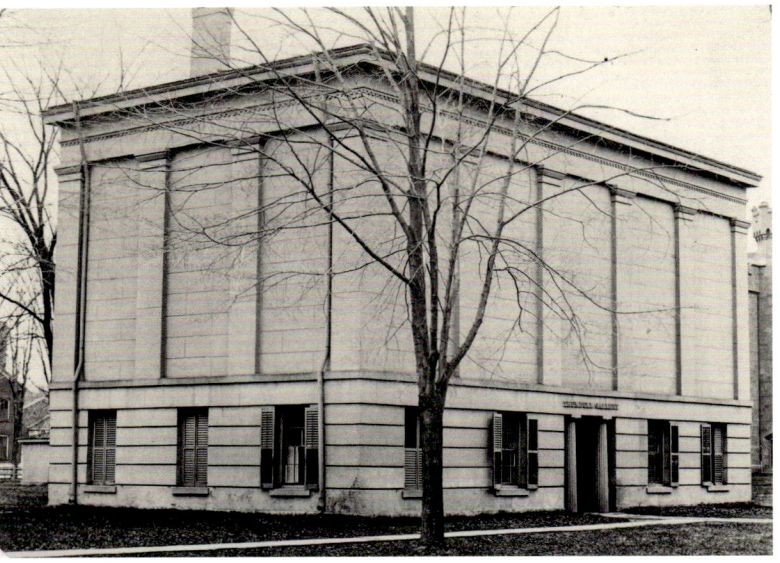

Fig. 38   Trumbull Gallery, Yale University, 1865. John Trumbull, architect; completed 1832. Sterling Memorial Library, Manuscripts and Archives, Yale University

unlikely to have the same high profile as the football stadium or the basketball arena, it also acts as a key point of intersection between the academic institution and the community that surrounds it. It serves as a welcome antidote to the isolation of the ivory tower, facing, as it were, both inward and outward, with a mission that is more subtle but no less demanding than that of the encyclopedic public art museum.

The Princeton University Art Museum, like every museum on a university or college campus, is a descendant of the Trumbull Gallery, the Neoclassical stone box erected in 1832 on the campus of Yale University (fig. 38). The first university art museum in the United States, it was created in one fell swoop when Yale purchased twenty-eight paintings and sixty miniature portraits from the artist John Trumbull, who then went on to design the building on the campus in which they were displayed. Trumbull's gallery is no longer extant, but it morphed into the Yale University Art Gallery, housed in a trio of buildings—one a Ruskinian Gothic structure from 1866 by Peter Bonnett Wight, one an eclectic Florentine and Romanesque Revival building of 1928 by Egerton Swartwout, and the third a modern building by Louis Kahn from 1953—that join together to create a majestic streetscape, not to mention a de facto seminar in American architectural history (fig. 39). The Kahn building was not only the architect's first important structure and a foundational moment in his career, it was also the first time that the program of the academic art museum was treated as the occasion to create a significant work of modern architecture.

Yale would be followed over the years by other academic institutions that, like civic museums, sought to house their art collections in buildings that would make a meaningful contribution to contemporary architecture—a list that includes, among others, art museums at Harvard by James Stirling and later by Renzo Piano; at the University of California, Berkeley, by Mario Ciampi and then by Diller Scofidio + Renfro; at Wellesley College by Rafael Moneo; at Purchase College, State University of New York, by Philip Johnson; at

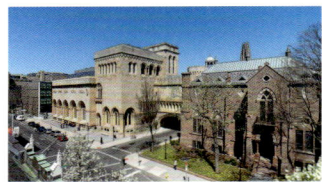

Fig. 39   Yale University Art Gallery. From left: Louis Kahn Building. Louis I. Kahn, architect; completed 1953 | Old Yale Art Gallery. Egerton Swartwout, architect; completed 1928 | Street Hall. Peter Bonnett Wight, architect; completed 1866

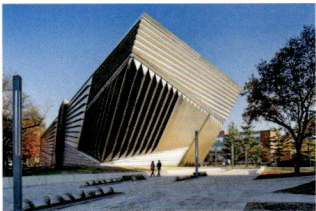

Fig. 40   The Eli and Edythe
Broad Art Museum, Michigan
State University. Zaha Hadid,
architect; completed 2012

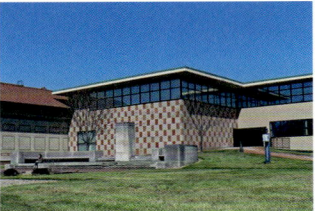

Fig. 41   Venturi addition, Allen
Memorial Art Museum, Oberlin
College. Robert Venturi, Denise
Scott Brown, and Associates,
architects; completed 1977

Fig. 42   Princeton University Art
Museum, 2012. Steinmann and
Cain, architects; completed 1966

Colby College by Frederick Fisher; at Dartmouth College by Charles
Moore and later by Tod Williams and Billie Tsien; at Michigan State
University by Zaha Hadid (fig. 40); at the University of Minnesota by
Frank Gehry; at Oberlin College by Venturi & Scott Brown (fig. 41);
and at Bowdoin College by Machado Silvetti.

Princeton, until now, has had no presence on this distinguished
list. The Princeton University Art Museum was initially housed in
an 1890 Romanesque Revival building by A. Page Brown, which was
expanded in the form of a Venetian Gothic addition by Ralph Adams
Cram in 1923 (see fig. 11), roughly contemporaneous with Swartwout's museum at Yale and not dissimilar to it, not only in terms of
architecture but also because it, too, was an academic building intended
both for the display of art and for teaching about it. Like Harvard and
Yale, Princeton before World War II reflected the tendency among almost all academic institutions to embrace traditional architecture,
a preference reinforced in the case of the Museum, surely, by the belief that art collecting was itself a fundamentally conservative pursuit.
Over the years Princeton's initial museum complex was expanded
and altered in innumerable ways by multiple architects, unfortunately
not to the urbane result achieved at Yale (fig. 42). Princeton's original
structure by Brown was demolished, and the Cram building partly
removed to make room for two less-than-graceful attempts at modernism, a banal International Style building by Steinmann and Cain in
1966 and a vaguely postmodern wing by the firm of Mitchell Giurgola
in 1989. Neither of these additions represented the high architectural
ambitions or the fullness of concept of any of the better modern academic museums, and the effect of both was to heighten the sense of the
museum as a messy jumble (fig. 43). Raymond P. Rhinehart, discuss-
ing the Museum in his 1999 architectural guide to Princeton, asked,
"What can you say about a building that seems to have been assembled from pieces rather than designed? Like Frankenstein, the sutures
are clearly visible."[1]

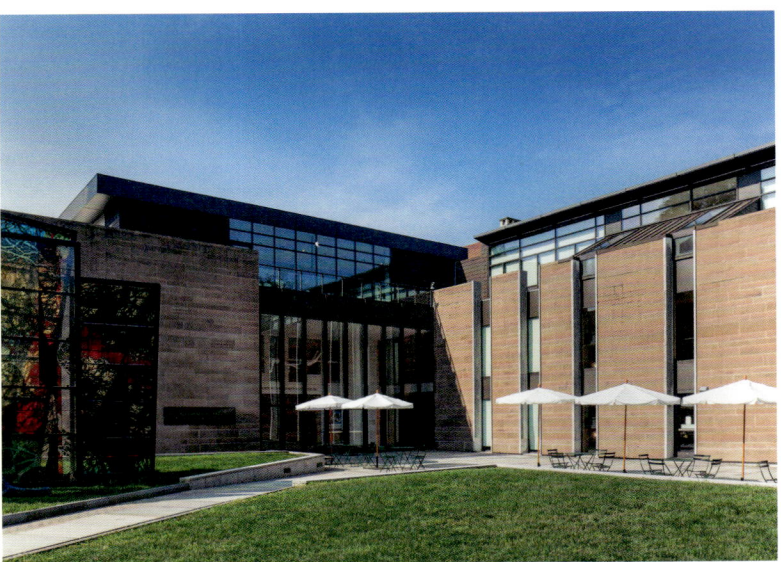

By then little of value within Cram's historic structure was left, even though a portion of it was nominally still a part of the awkward hybrid of old and new. It was not surprising that as the Museum envisioned its future the University decided that it had no choice but to embark on another rethinking of the complex and retained the architect Frederick Fisher to study the possibilities. The conclusion of Fisher's studies was that the incoherence of the existing hodgepodge of buildings containing the Museum and its related academic programs would not be easily correctable by any means other than entirely new construction and that an expansion in the form of yet another addition would only make the problem worse.

But if the situation called for an entirely new art museum, should it be on the same site as the existing museum? That would be an especially challenging undertaking, given the Museum's historic site. The Princeton campus is not urban in a technical sense, and most of it is not crisscrossed by public streets. In comparison to the settings of Yale or Harvard or Columbia, it could surely be called suburban if not rural. But Princeton's campus is in fact densely built up and has been getting denser by the year, and the site that the University's art museum has occupied since its first building was constructed in 1890 is set behind two of Princeton's most famous buildings, the nearly twin classical temples built in 1889 for the Whig and Cliosophic Societies, near the venerable nineteenth-century stone dormitories Edwards Hall and Dod Hall and roughly on an axis with the University's oldest building, Nassau Hall, a sprawling Georgian structure from the eighteenth century. The Museum is on a straight line from what is traditionally seen as Princeton's front door, and McCosh Walk, the best known of the many pathways that form a network of pedestrian paths through the campus, runs beside it.

Inserting a vastly expanded new museum structure into this central, heavily built-up setting was going to be, at the very least, an act of architectural microsurgery; space was tight, and the older buildings around the site already gave it strong definition. It was reasonable to question whether the architect of this new project, whoever it would turn out to be, would have enough room to maneuver either conceptually or physically. Before this project began, Princeton considered relocating the Museum to a site at the western edge of the campus where it would have been a neighbor to a new arts center designed by the architect Steven Holl, as well as to Princeton's McCarter Theatre, joining with them to create what could have been a campus arts district. But unlike the arts center, which has few public spaces, the Museum at Princeton—like its peers at Yale, Harvard, and many other academic institutions—is intended for a general audience as much as for students and faculty. It has never been anywhere other than the center of the campus since its founding in the nineteenth century, and it plays a critical role in the University's public outreach. James Steward, the director, argued strongly that the Museum's role as part of Princeton's public face justified keeping it where it had always been.

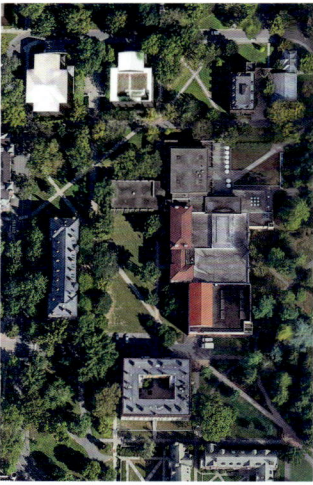

Fig. 43   Aerial view of Princeton University's campus, at center right the Princeton University Art Museum, McCormick Hall, and Marquand Library, 2019

Steward's view carried the day, and that, in turn, began to define and focus the architectural problem. Locating a vastly expanded art museum in the center of a dense campus seemed to call for a choice: The Museum's architect (who at that point had not been selected) either would have to be willing to make a significant degree of accommodation to the complexities of the building's context or would have to make a conscious decision to ignore the surroundings in favor of an autonomous, purely sculptural object. There were risks to both options. The former choice could yield a dull building that—by virtue of trying too hard to defer to the multiple nearby buildings of varying periods, styles, and quality around it, not to mention the requirement of fitting a large and complex program into a tight site—would have little character of its own. The latter choice, a more sculptural building that did not appear to pay much heed to what was around it, posed the risk not of too little character but of too much. If Princeton placed a dramatic building that had the potential to be a powerful cultural magnet at the center of its venerable campus, however compelling it might have been as an object in its own right—and however much it could be said to be in tune with trends in contemporary museum design—it could challenge, not to say overwhelm, the plethora of old and sometimes distinguished structures all around it, competing with them for attention and, ironically, replicating in different form the discordancy that has long plagued this museum.

In 2018, after an extensive search process, Princeton awarded the commission for the building to Adjaye Associates, the firm founded and led by David Adjaye, the Ghanaian British architect who was the lead designer on the team that built the Smithsonian's National Museum of African American History and Culture on the National Mall in Washington, DC (see fig. 28), with the firm of Cooper Robertson appointed as executive architects.[2] The design Adjaye produced, with the assistance of his colleagues Joe Franchina and Marc McQuade, was unveiled in 2020. It makes clear not only that Adjaye was aware of the unusual challenges of this site but also that he chose to respond not by selecting either the option of deferring to context or that of producing an autonomous and assertive design. He instead decided to demonstrate that these two approaches need not be mutually exclusive. The design of the Princeton University Art Museum at once follows the paradigm of the contemporary museum—it is surely a distinctive and memorable object—and departs from it, since it makes no effort to separate itself from its surroundings and, in fact, allows aspects of the campus to dictate much of its form. This new museum is both an elegant object central to the Princeton University campus and a set of pathways and connections subtly woven into the daily life of the campus. It is both prominent and understated, both a foreground object and a large structure that recedes into the fabric of the campus. Adjaye made the decision, in effect, to attempt to have it both ways.

But it was unquestionably the first option, responding to context, that set forth the basic parameters of Adjaye's design. He made the

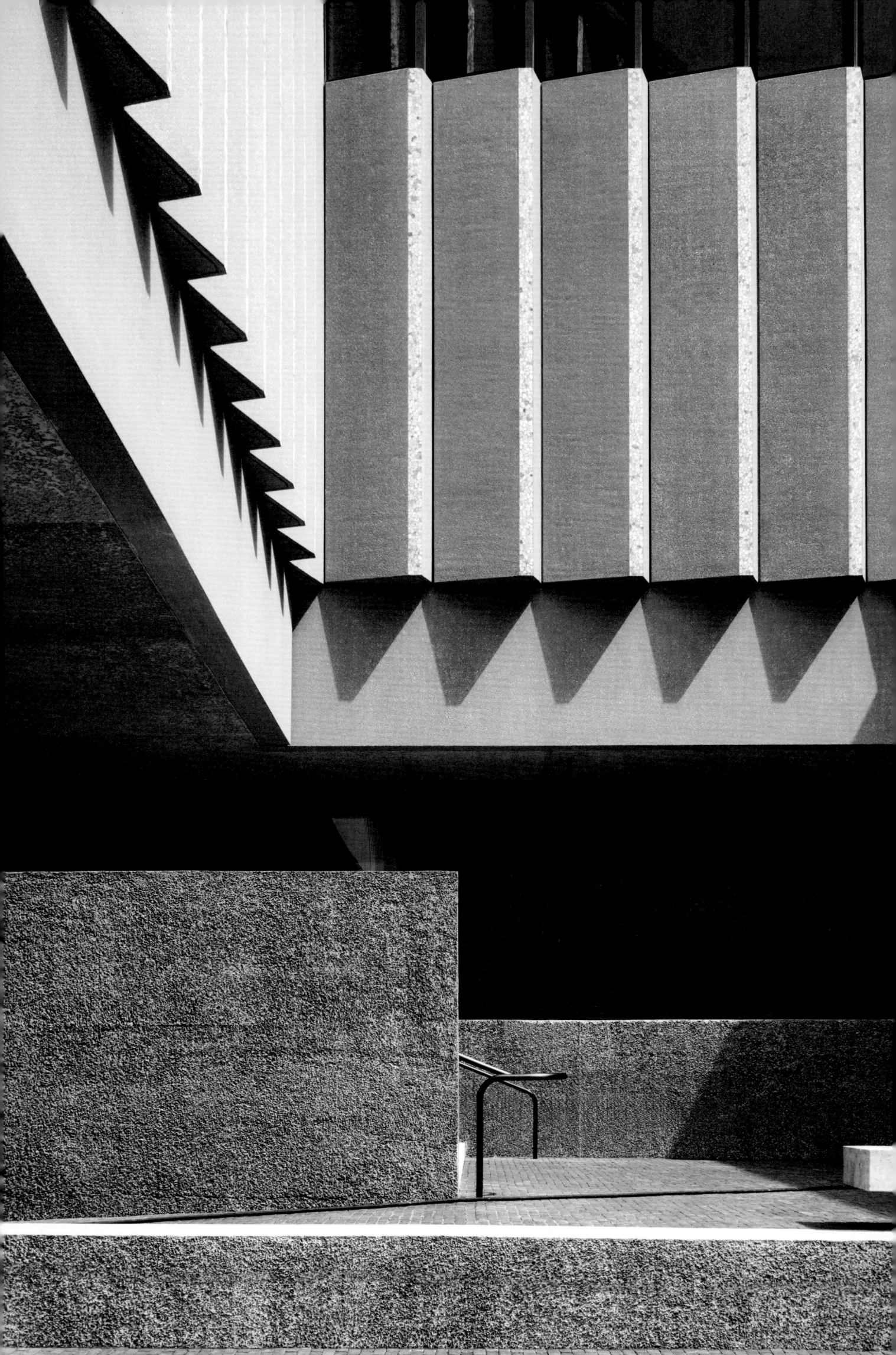

Museum's complex surroundings, not just the existing architecture of the campus but even more its various pedestrian circulation patterns, into the primary formal generator for the project, which he conceived as consisting of nine separate gallery pavilions for the display of art, all of which are elevated slightly above ground level to allow pedestrian circulation to pass beneath the building's overhangs. Eight of the pavilions are entirely new; one is a portion of the 1966 building that was retained and resheathed to conform more closely to the architecture of the new building. The multiple pavilions serve both to break up the scale of the building, which more than doubles the size of the previous museum, and to give the various portions of the Museum's diverse collection a degree of individual identity.

Elevating the pavilions allowed them to appear, at least in part, to float over the outdoor pathways and terraces, and it also gave Adjaye the opportunity to give the building an elaborate, even majestic, canyon-like entry court that leads to a grand staircase to the gallery pavilions above. The court, which is defined in part by a monumentally scaled piece by the artist Nick Cave that was commissioned for the building, doubles as a main north–south pedestrian route through the site, connecting with existing pedestrian paths on the campus. There are other routes as well that slip under the building—though a better description would be "across the site"—offering glimpses of the art and activity within. The Museum at ground level is a network of pathways, landscaped terraces, and public spaces, giving nearly equal priority to those who intend to enter and go up to the level of the gallery pavilions and those who are just passing through.

It is hard not to think here of Le Corbusier's extraordinary Carpenter Center at Harvard of 1963 (fig. 44), not an academic museum but more of a studio building designed for film and the visual arts. Le Corbusier exploited a tight site between Quincy and Prescott Streets on the Harvard campus by weaving a pedestrian ramp through his concrete structure, creating a connection between the two streets that would serve as a shortcut as well as an opportunity for passersby to see the work being done by artists in the building. Adjaye, like Le Corbusier, uses circulation as a device to expose his building and the activity

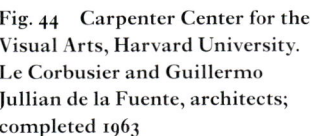

Fig. 44   Carpenter Center for the Visual Arts, Harvard University. Le Corbusier and Guillermo Jullian de la Fuente, architects; completed 1963

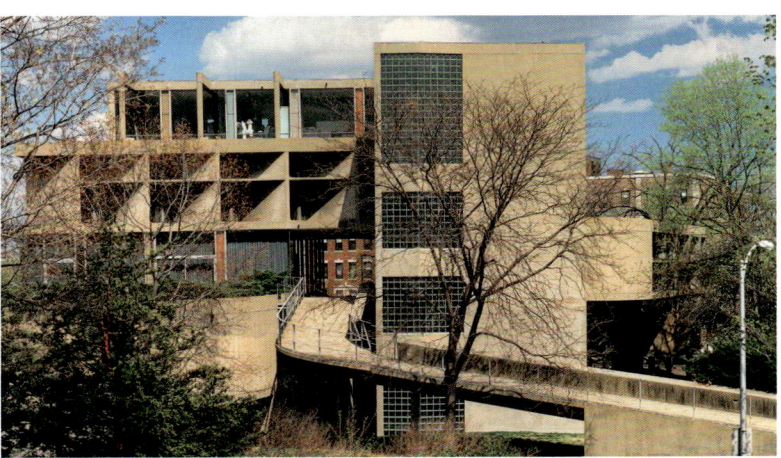

within it to a broader community than its actual users and, in doing so, strengthens the connection between the building and its surroundings. In both buildings, the notion of urbanistic connection is treated as real physical experience and as a metaphor for engagement.

The Princeton University Art Museum also shares with the Carpenter Center an intentional ambiguity about what constitutes its primary facade. Adjaye has referred to his design as being a composition consisting of all fronts and no backs, and Le Corbusier could have made much the same point about his building. Both are meant to be approached from any direction and to present a first impression of equal value no matter what the vantage point—though Le Corbusier's building is conceived far more as a freestanding sculptural object than Adjaye's, which seeks to show a degree of deference to its neighbors.

Still, both buildings in their way remind us that a work of architecture need not look like the buildings around it to be responsive to them. To speak of Adjaye's architecture here as contextual, then, is not to say that it closely resembles anything else on the Princeton campus. It does not, but the exterior that Adjaye has designed acknowledges the complexity of its highly varied architectural surroundings in meaningful ways. Although the facade of the Museum is not precisely like anything around it, it echoes several key aspects of many of its neighbors: it is built of masonry, it is richly textured, and its articulation is largely vertical. It bespeaks a solidity, even as it embodies openness and circulation, and it is in the balance of these different things that the strength of the design lies. The vertical emphasis of the facades is key. Many of the facades of buildings at Princeton are dominated by vertical elements—obviously the Gothic ones but also more recent buildings that Minoru Yamasaki, Rick Joy, and other architects have given this campus (fig. 45), which has no tall buildings but so many smaller ones whose facades emphasize verticality that one might almost describe Princeton as a horizontal assemblage of vertical elements. Adjaye's facades consist for the most part of vertical panels of medium-gray reinforced concrete mixed with granite aggregate, which are slightly canted—that is, set at a slight diagonal—with their long sides left rough and their short ends highly polished, making the two finishes read almost as different materials. Crafted to look almost like slats, they are alive in the play of light, with a quiet reserve and measured rhythm that relates both to the Museum's classical neighbors, such as Whig Hall and Clio Hall, and to the heavier, more textured stone of the Romanesque and Gothic Revival buildings nearby (fig. 46).

If Adjaye's careful composition of windowless boxes floating above an entry plaza even loosely evokes any other piece of architecture, it is one that was much farther from Princeton than the Carpenter Center is: the striking but *retardataire* campus from 1965 of the Los Angeles County Museum of Art designed by William Pereira, a set of vaguely classicizing pavilions that are remembered now as having had a certain midcentury modern panache (fig. 47). The resemblance is only superficial, to be sure; Adjaye's building is vastly more sophisticated

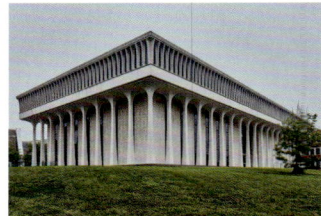

Fig. 45   Robertson Hall, Princeton University. Minoru Yamasaki, architect; completed 1965

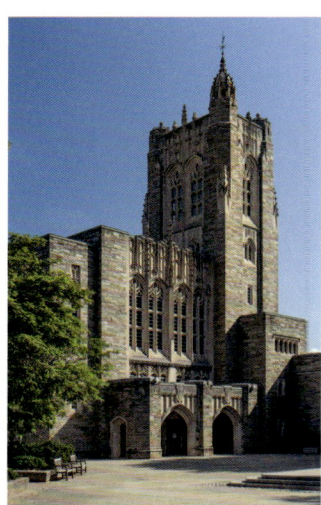

Fig. 46   Harvey S. Firestone Memorial Library, Princeton University. Robert B. O'Connor and Walter H. Kilham Jr., architects; completed 1948

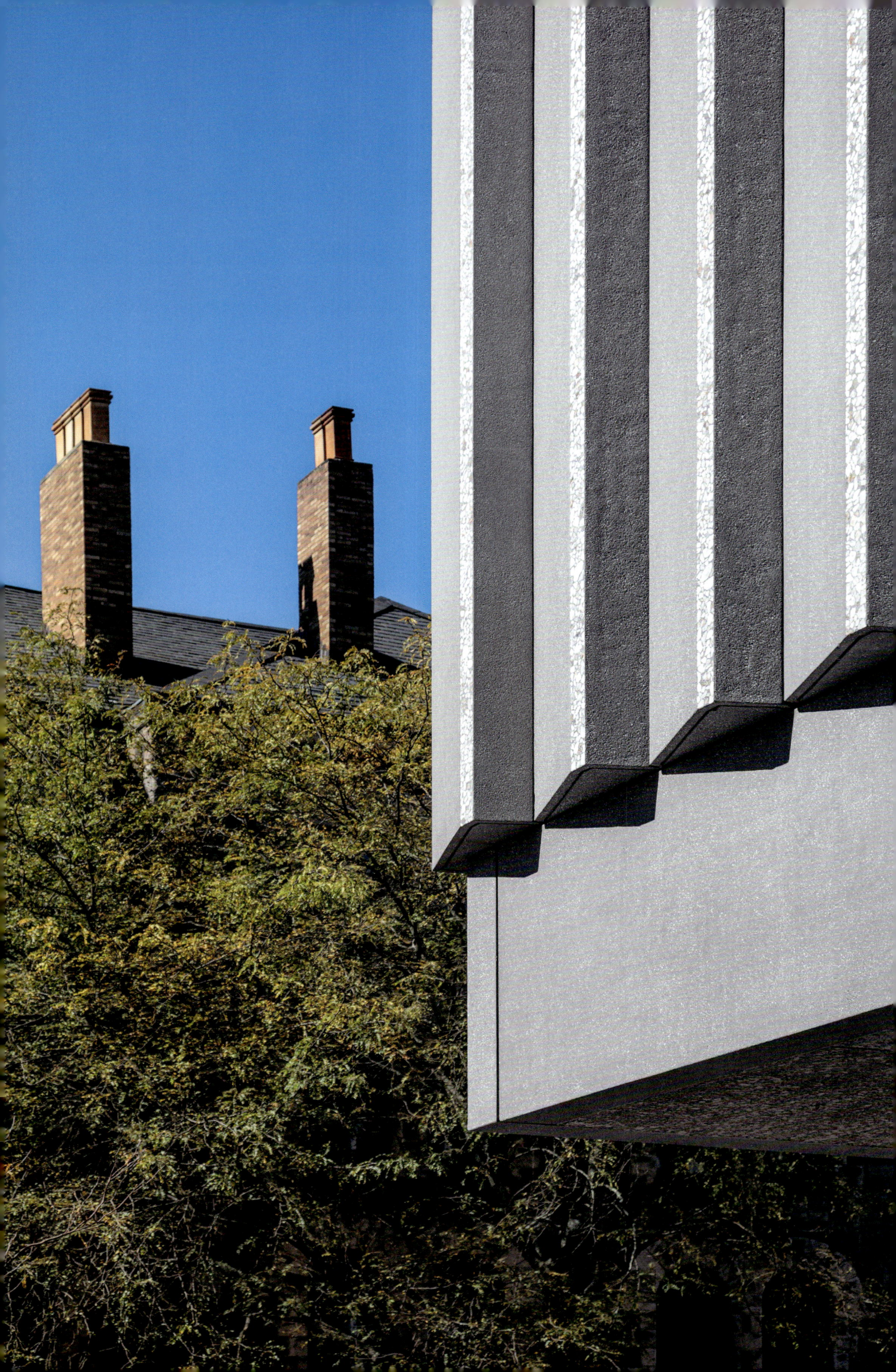

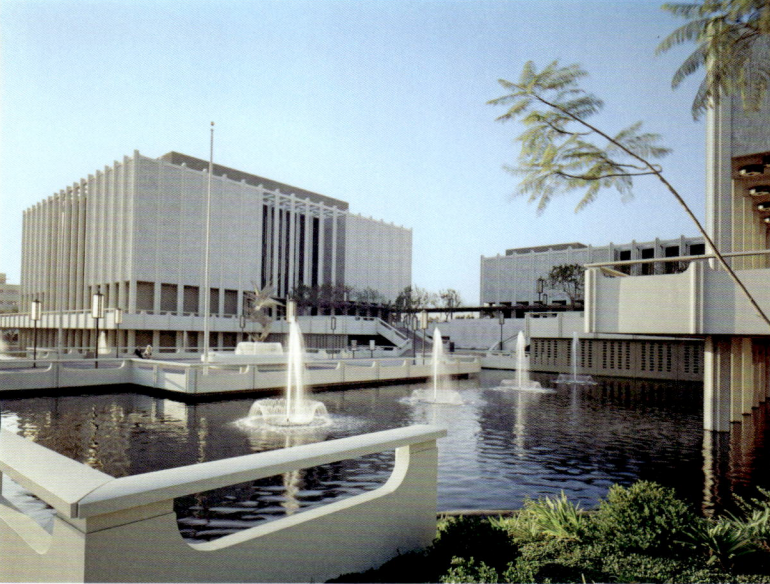

Fig. 47   Los Angeles County
Museum of Art. William Pereira,
architect; completed 1965

than Pereira's, both without and within, and it indulges in none of the decorative pseudoclassicism that weakened the Los Angeles buildings. Moreover, because the Princeton University Art Museum, like the Carpenter Center, is organized around the idea of facilitating connections with its surroundings, it is fundamentally in opposition to Pereira's pavilions, which aspired more to be like an Acropolis floating above Wilshire Boulevard than a work of architecture that acknowledged the city around them. Still, Pereira's Los Angeles County Museum of Art (which was demolished in 2020 to make way for a new museum designed by Peter Zumthor that is very much a foreground building) did exude a kind of pictorial verve, and it is this memorable quality that Adjaye has managed to call to mind.

The Princeton pavilions are large and mostly opaque, but their texture and elevation above the ground make them seem relatively light nevertheless, and the building sits comfortably in its tight quarters. The entry court, which offers views into the building, leads both to a central hall that rises through the height of the building, called the Grand Hall, which will double as a lecture hall and event space, and to the handsome monumental staircase that brings access to the gallery pavilions themselves, which constitute a sort of *piano nobile*.

Here the references are clear to another significant work of museum architecture, Louis Kahn's Yale Center for British Art (fig. 48), which opened in 1977 across the street from Kahn's celebrated building for the Yale University Art Gallery. This is the one instance in which Adjaye's inspiration seems to have been conscious, not to say almost literal in some cases: you can imagine him walking through Kahn's galleries, which like those at Princeton are on the second floor and lit from above by natural light coming through a deep coffered ceiling framed in wood, and taking note of how brilliantly Kahn combined the strength and solidity of masonry with the warmth of wood. Adjaye did the same, with different wood and different details and, in the case of many of the gallery pavilions, a larger, more institutional scale. Adjaye, like Kahn, understood how the interplay between wood and stone could be both subtle and sensual, and he let that set the tone for the galleries and, indeed, for the entire interior.

The gallery pavilions generally have no natural light except through the rooftop solar tubes that diffuse light from above, and they vary in size to accommodate the needs of different portions of the Museum's collection. The larger pavilions for contemporary art will have temporary dividing walls that can be reconstructed in response to changes in what is on display, as in most museums. The circulation spaces between the pavilions—many of which are used inventively to display portions of the collection—do not turn inward to the same extent and have frequent openings, offering views outside that frame key aspects of the campus landscape as well as the surrounding architecture and, in one case, works of monumental sculpture, all of which enhance the larger goal of deepening the sense of connection between the Museum and the rest of the campus. The interior also includes a small, elegant restaurant perched on the top of the building; a shop; and the usual array of spaces for art storage, conservation, and administration. There is also a large outdoor sculpture terrace, and

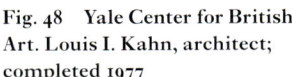

Fig. 48　Yale Center for British Art. Louis I. Kahn, architect; completed 1977

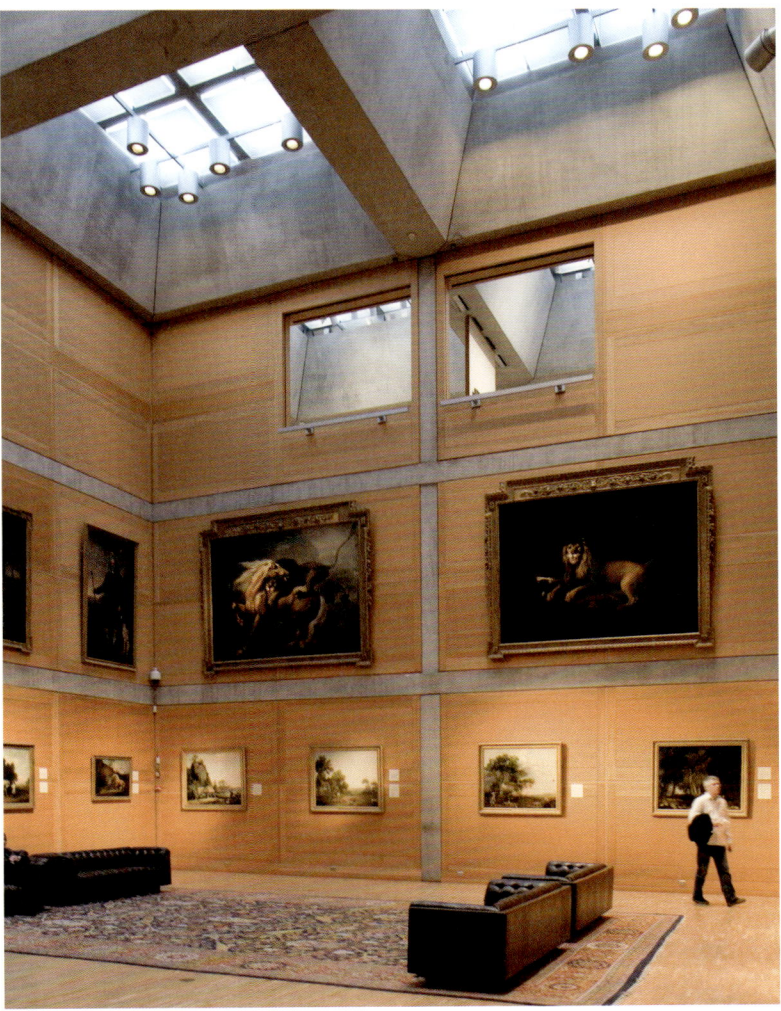

some of the areas below the raised pavilions are intended to serve as public event spaces.

At one point there is also an exquisite room lined entirely in wood, with built-in benches and views to the campus landscape. This space, smaller than any of the galleries, contains bare walls and a single work of art on the ceiling—a site-specific painting by Jane Irish—and yet it embodies Adjaye's ideas for this building more fully, and expresses them more concisely, than any other space in the Museum. This elegant room is a space for contemplation, a place poised between the art and the architecture, between the inside and the outside, between the public and the private, and between this building and the campus around it. It is a space to ponder what is, in the end, the essential idea underlying the design of this museum: the notion of balance and what it can mean in the making of architecture.

1   Raymond P. Rhinehart, *Princeton University: An Architectural Tour* (Princeton Architectural Press, 1999), 100.

2   In 2023, after the design had been fully completed and the building was under construction, Adjaye was accused of sexual misconduct by three women who had formerly been in his employ, and he withdrew from active involvement in the day-to-day supervision of the project. The Museum's completion was overseen by Joe Franchina and Marc McQuade, senior architects in Adjaye's New York office, who had been involved in the project from its beginning.

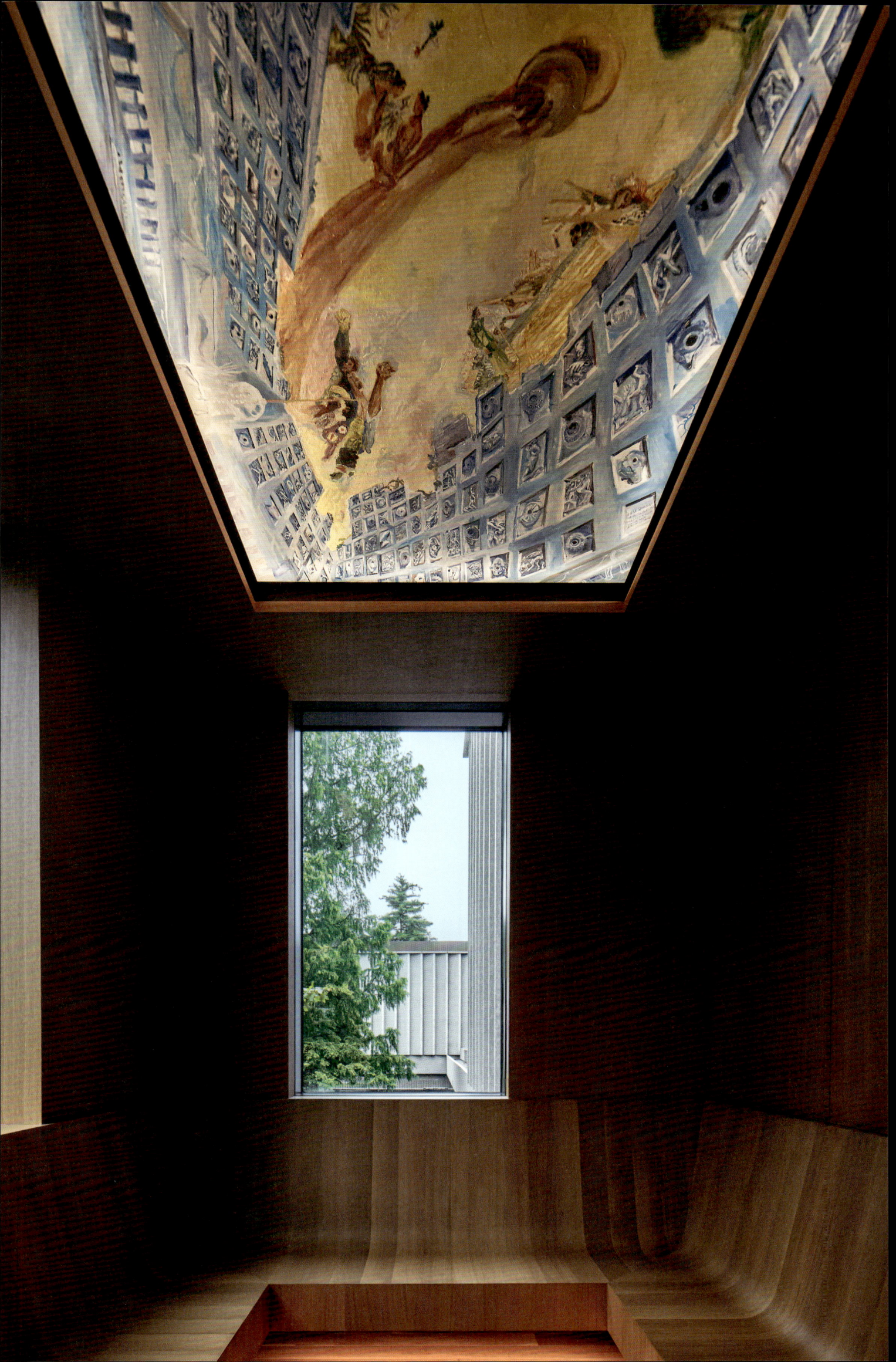

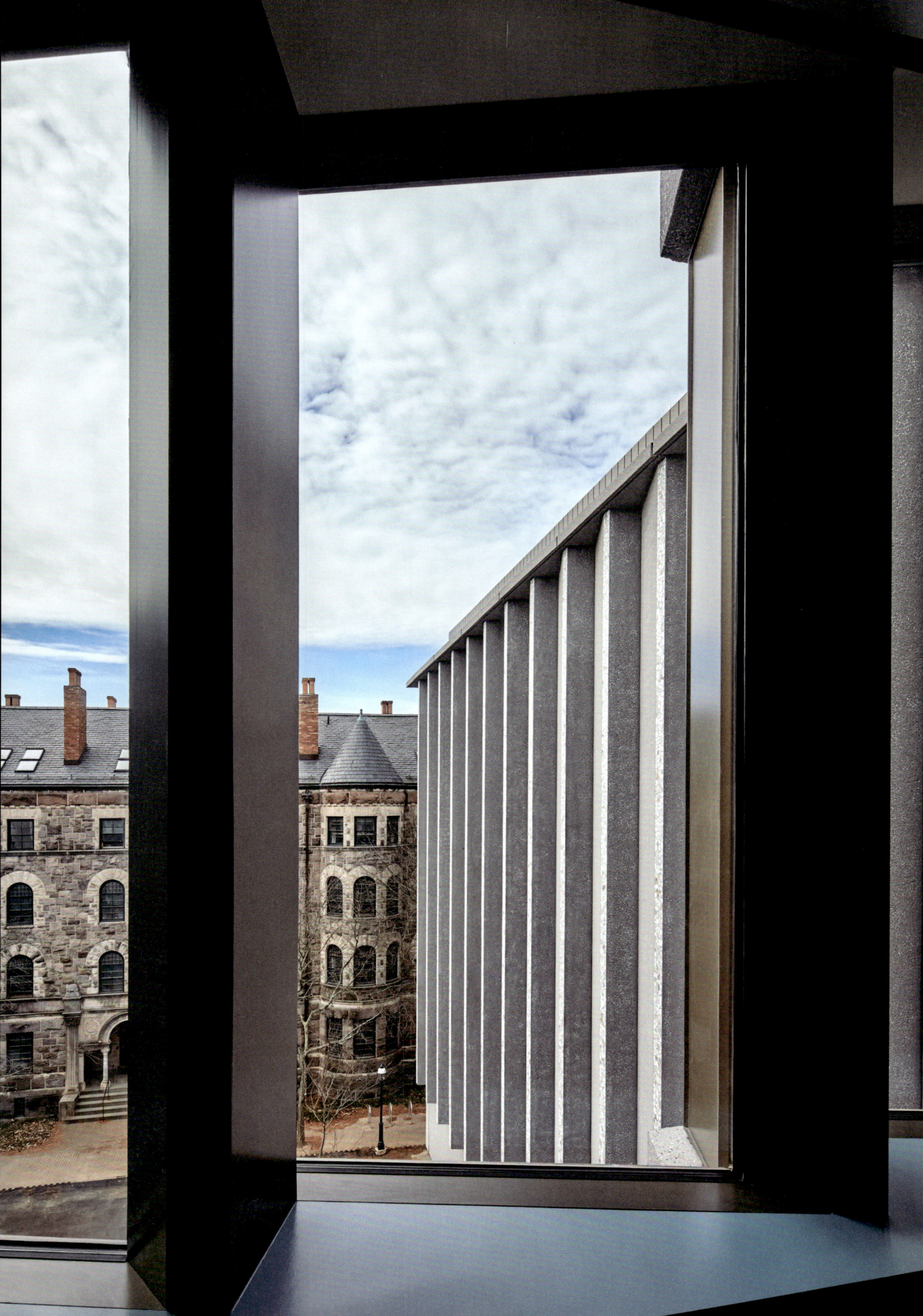

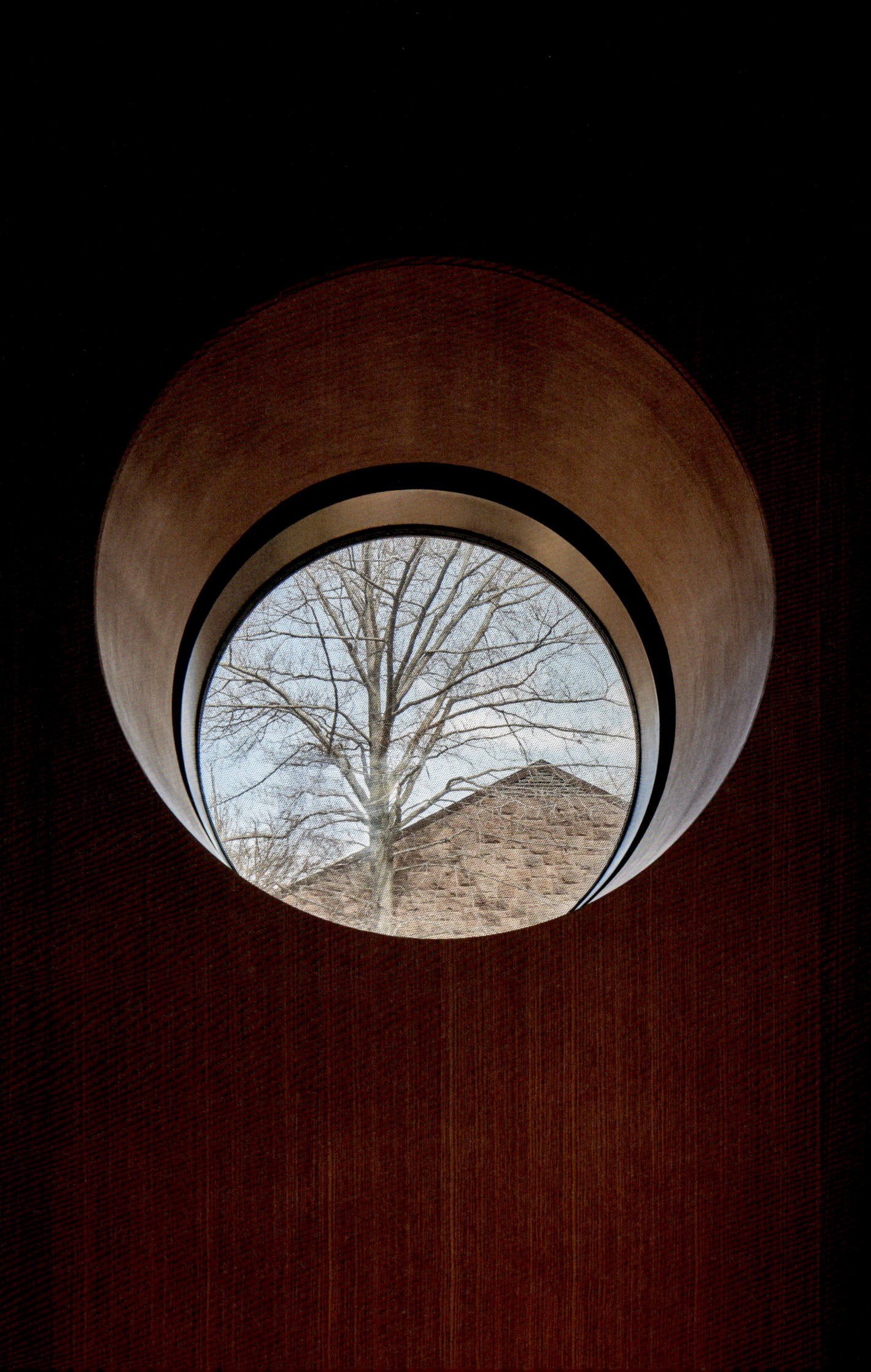

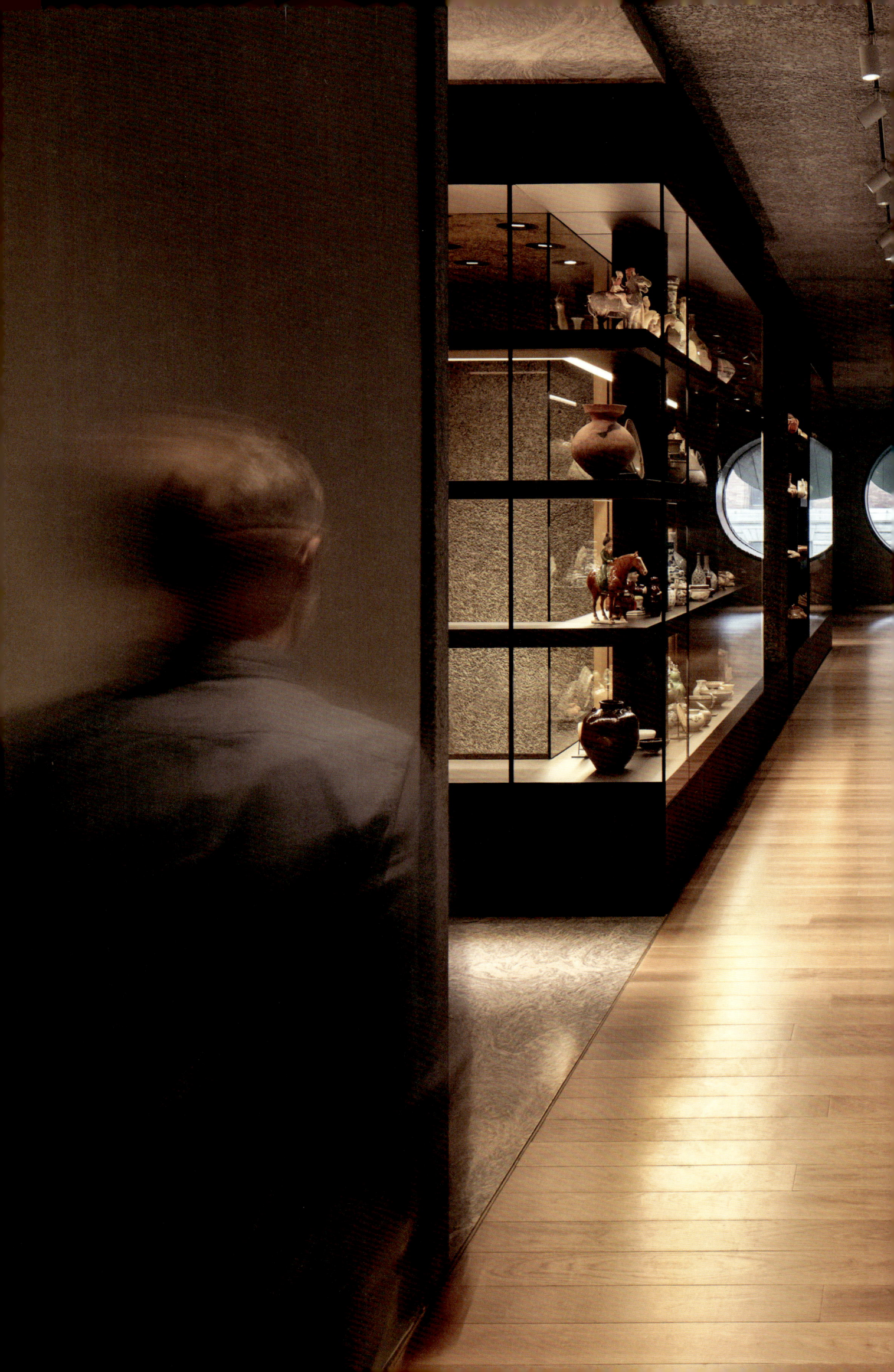

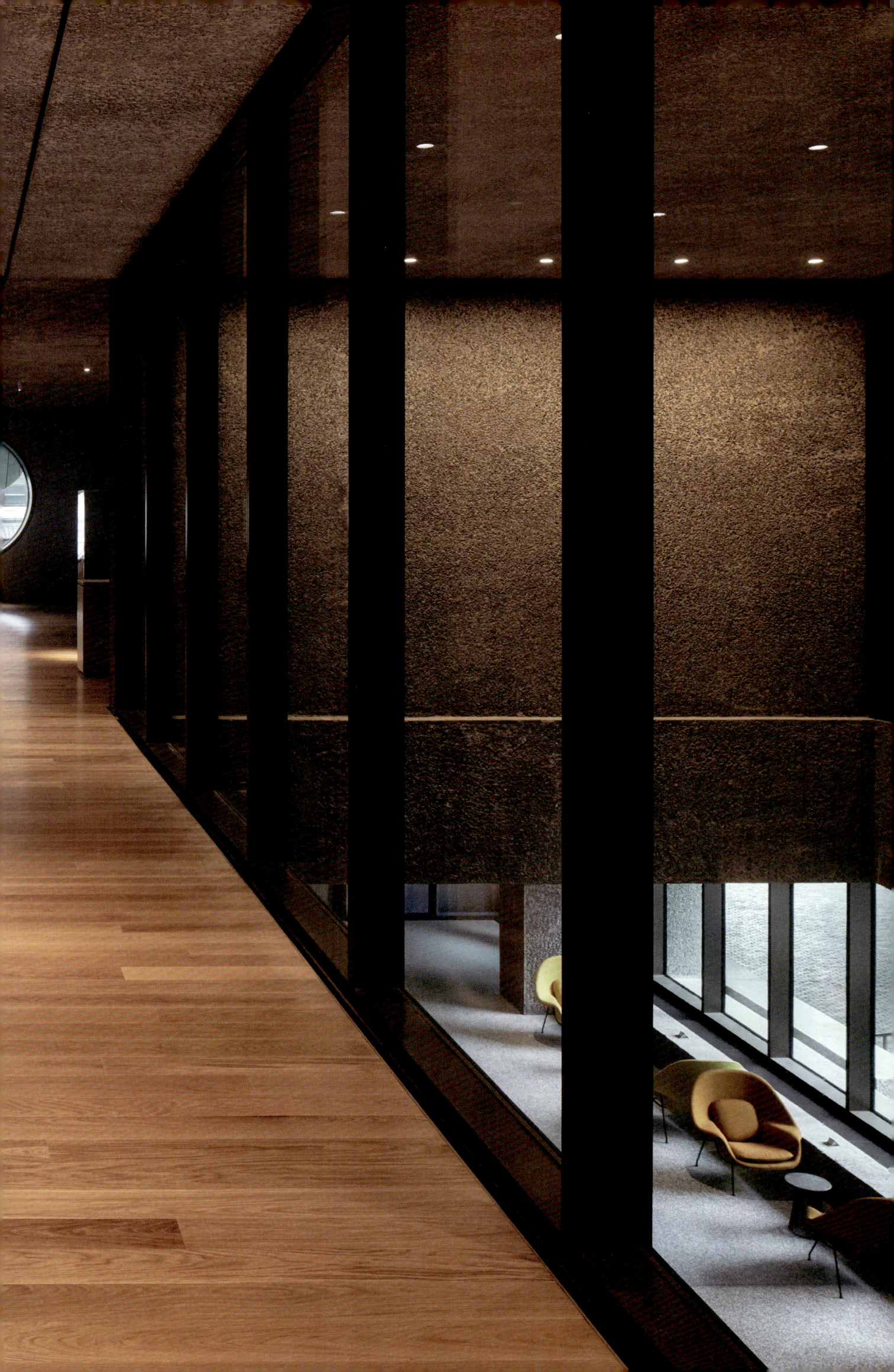

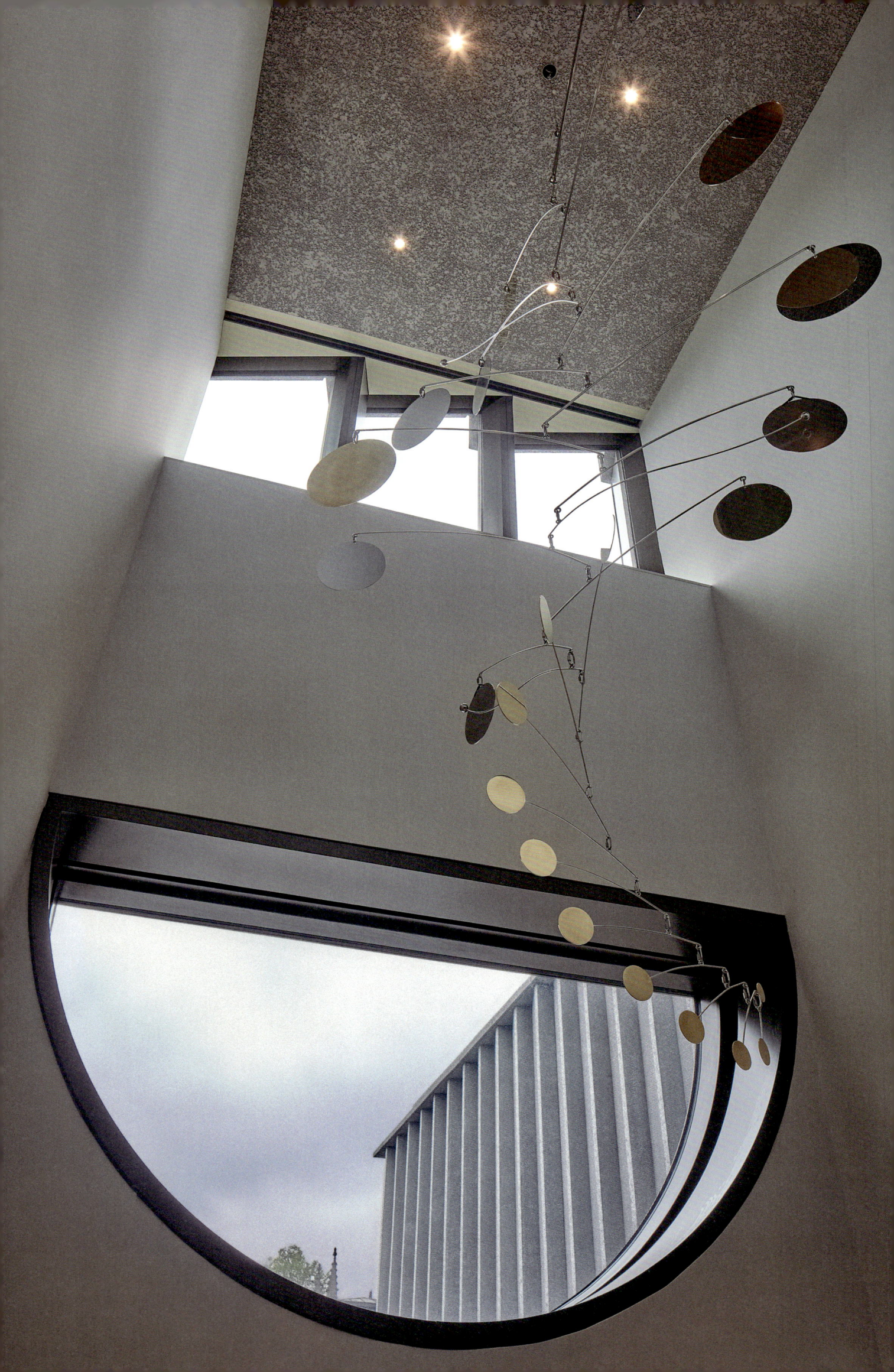

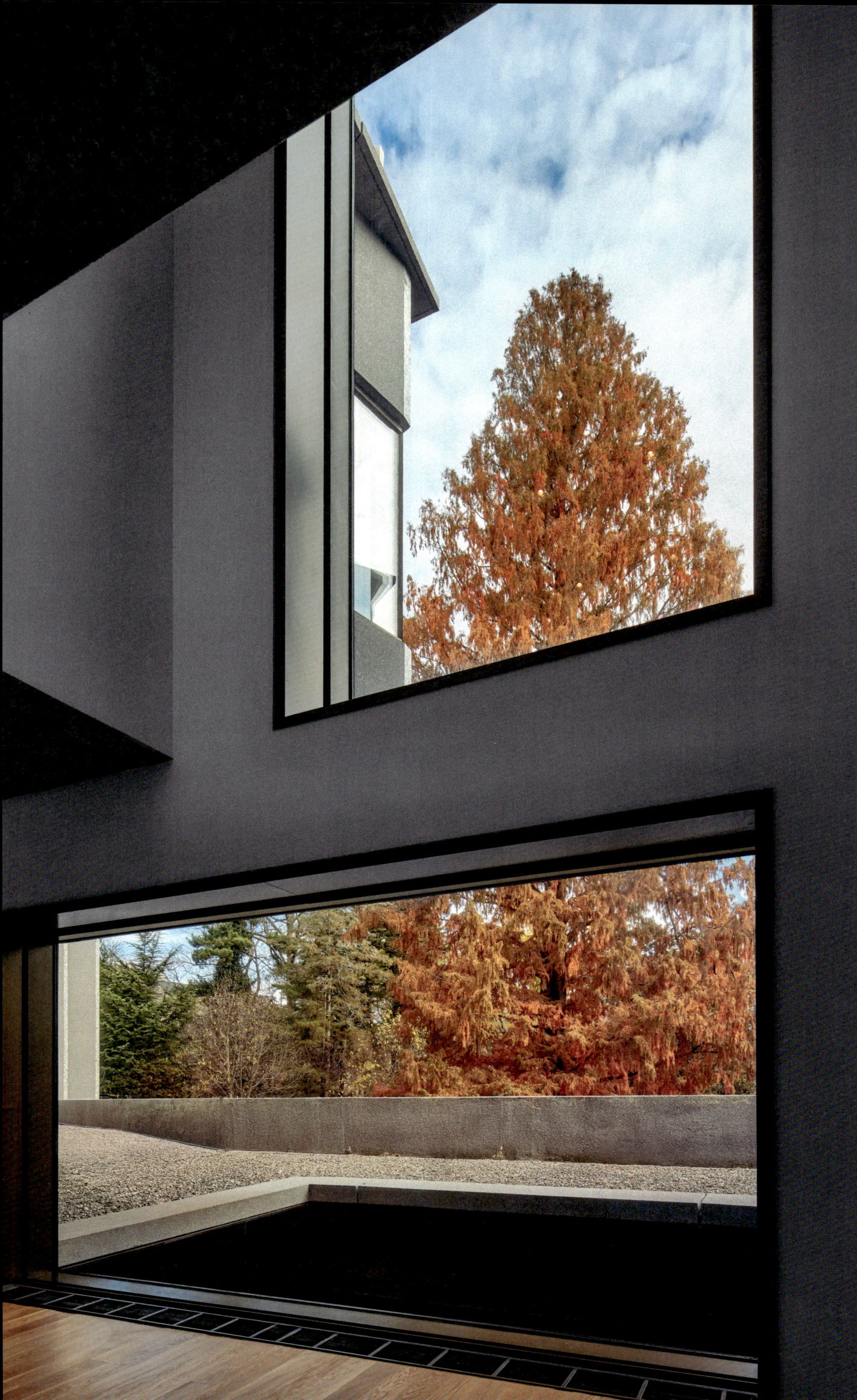

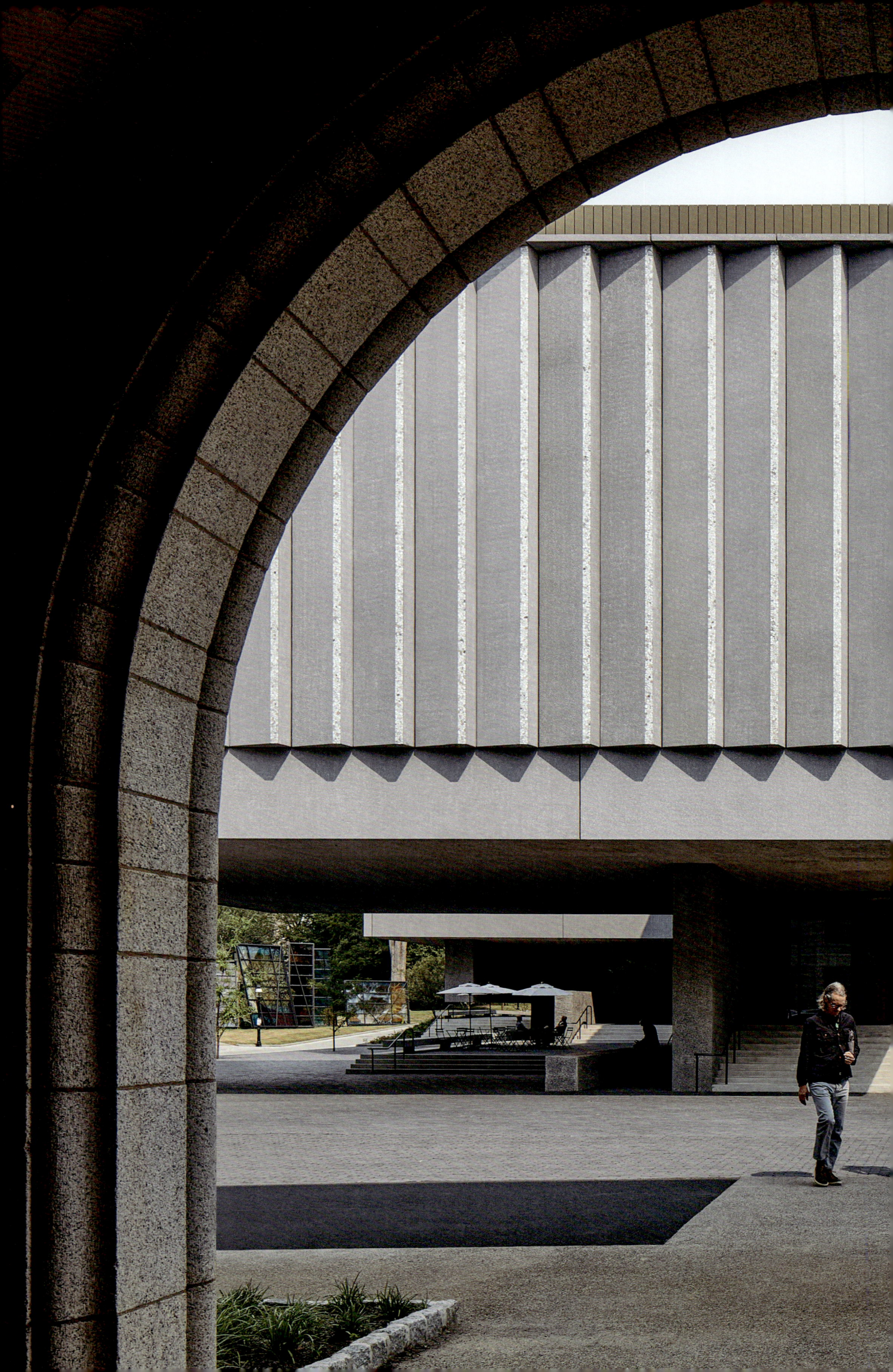

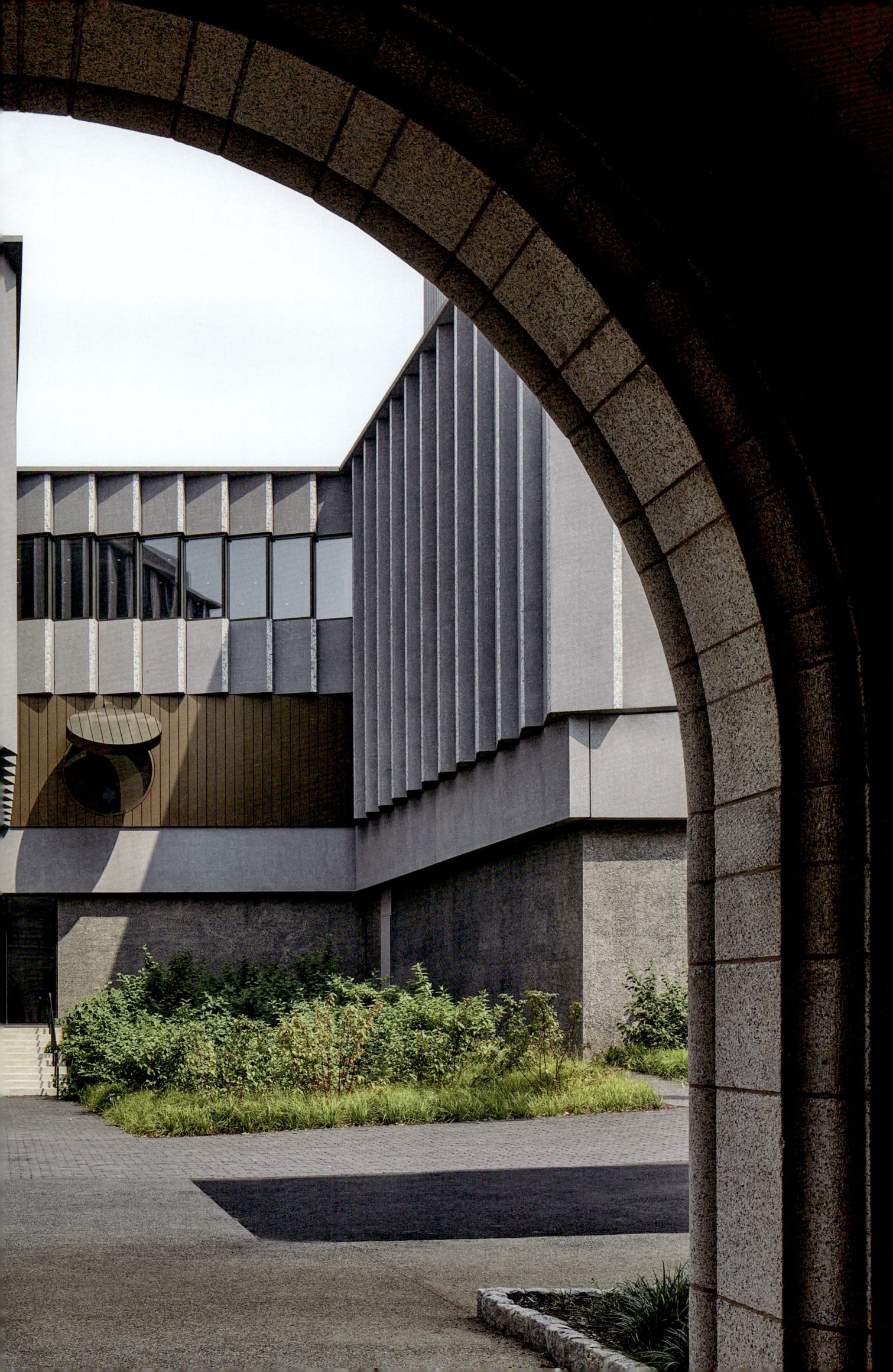

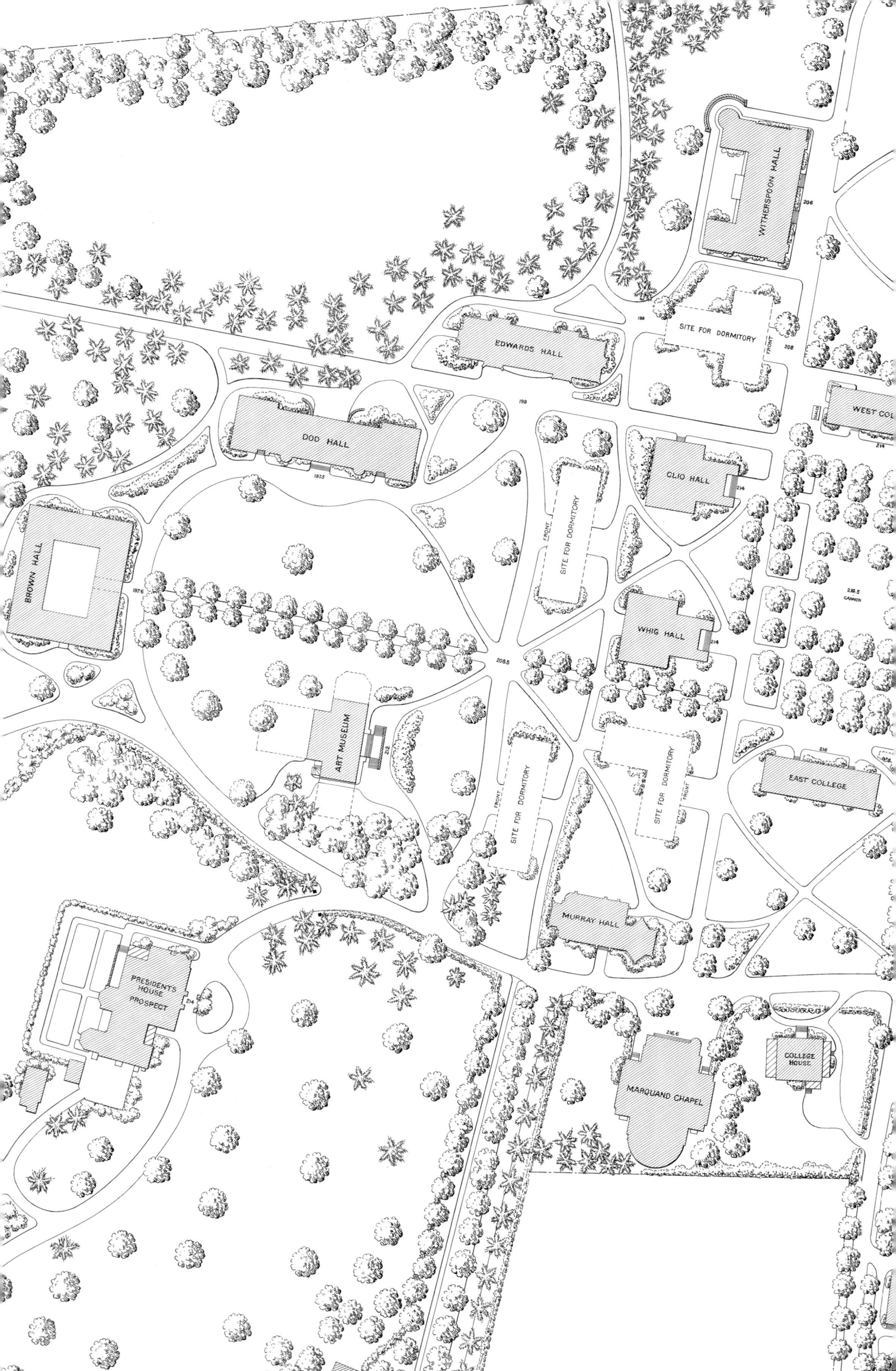

WITHERSPOON HALL

206

SITE FOR DORMITORY

FRONT

208

EDWARDS HALL

199

WEST COL

DOD HALL

197.5

CLIO HALL

214

FRONT

SITE FOR DORMITORY

BROWN HALL

197.6

216.5
CANNON

WHIG HALL

214

208.5

ART MUSEUM

212

SITE FOR DORMITORY

FRONT

FRONT

SITE FOR DORMITORY

EAST COLLEGE

216

MURRAY HALL

PRESIDENT'S
HOUSE
PROSPECT

214

216.6

MARQUAND CHAPEL

COLLEGE
HOUSE

A Tapestry Unfolding

RON McCOY

1. The Sense of Place

Vincent Scully, the influential architecture historian, described the American college campus as a unique environment "in which buildings are designed to get along with the others and to shape a space—a theater for human action."[1] The Princeton campus is a vivid manifestation of precisely this type of theater, graced with a remarkable sense of place resulting from certain salient beauties: the natural landscape, the materials and craft of its buildings, and the movement of the body in space.

Landscape features of the campus are evident in the subtle yet constant presence of the terrain, the wooded stream corridors, the vaulted tree canopies, the hidden sky, and the dramatic and often mysterious quality of light and shadows. Within this setting, the buildings remind us that architecture is temporal as well as spatial. The eighteenth- and nineteenth-century Princeton campus is defined by distinct individual buildings appearing in a parklike setting. As one explores the campus walkways, vistas of buildings are slowly revealed. We understand the campus to be loose but cohesive, varied and episodic. Successive layers appear, inviting a sense of wonder, reflection, and inspiration. Memories are carried with us over time, so that emotions from one moment are reawakened by another.

And while the architecture of the campus is stylistically eclectic, there is a unifying material culture that emerges from traditions of craft. Sandstone, argillite, and schist have been pulled from local quarries and chiseled into form. A powerful sense of authenticity and permanence resides in these materials and the details of their construction, whether in a rough fieldstone wall or a finely carved ogee arch. The individual units of stone are used to create buildings of any size. Buildings can be large, even monumental, and convey a level of intimacy—made by the hand of an artisan. All of these specific qualities create a unique atmosphere, one that we experience through the full range of our senses, through ritual reencounters with the built and natural landscape inside the revolutions of the seasons.

The campus is also an expression of the ideals and values of a community. Unlike a contemporary metropolis, which is often a cacophony of competing voices, the organization and form of a campus are an expression, created over time, of a single institution. Thus the Princeton campus presents itself today as a record of ideas and community aspirations rendered in space and form.

2. Three Centuries of Change

No site on the Princeton campus has been planned and built upon as much as that of the Museum. In 1890 the first purpose-built museum, designed by A. Page Brown in the style of a Romanesque Revival pavilion, was completed (fig. 49). This elegant two-room gallery was followed by five generations of change, each adding to, modifying, or removing the work of the previous generations. The original Romanesque Revival building was demolished in 1966. Venetian Gothic wings came and went as generations of architects transformed the Museum with modern, postmodern, and modern (again) additions. All were designed to serve the changing needs of the Museum, the Department of Architecture, and the Department of Art and Archaeology. The end result was compromised ambitions and a large and fragmented assemblage of spaces.

With a careful eye for detail, a visitor can see that the Museum is surrounded by three distinct generations of campus making. Nassau Hall, situated directly to the north of the Museum, was erected in 1756 to accommodate the entire College. Over the next century the first generation of the campus emerged as a community of buildings in Colonial, Federal, and Greek Revival styles (fig. 50). Classical principles of symmetry and balance, along with traces of planning inspired by

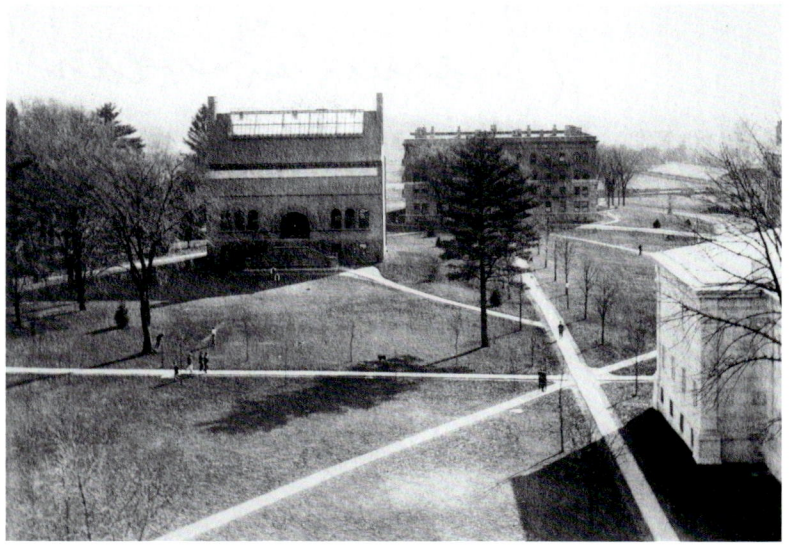

Fig. 49 Museum of Historic Art, 1893. Arthur Page Brown, architect; completed 1890. Collection of the Historical Society of Princeton

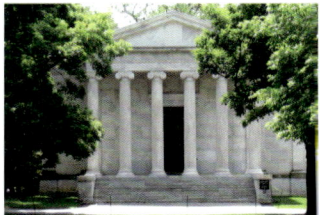

Fig. 50 Clio Hall, Princeton University, dedicated 1892

Fig. 51   College of New Jersey General Plan, 1893. F. L. Olmsted & Co., landscape architects. National Park Service, Frederick Law Olmsted National Historic Site. The plan shows the diagonal escarpment connecting Brown Hall, Dod Hall, Edwards Hall, and Alexander Hall

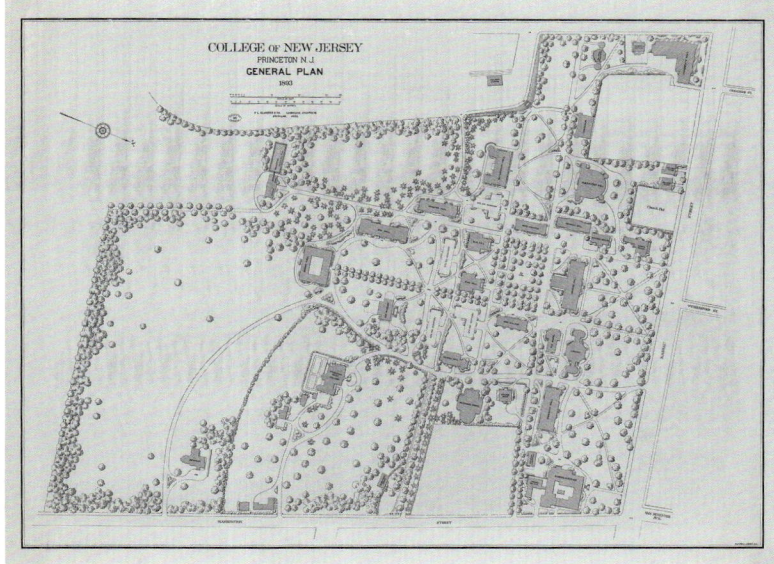

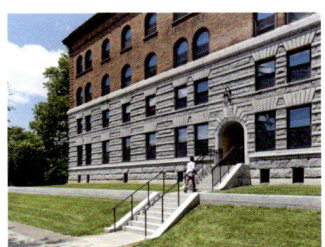

Fig. 52   Brown Hall, Princeton University. John Lyman Faxon, architect; completed 1892

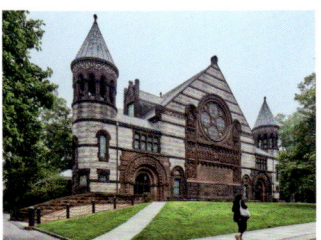

Fig. 53   Alexander Hall, Princeton University. William A. Potter, architect; completed 1894

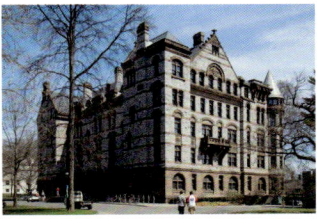

Fig. 54   Witherspoon Hall, Princeton University. William A. Potter and Robert H. Robertson, architects; commissioned 1875

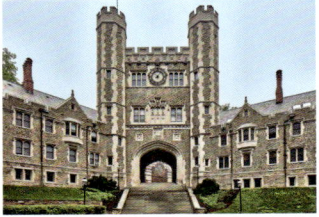

Fig. 55   Blair Hall, Princeton University. Cope & Stewardson, architects; completed 1897

Thomas Jefferson's new campus at the University of Virginia, established unity and coherence.

To the immediate west of the Museum, along a natural diagonal escarpment (fig. 51), the second generation of the campus emerged, reflecting distinctly different values. Here one finds individual buildings of intentional variety—Neo-Renaissance (fig. 52), Richardsonian (fig. 53), and High Victorian (fig. 54)—inspired generally by the ideals of Romanticism, Romantic landscape gardens, and the nineteenth-century battle of architectural styles. All were intended to evoke a specific image, which, in the words of Princeton's eleventh president, James McCosh (1811–1894), would be "somewhat on the model of the demesnes of English noblemen."[2]

Also within sight, to the west and south of the Museum, are the neighborhoods of the Collegiate Gothic campus, Princeton's definitive style, declared so by the trustees in 1896 (fig. 55). Serene three-sided quads and linked landscapes represent yet another distinct and conscious concept of campus. The architects of this generation looked toward Oxford and Cambridge as icons of learning and symbols of community. Ralph Adams Cram (1863–1942), Princeton's consulting architect and voice of this era, was particularly critical of the University's superficial preoccupation with questions of architectural style, proclaiming: "It is curious that Princeton should thus far be the only university, so handicapped by the defiant individualism of a light-hearted past, to realize that architecture and aesthetic organization are not matters of predilection, but are fundamental necessities."[3]

Cram and his colleagues embarked on an effort to transform the openness of the parklike setting into a unified community and a continuous fabric of courtyards, vistas, and landmarks. The architecture is intimate and picturesque, with colliding forms and rooflines shaping dramatic silhouettes against the sky. It is an architecture of anticipation, in which one is held by the space of a courtyard and offered

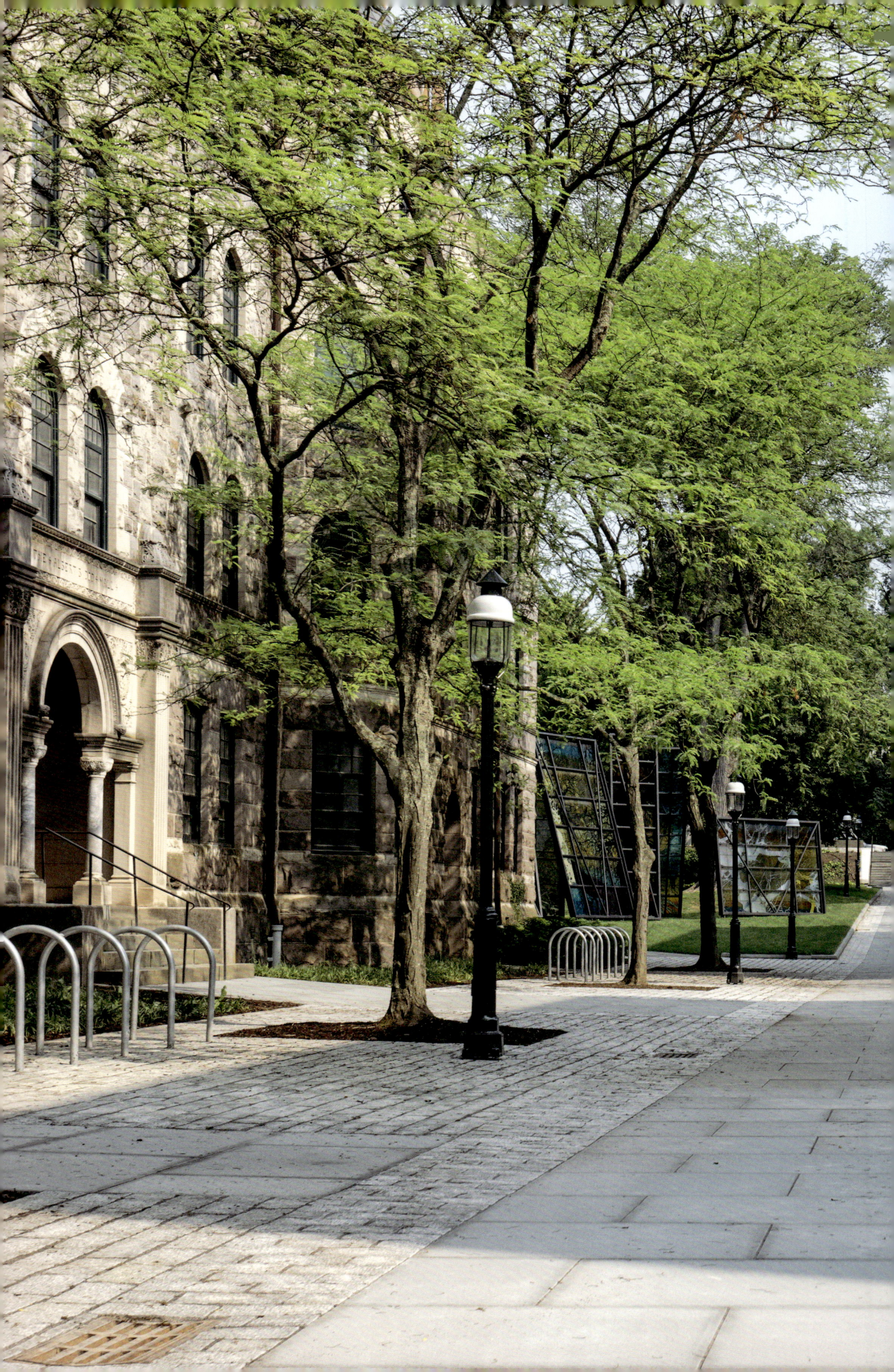

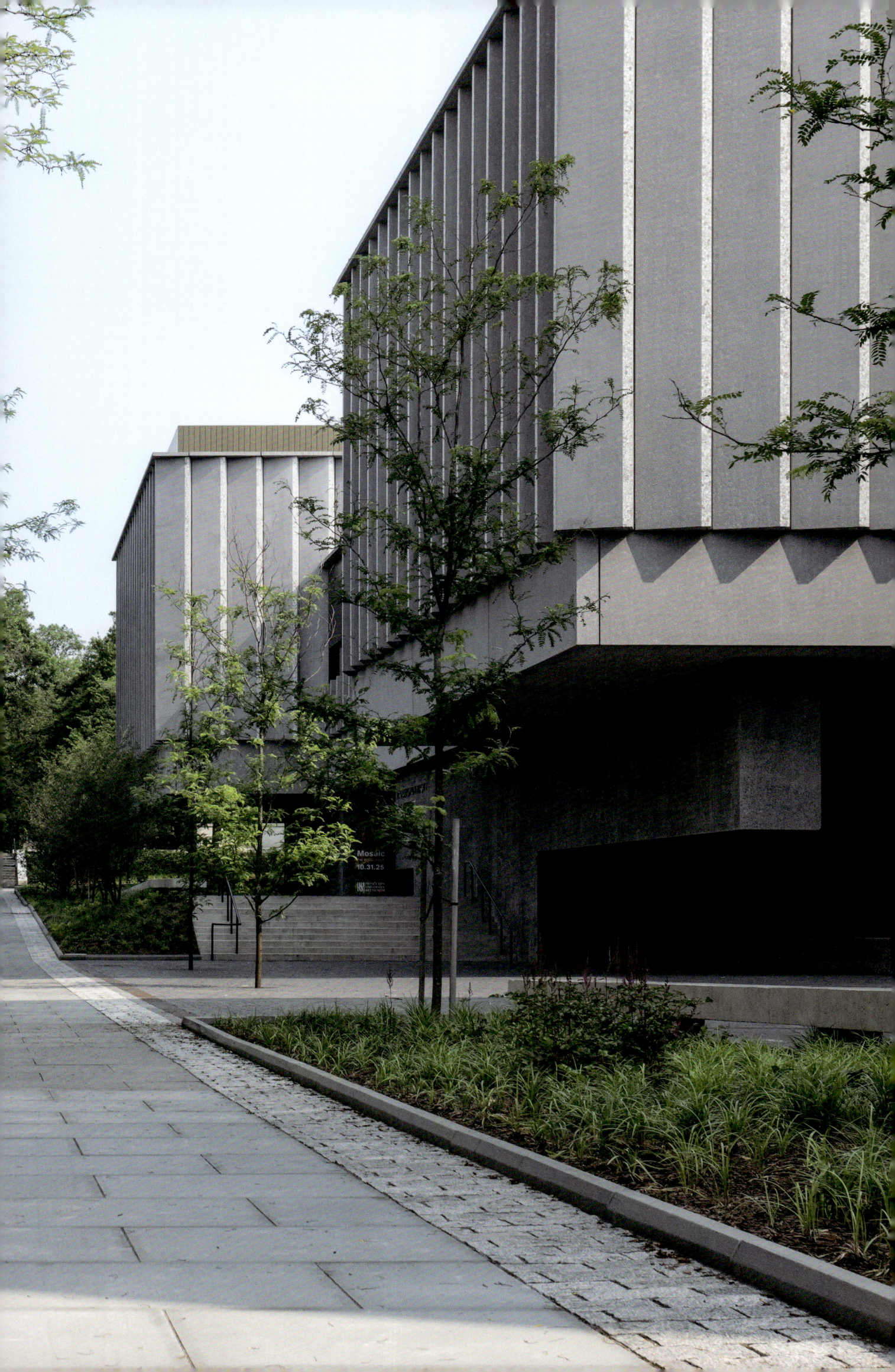

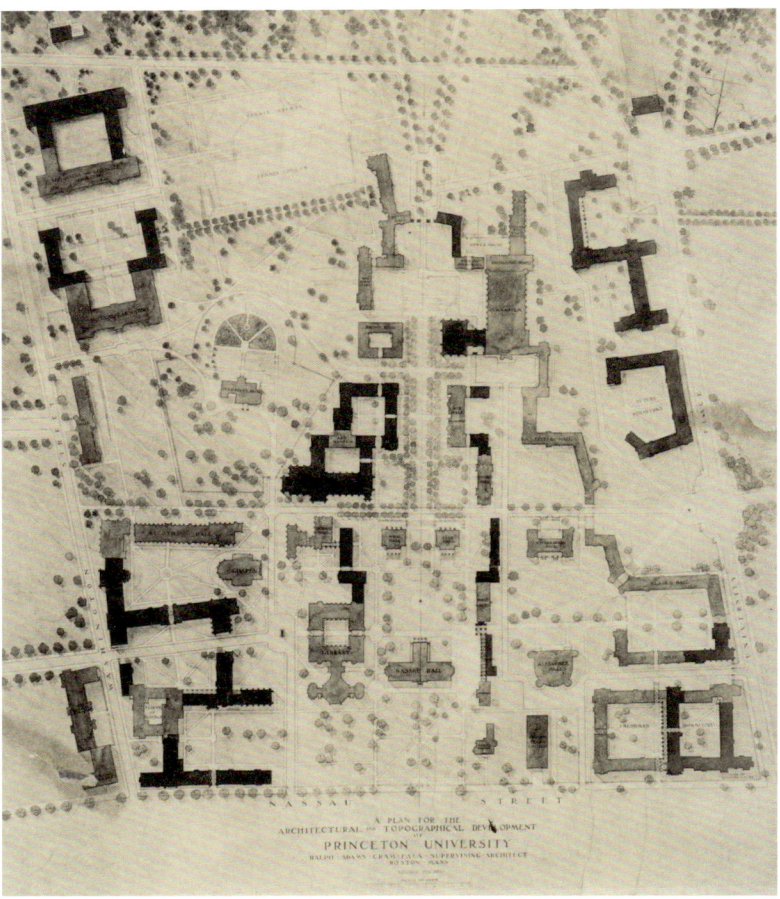

Fig. 56 A Plan for the
Architectural and Topographical
Development of Princeton
University, 1911. Ralph Adams
Cram, supervising architect.
Princeton University Library.
Department of Special Collections

curated vistas. The episodic sequence of discovery repeats organically, as new portals frame enticing features and spaces beyond.

I am drawn to the idea of the campus as a tapestry unfolding across time, in which the patterns of built and unbuilt work from each generation inform the next. Throughout three centuries of change, two essential planning principles have anchored the coherence and legibility of the evolving campus, both of which are now incorporated into the design of the new Museum. The most important of these principles, the central axis of Nassau Hall, was strengthened by Cram, in his campus plan of 1911, as a grand, tree-lined allée. The new Museum embraces this axis along its western edge, shaping the sloping ground into a series of cobblestone terraces.

Less obvious but ever present in the growth of the campus is the secondary axis located along the east side of Nassau Hall. In his unbuilt plan of 1893, Frederick Law Olmsted identified this axis, rather than the central axis of Nassau Hall, to be the primary campus allée, beginning at the gate on Nassau Street and terminating at Brown Hall (see fig. 51). Cram, in an unrealized aspect of his plan, imagined this path differently, as a sequence of Collegiate Gothic portals and courtyards (fig. 56). The new Museum adapts Cram's episodic pathway into a public walkway through the building, reasserting the connection to Brown and allowing the pathway to tumble and weave its way to the southernmost edge of campus. While the campus invites one to wander, these two axes provide a reassuring balance to the experience, creating a sense of emotional comfort within a milieu for discovery.

3. Seeing the Museum

In this context of the campus history and sense of place, how might we understand and experience the new Princeton University Art Museum, designed in a collaboration between Adjaye Associates, Cooper Robertson, and Field Operations? It is immediately obvious that the primary challenge facing the designers was to resolve the tension between the significant space requirements of the Museum and the intimate scale of the early campus. The program for the new building is nearly twice as large as the previous complex. Additionally, the opportunity to democratize the encyclopedic collection by presenting all of the galleries on a single level led to a floor plate that is the second largest on campus, surpassed only by Level A of Firestone Library.

The new building resolves this tension by creating a composition of seven semi-independent gallery pavilions on the second floor of the Museum. Each pavilion connects to but projects outward from the body of the building. These raised pavilions, with their crisp, volumetric clarity, adhere to classical principles of composition found throughout the historic campus and respect the scale and the figure-in-field character of the neighboring buildings. A delicate, vertical pattern of concrete panels, extruded from a serrated profile, wraps the pavilions and the upper body of the Museum, floating above the campus yet sitting comfortably within the boundary established by the cornice lines of the surrounding buildings.

While the second floor of the Museum is dedicated to the galleries, the ground level belongs to the campus. Here the building is transparent, public, and porous. Unconstrained by the geometry and functional requirements of the galleries above, the Museum embraces the campus along its edges and invites the community into the building. "Artwalks" serve as public passages, connecting to the everyday network of campus walks, inviting routes through the building rather than around it, and allowing one's thoughts to be gently interrupted, touched, or inspired by art and the power of the human imagination.

The north-facing portal, the primary entry to the Museum, respects the legacy of Cram's episodic sequence of spaces and contributes to the unfolding tradition of place making at Princeton. This portal leads to a small entry court, an outdoor space captured in the void between the new Museum and the existing Marquand Library of Art and Archaeology. This tall, dramatic room is covered by skylights and framed by a monumentally scaled timber structure. This is a welcoming area—a classic space of transition and preparation—introducing the defining architectural elements of the spaces beyond. The court is both energetic and contemplative, animated in all directions by views into galleries and surrounded above by Nick Cave's heroic mixed-media mosaic (see page 111).

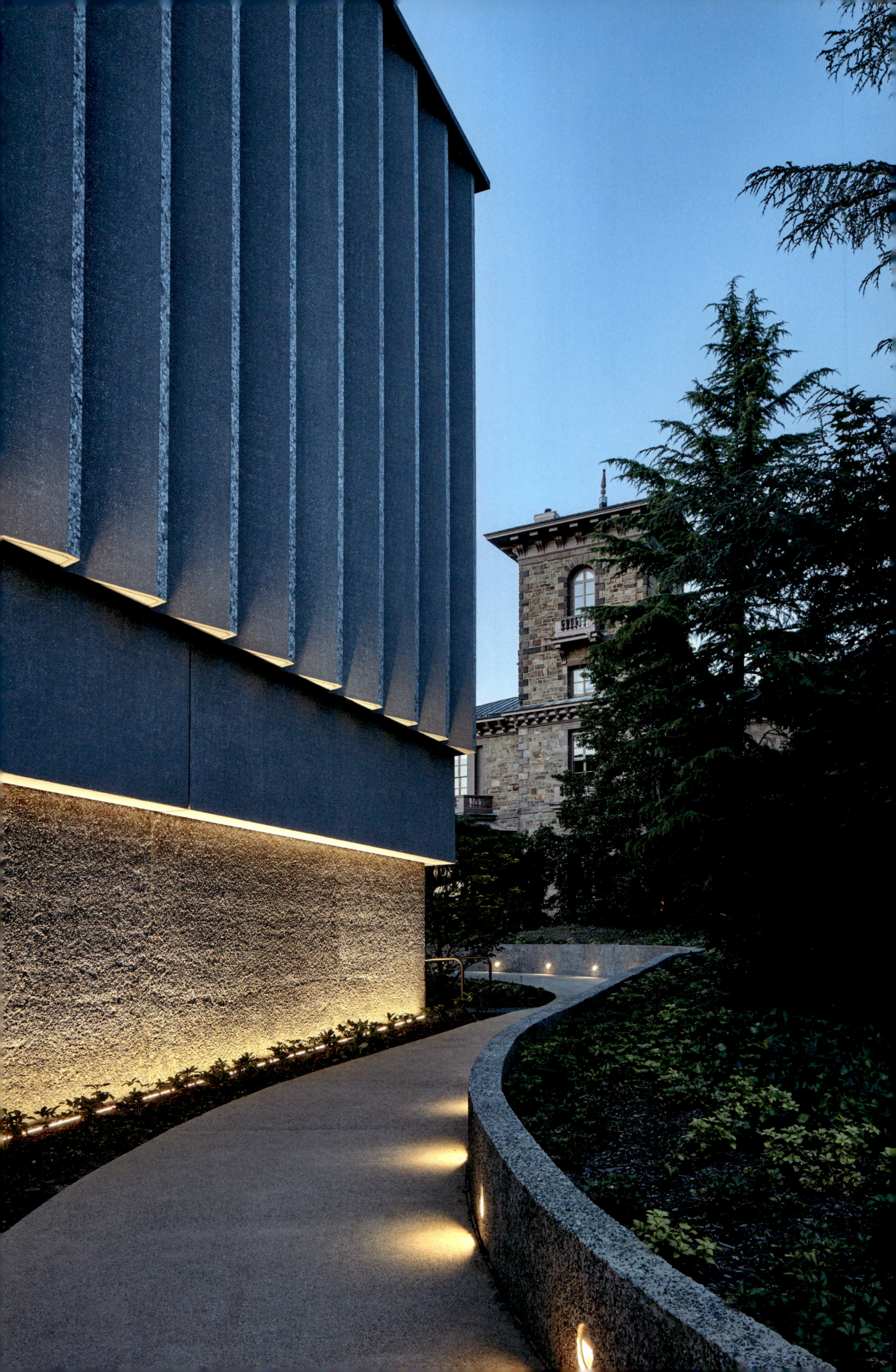

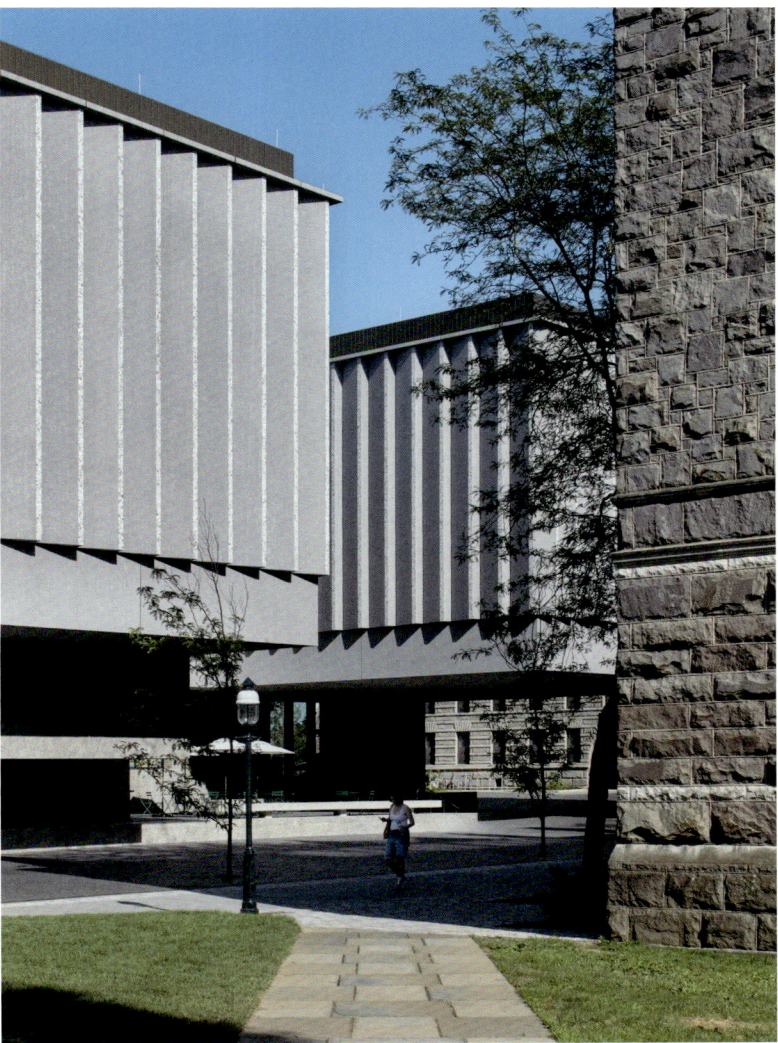

To the west, the Museum absorbs the gentle intersection between the formal axis of Nassau Hall and the diagonal escarpment, framing historic vistas while creating a stepped sequence of outdoor rooms. These, too, are spaces of transition, knitting the building to the campus and sheltering, porch-like, the western entrances to the Museum (fig. 57). These features have created a remarkable new family of campus spaces, folded and shaped by deep beams, parapet walls, and the soffits of the gallery pavilions above.

I have learned to see the Museum as a stone building rendered through contemporary methods of construction. Heavy walls anchor the building to the earth, and the dark stone aggregate of these cast-in-place concrete walls is revealed through a technique of heavy sandblasting. Above, precast panels of concrete "fins" reveal a mist of white stone aggregate and play endlessly with sun and shadows. The tips of these fins are hand-seeded with fragments of white marble, recalling the classical fluted columns of the adjacent Whig Hall. Inside, the family of stone materials expands as the expressive concrete aggregate is complemented by polished terrazzo and the atmospheric grain of granite details employed on the Grand Stair and the gallery portals.

When I was a young student learning about works of architecture, I would spend hours examining buildings from a distance, exploring their relationships with the surrounding context. As I have observed the construction of the Museum, I have been able to enjoy this way of understanding again, taking care to place one or more layers of the campus between myself and the new building. I stroll the campus pathways and experience the slow-moving vistas and atmosphere that have been shaped over 268 years of campus making. I am excited to frame a view of the Museum's marble-tipped stone panels between the fluted white marble columns of Whig Hall (fig. 58); to hold the memory of Collegiate Gothic portals and courtyards in my mind as I approach and enter the Museum from the north; to walk along the diagonal from the northeast toward Brown Hall and beyond, where I feel the subtle attenuation of this picturesque landscape. As I approach from the south, between Brown and Dod Halls, I appreciate how the museum unifies the spaces captured between the stone bases of these three buildings, framing the vista of Nassau Hall (fig. 59), and I recall that I am witnessing the evolution of three centuries of a community speaking across time. From the east, from Prospect House, I admire how the design respects the historic gardens cared for by Beatrix Farrand (1872–1959) and generations of campus stewards. While landscape and architecture are equal parts of the campus experience, the enduring visual power of Princeton is a complex totality of features, far more than the attributes of any individual building.

I also remind myself that architecture is an evolving creative discipline with an inherent ambition to seek meaning, employ symbols, and express our values and our understanding of who we are in the

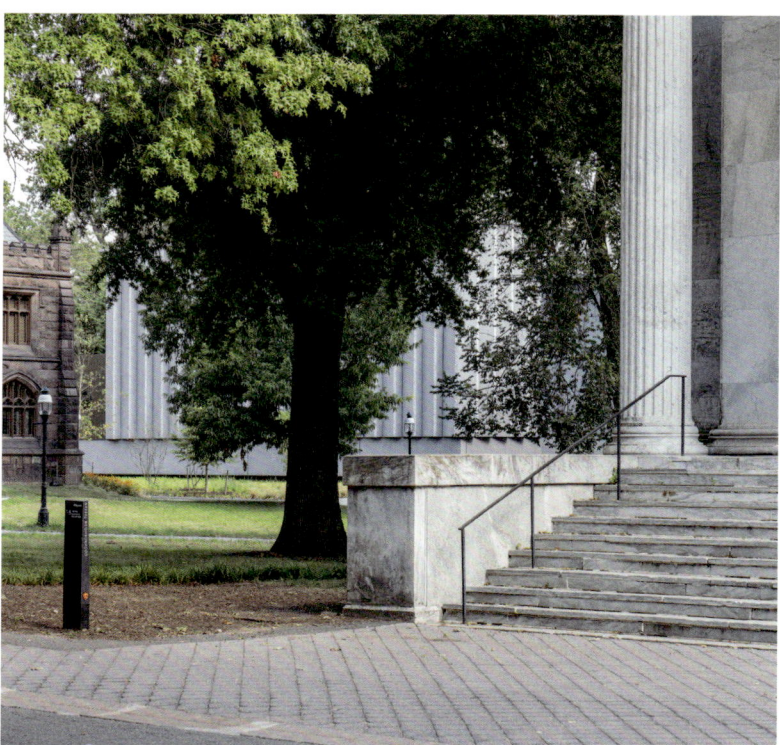

Fig. 58   The Museum seen through the columns of Whig Hall

Fig. 59 View of Nassau Hall
from the south

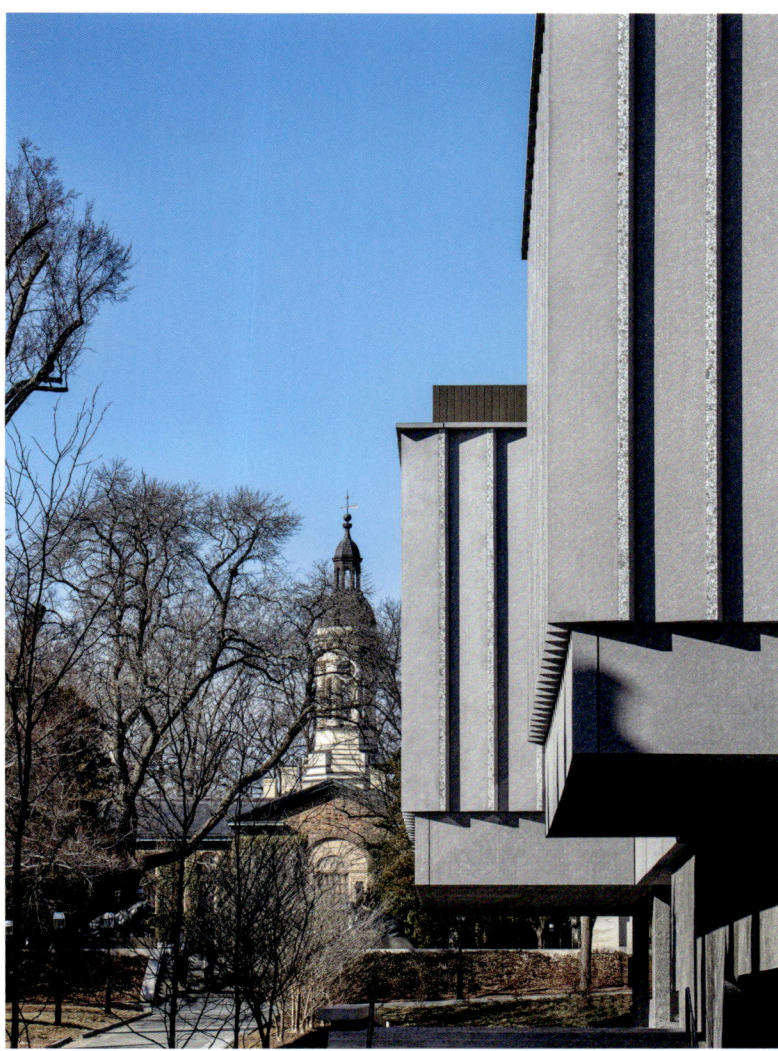

world through space, time, and material. At its best, architecture contributes to the unique characteristics of place while it explores, tests,
and adds new layers of memories and experiences. The Museum is
surrounded by more than a dozen different architectural styles; none
of them are "right," yet all contribute to the beauty of the campus. As
I imagine the Museum becoming a new heart of arts and humanities at
Princeton, I recall this, written by Ada Louise Huxtable: "I am devoted
to the principle that every age produces its greatest buildings in its own
image.…Ultimately, it is the addition and absorption of this continuous record of changing art, technology, ideas and uses that make cities
unique repositories of the whole range of human endeavor."[4]

1   Vincent Scully, "Louis I. Kahn and the Ruins of Rome," *Engineering and Science*
    (California Institute of Technology) 56, no. 2 (1993): 3.
2   James McCosh, quoted in William Milligan Sloane, ed., *The Life of James
    McCosh: A Record Chiefly Autobiographical* (Scribner, 1896), 196.
3   Ralph Adams Cram, "Princeton Architecture," *American Architect* 96, no. 1752
    (July 21, 1909): 21.
4   Ada Louise Huxtable, "The Way It Never Was," in Huxtable, *On Architecture:
    Collected Reflections on a Century of Change* (Walker, 2008), 426.

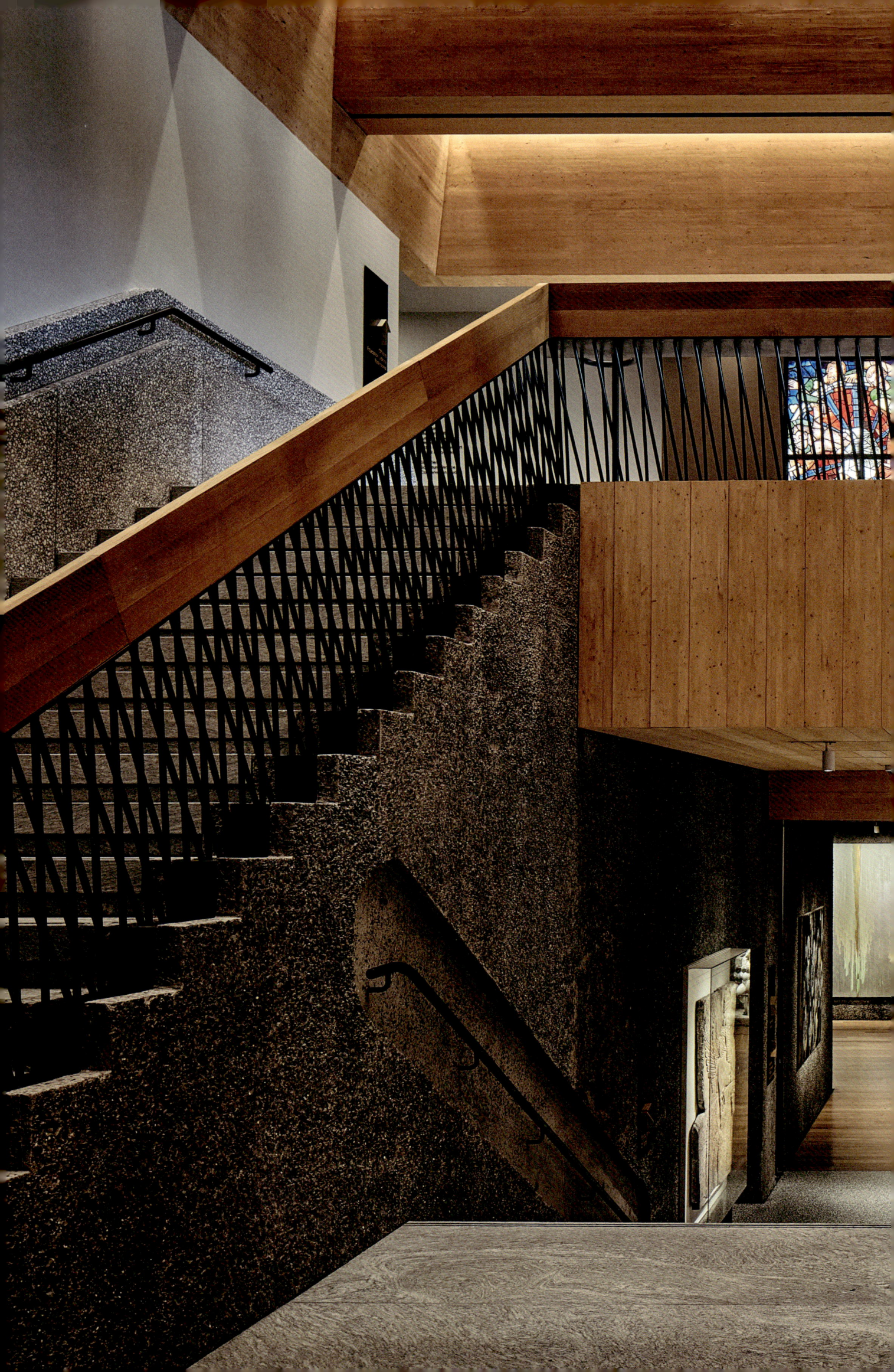

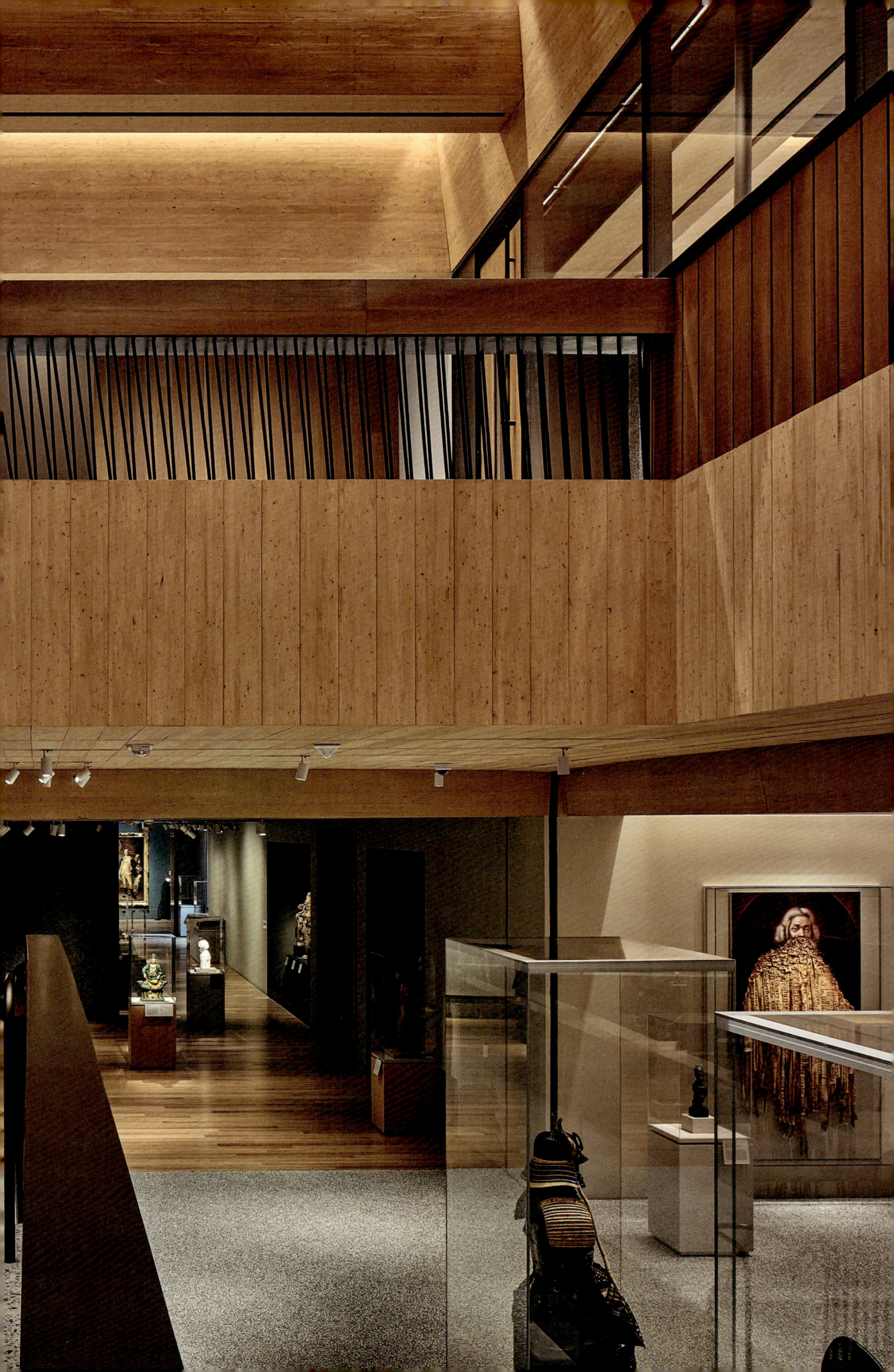

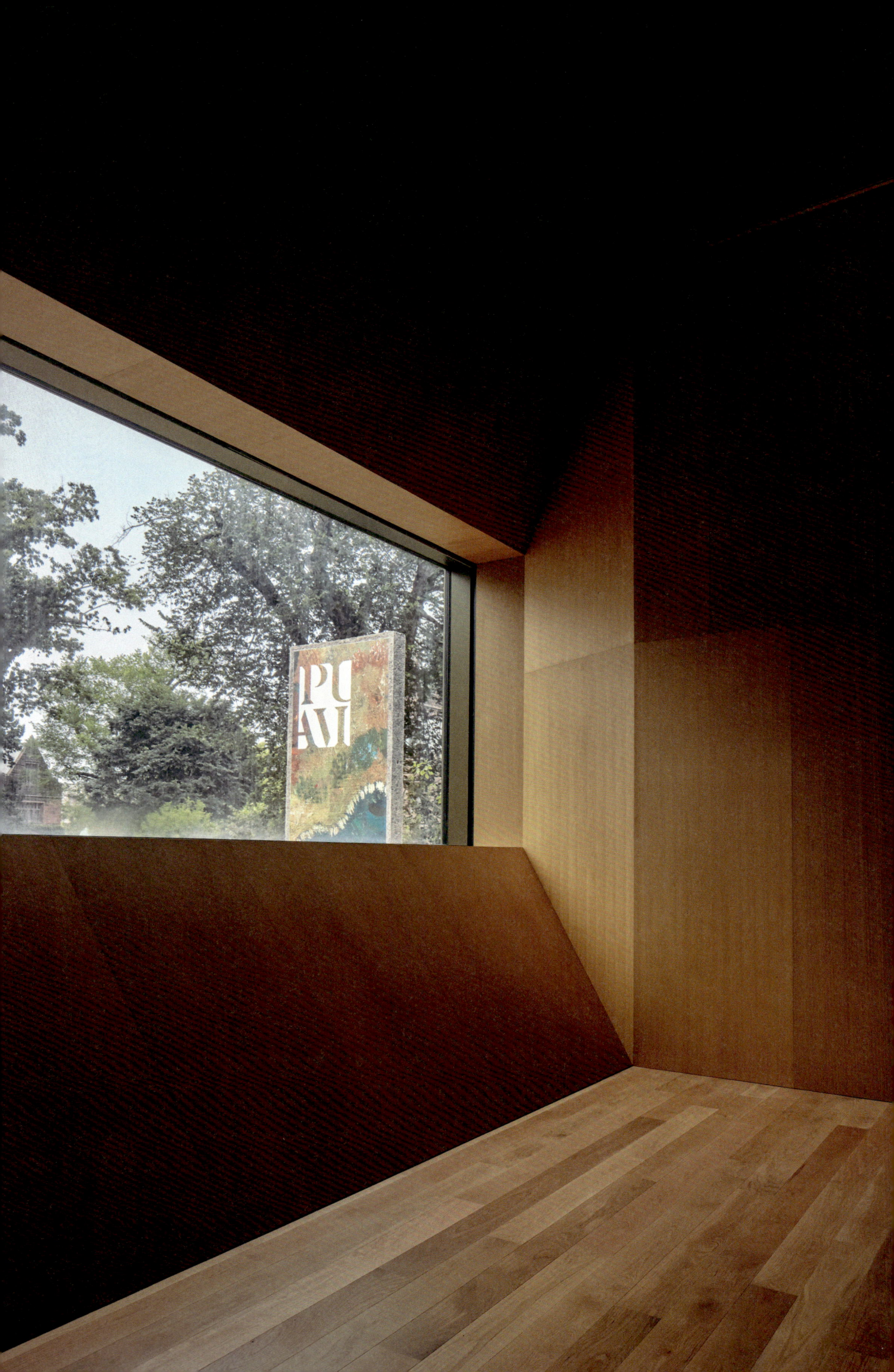

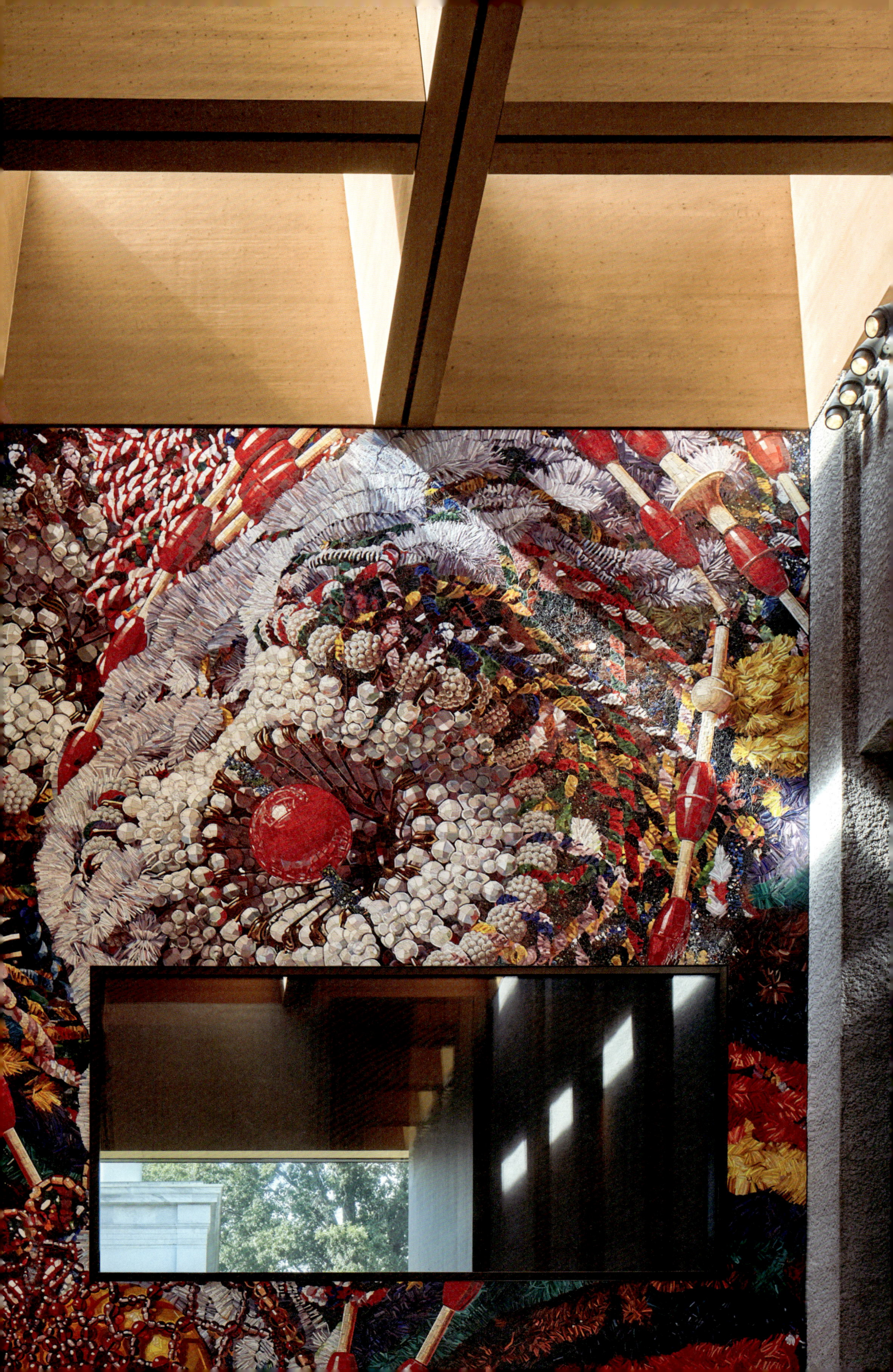

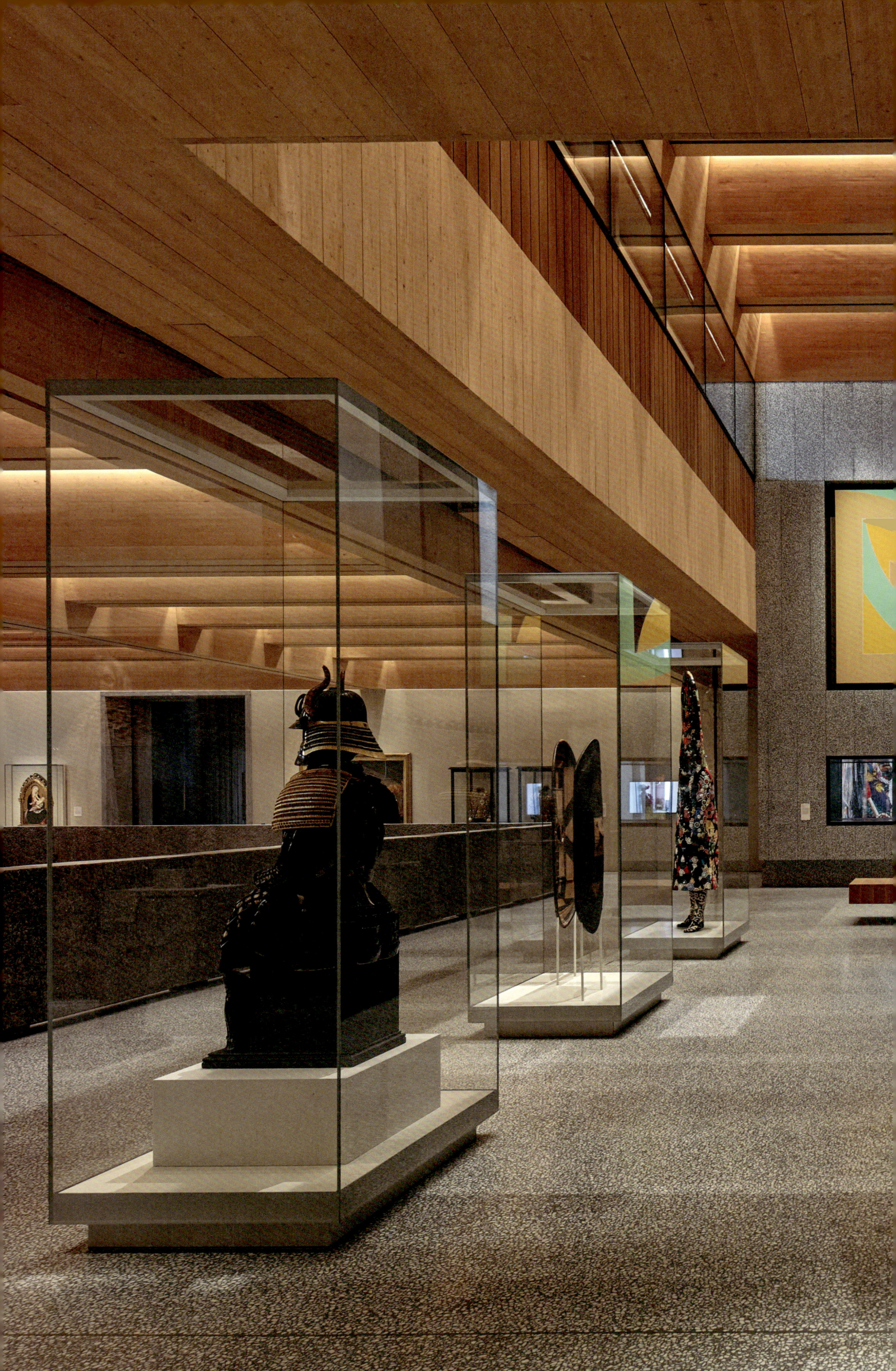

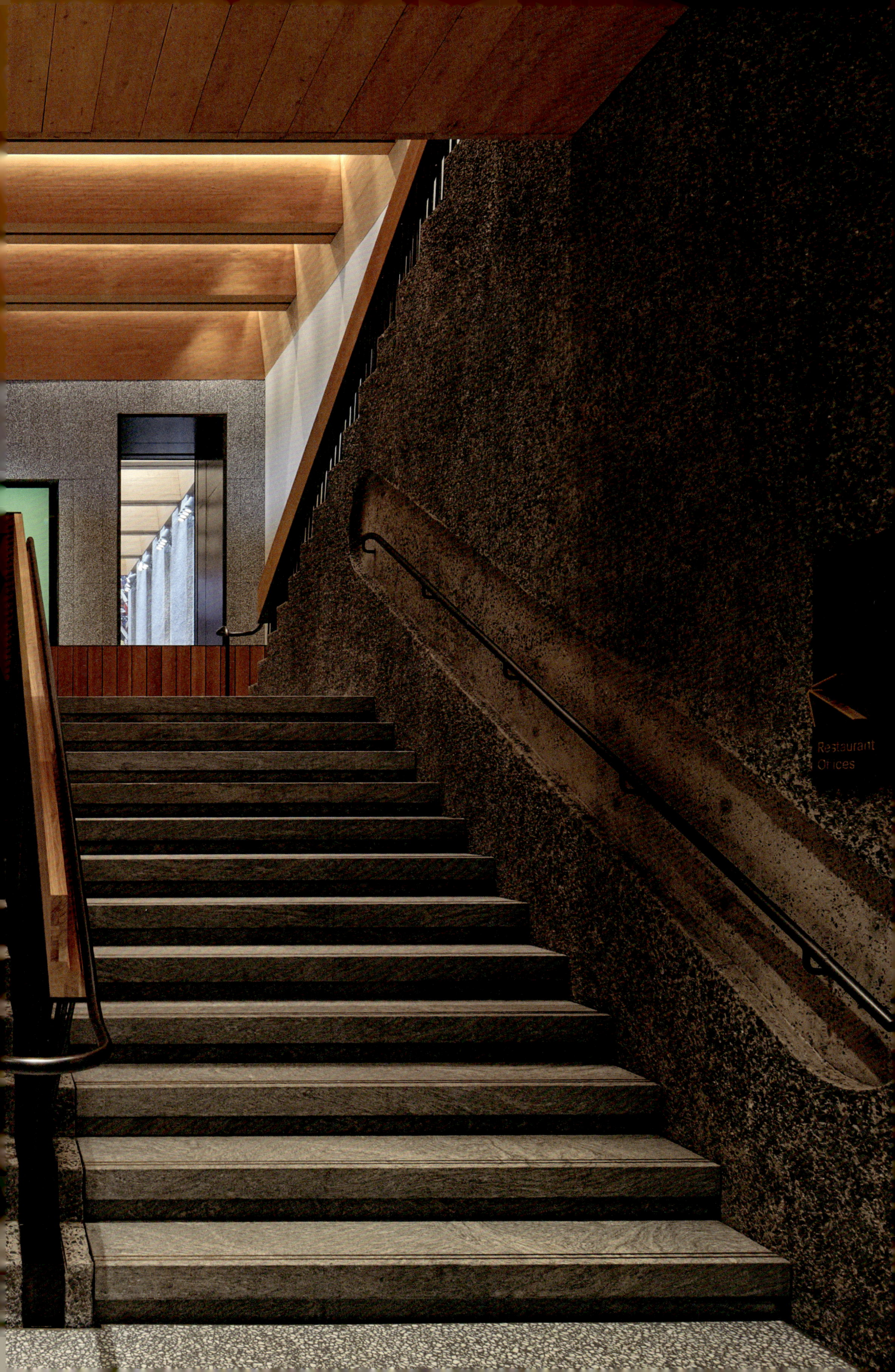

Restaurant
Offices

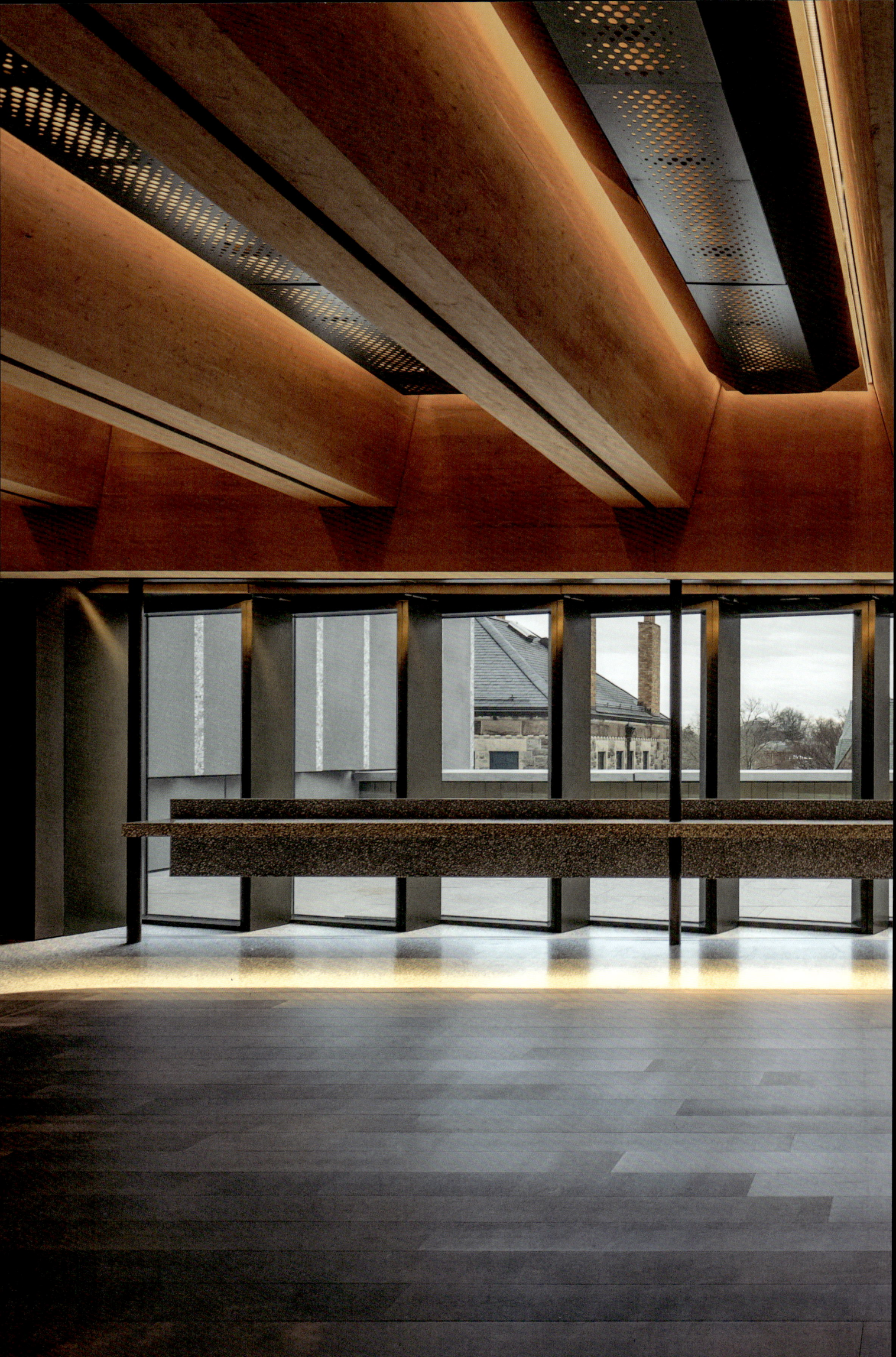

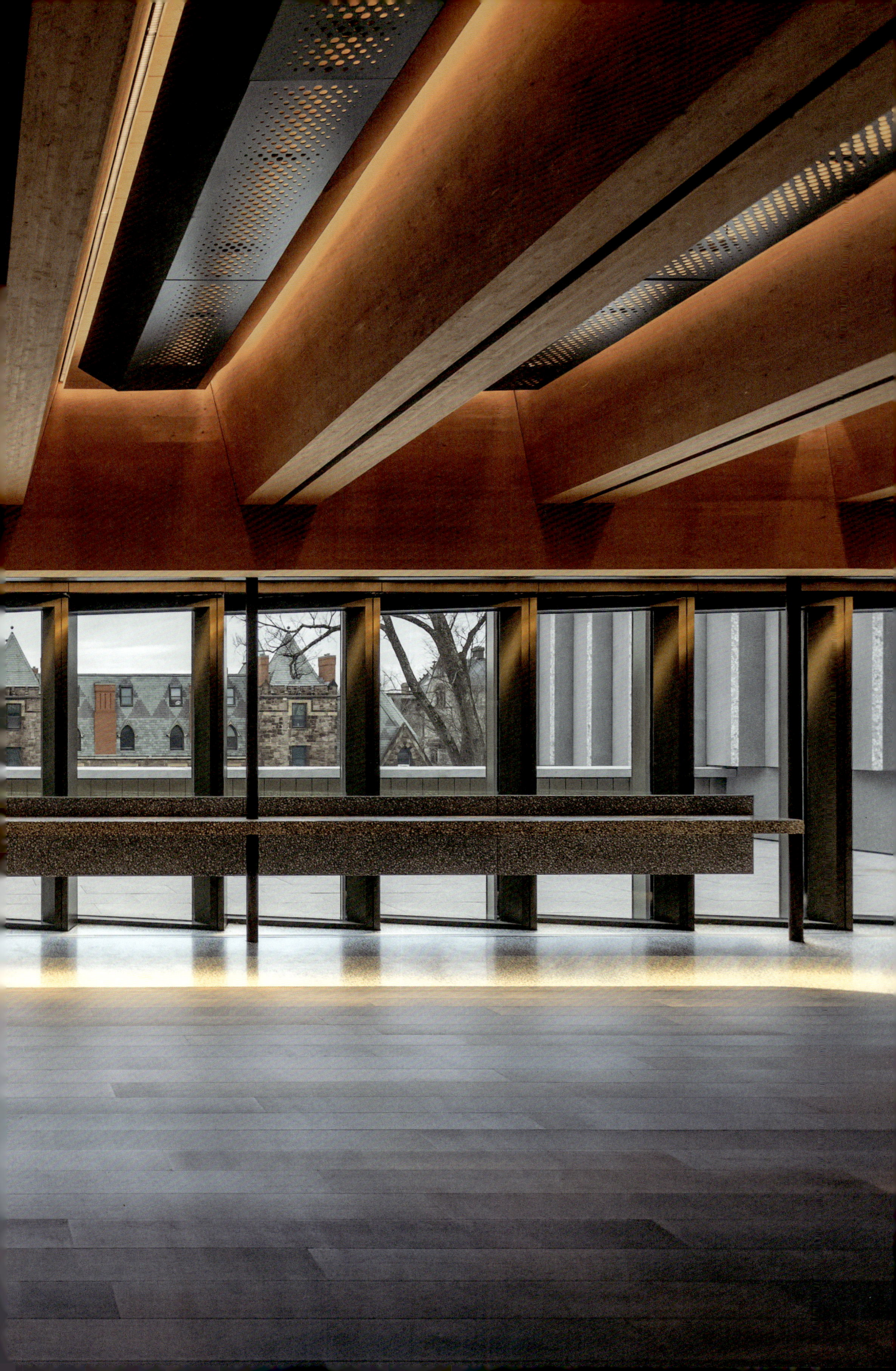

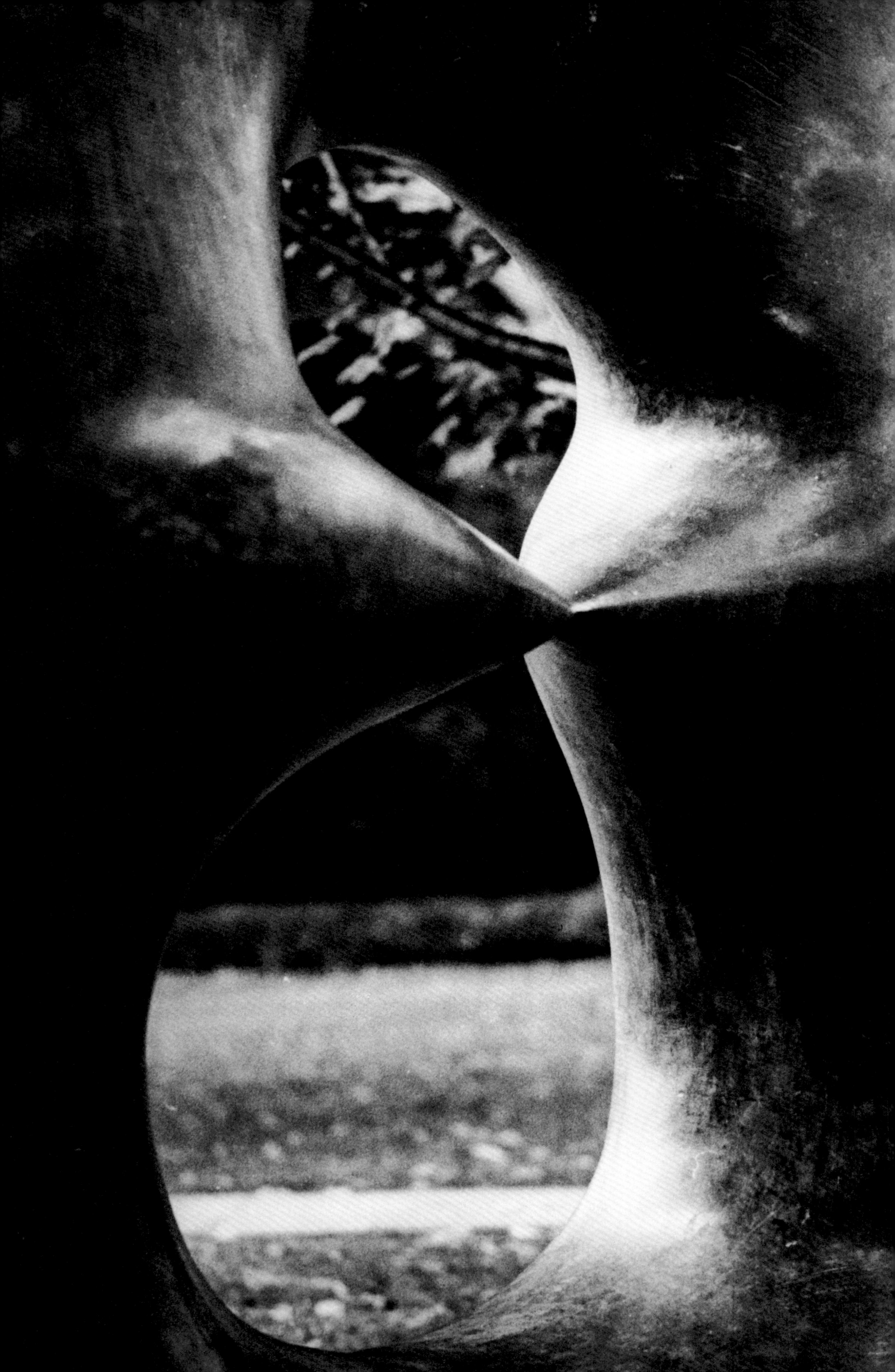

The Secret Life of a Museum

MARK STEVENS

When I was a child, I spent rainy days at the local library. I loved the smell of old books and admired the librarian with red hair who could raise her finger to her lips and go shush without making a sound. I'd like to say I was reading Tacitus in Latin, but mostly I raced through adventure books and rummaged barbarously in the shelves looking for … I could not have said. (Not once did the red-haired librarian discourage me.) A particular treasure was an early collection of cartoons by *The New Yorker*'s Charles Addams, whose métier was secrets, mischief, and the charmingly wicked. One of my favorite cartoons, from 1950, depicted the night watchman at the Museum of Natural History standing under the darkly looming skeleton of a *Tyrannosaurus rex*. He points his flashlight down at a vitrine holding an ancient dinosaur egg. *Which has just hatched* (fig. 60).

I remember this cartoon whenever cultural watchmen ruminate on the role of museums. Their daytime musings ring true (I'm a dues-paying member of the guild), but a museum, apart from tending to the bones—the revelatory bones—also performs many complementary "nighttime" roles, especially at a university where young minds form. Not by hatching monsters but by creating an unorthodox arena outside the lecture hall where personal discoveries, sparked by serendipity and unanswered questions, can strengthen an individual sensibility. At Princeton, the lessons of professor, book, and class come first, but teachers, too, hope to inspire less traveled ways of thinking. The Addams cartoon depicts a secret awakening, the lonely guard having discovered with his pencil of light—which is all any of us has—that the past is neither dead nor buried. Our skin's in the game.

* * *

The new Princeton University Art Museum opens with two bold declarations. Set on a crossroads in the heart of the campus, it highlights the

University's ongoing commitment to the humanities, a worthy resolve in a period often stifled by technocratic dreams of money. The building itself reflects elements of the surrounding architecture but does not flatter the past and, while elegant, is unavoidably large. This may trouble some people but also sends a useful signal. Should the humanities today retire to a corner? Aspire to fit in? Sometimes, perhaps. But the humanities must also interrupt and challenge. (Princeton will still have plenty of paradise.) The second bold declaration, as the Museum opens, lies embedded in its "nine-pavilion" design, which represents the desire of Western society to assign equal weight to art from different cultures. Parsing space into connected pavilions is a way to acknowledge distinctive civilizations while remaining porous enough to convey the cross-fertilization that invigorates art. A tradition may have a house but only one closely joined to others in a worldly village, implicitly asking the knottiest (and airiest) "compare and contrast" question ever to face a Princeton student. Or, for that matter, professor.

With this new museum, Princeton also creates something quieter but no less important: a fresh contemplative space. One very different from those found in Firestone Library or the Princeton Chapel. Art has spiritual and bookish dimensions, of course, but this museum's design—while tidy—permits no churchy or scholarly refuge from the visual cacophony and crazy-quilt patterns of history. The art on display cannot unfold with the measured cadence of a book or library. No matter where a student stands in this museum, a work of modern or contemporary art will be close at hand, sometimes as a commission given to a living artist. As students look at the past, the present will look at them. And the other way around. In contrast to most encyclopedic museums, in which art often appears geographically rooted, the spaces here are more permeable. The varied traditions appear slightly afloat, a disorienting but telling sensation that reflects a period when boundaries are no longer what they were.

The Museum hopes to beguile students into a place where they can spend twenty minutes before a class, while away an afternoon, drink coffee with friends, or gather at parties and theatrical events. Over time, some will then make more serious use—including solitary use—of this new contemplative space. They will be changed. No such museum existed when I was at Princeton, but I had the advantage of being friends with a small group of students intensely drawn to art, and I can testify to what can happen when art and students collide at a university. I arrived with strict views on art, having left the red-haired librarian far behind. But I became one of the many students spellbound by the way in which the historian Carl Schorske opened up Viennese art—and much else—to create a dynamic social portrait of Vienna during the late nineteenth and early twentieth centuries. Schorske presented art as a revealing cultural artifact, embodying the tensions of a particular society, but he did something else besides. It was obvious that he personally *relished* the art. In front of a picture, he lit up like a candle.

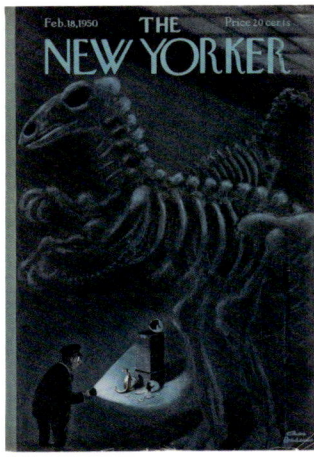

Fig. 60   Charles Addams
(1912–1988; born Westfield, NJ;
died New York, NY), Cover
illustration for *The New Yorker*,
February 18, 1950

How could I regard art as merely a historical artifact if a professor so omnivorously intelligent began to glow? I started to examine Gustav Klimt and Egon Schiele, whom I pompously considered decadent, in a more personal way. I was repelled. I was intrigued. And a kind of secret education began, one without grades. I spent hours in museums, alone or sometimes with a close friend or two. Often I had the Museum at Princeton to myself. I soon became less strict. Art developed the power to delight, disturb, and also bore me, appearing fleshy here and ineffable there, its meanings contrary and tenuous—a tough fluttering thing that eludes the net.

One classmate intrigued me. She regularly visited a certain pot, quite a small pot, in the basement of the old Museum. I remember very little about this pot—"a pot is a pot is a pot" was probably my view—but I did ask her once why she kept going back. She shrugged and cupped her hands. What could that mean? She also liked something broken or uneven about the pot. I would guess now what I didn't know then: that she was attracted to the Japanese concept of *wabi-sabi*, the Buddhist-centered belief that acknowledging chance, transience, and imperfection brings us closer to the truth than a self-centered desire for perfection. Perhaps she found this idea in a class or book and then took it personally, keeping the pot as a touchstone. She was developing a mirroring relationship with a particular work of art, initiating a kind of internal conversation different from but related to my own.

I've seen many such personal "relationships" flourish. They have no scholarly significance, of course. What of substance can be made of the disordered and ill-informed projections of young Joe Blow beaming around a museum? Except, perhaps, if one analyzes the social phenomenon itself. Is the epiphany in front of an expensive Van Gogh the result of a consumer society providing certain forms of titillation? Of course, in part. But these relationships also matter in other ways, as many scholars know. Artists themselves develop very personal relationships with particular works of art. Among students, these relationships can serve both private and social ends, often coming together in ways that may help individuals and their larger society.

The student with such a relationship may, for example, develop a nuanced rather than official empathy for what people now call "the other." The Mesoamerican who made *Two seated figures engaged in animated conversation* (fig. 61), one of the Museum's treasures, lived about two thousand years ago and came from a culture now unimaginably remote. But the two conversing figures do not appear the least bit foreign. They could be two characters in a generational drama opening next week off-Broadway. With repeated viewing of the same works, made possible by the Museum's easy availability, a student may learn how meaning continues to unfold and how the "eye"—that mysterious jelly—can begin to sharpen and clarify. Then the obvious content of a work will no longer be everything: The student will begin to respond to visual play and inspiration, to what the critic Clive Bell called "significant form." The other can become a pleasure, not just an obligation.

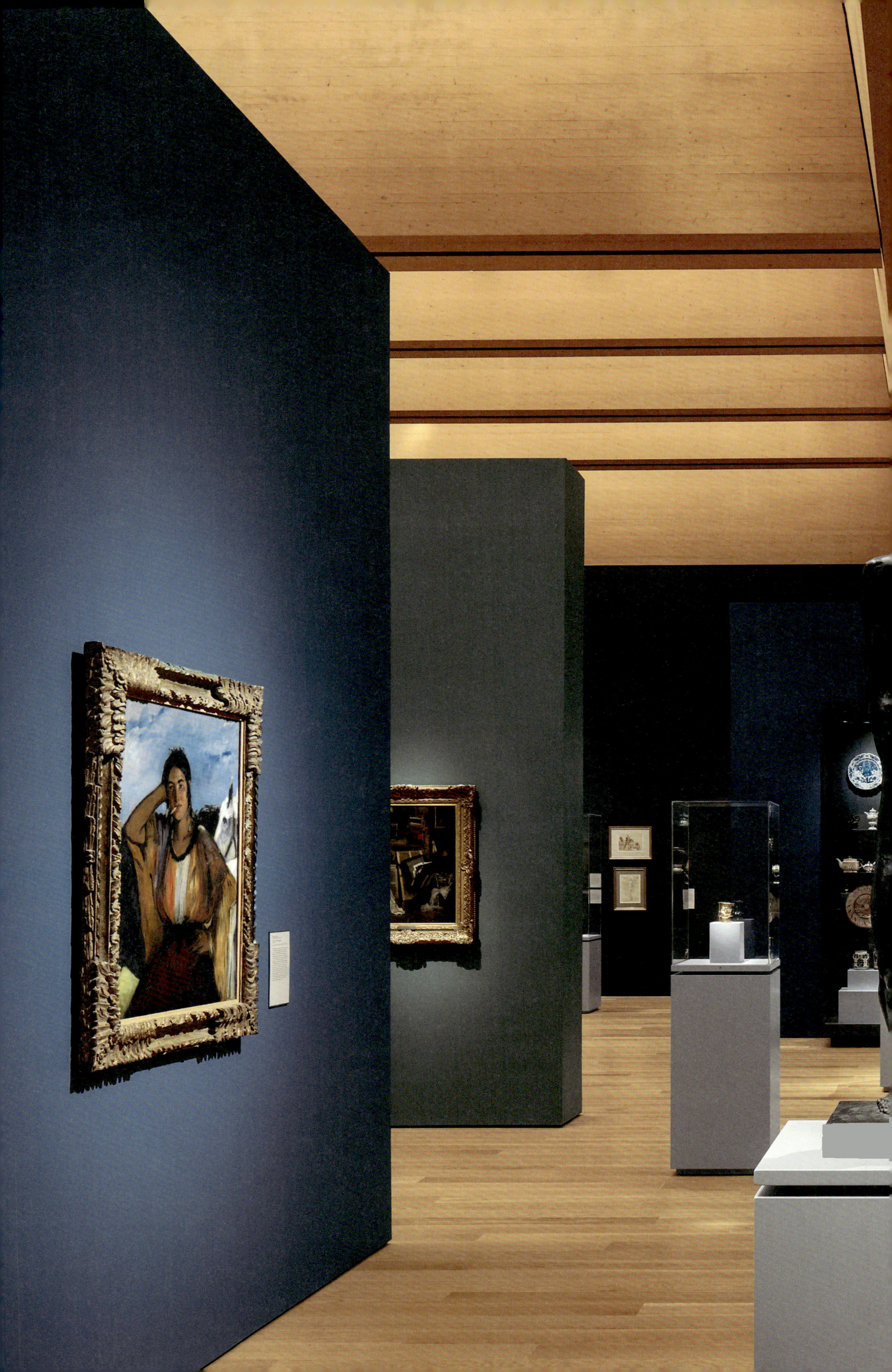

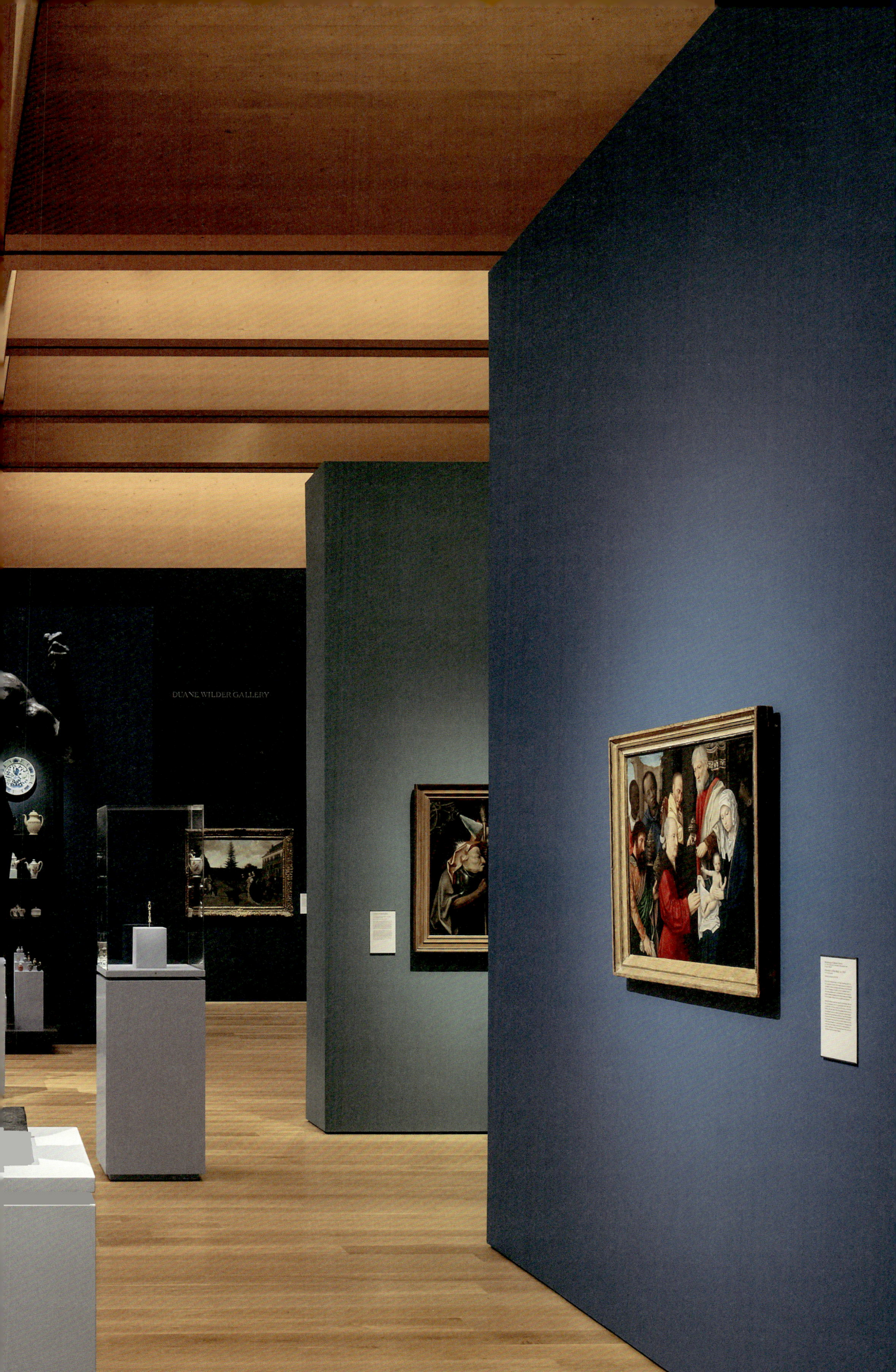

DUANE WILDER GALLERY

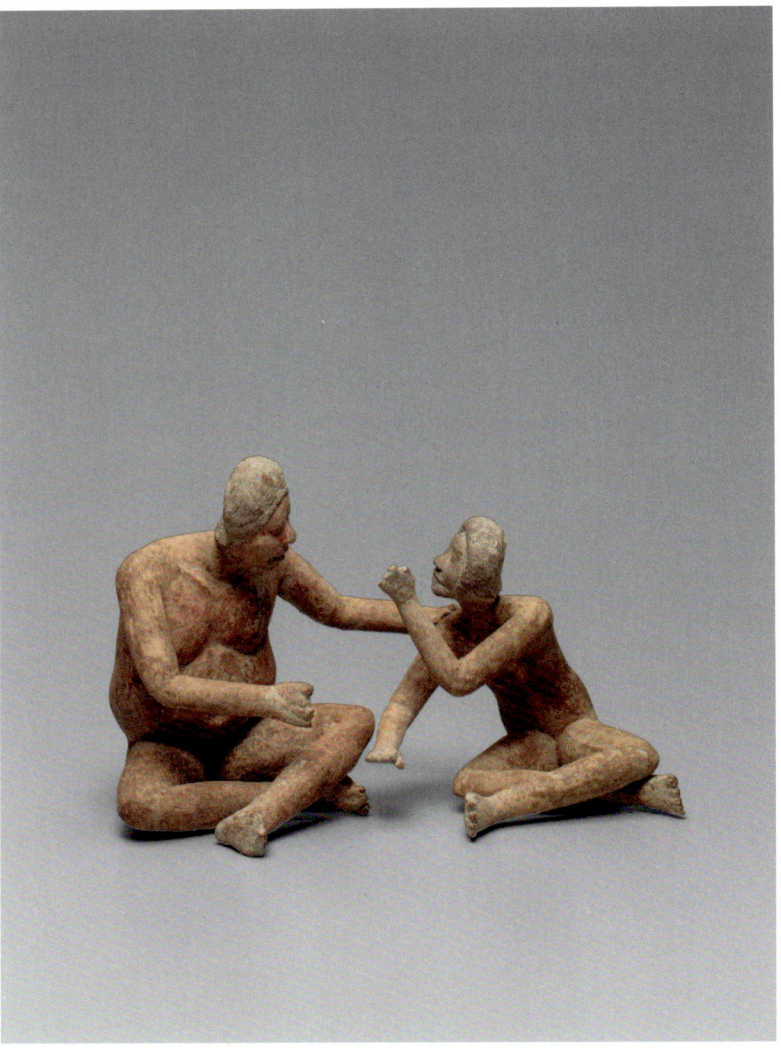

Fig. 61 Xochipala, Late
Formative Period to Early Classic
Period, *Two seated figures
engaged in animated conversation*, 400 BCE–500 CE. Ceramic
with traces of red and peach
slip-paint, h. 13.5 cm. Princeton
University Art Museum. Gift
of Gillett G. Griffin in honor of
David W. Steadman, Graduate
School Class of 1969 (y1972-38, -39)

What gives *Two seated figures engaged in animated conversation* its
pleasing power? The artist was not only a keen observer of individuals
but also a choreographer of shape who used weight and mass (the heft
of the contrasting bodies) and crisscrossing lines (the arm play above
the settled legs) to capture the emotional tenor of an intense back-and-
forth. "Significant form"—a dodgy phrase difficult to define—is hard
to teach, but pleasure is one of its essential parts. I was once told that
the art historian Meyer Schapiro, no slouch when it came to the social
analysis of art, liked to place a Piet Mondrian painting next to one by
Ilya Bolotowsky and then ask his students why the one was good but
the other better. Significant delight? Meaningful pleasure?

The language we use around art, typically too sterile or too
poetic, rarely conveys the secret life of pleasure. *Aesthetic* sounds
medicinal—*diabetic*, *emetic*, *prosthetic*—and *formal* suggests an excru-
ciating party. I once likened a color to a "lemon picked off the tree" and
was rebuked for being an aspiring poet with bourgeois inclinations toward connoisseurship. I should write, *cadmium yellow*. Even so, artists
and certain teachers like Schorske can be wonderfully good at awakening people to the joy of form, color, and light—even as they discuss

more sober matters. (Suddenly, within a student's face, the blinds snap up.) There have been times when, wearied by a museum plod-around, I have yielded to a fantasy that a museum is actually a shackled creature with two secretive passions, the first being a love for pleasure. (I'll get to the other in a moment.) Behind the nonreflective glass and wordy wall panel lies a pagan temple to visual escape—morals left momentarily at the door. Princeton students who think too much of grades and the future would take, as a requirement, Pleasure 101 followed by Significant Form 202.

Of course, nobody now uses the *b* word, which is as stale as an old closet and almost as bad as its appalling relative, *beauteous*. We know very well that visual pleasure can be used to promote elitist distinctions and evil ends. The best-known example of the latter is Leni Riefenstahl's celebration of Nazi rallies. But visual pleasure can also be socially useful, even virtuous. A student with a pleasure-loving but sharp eye is better prepared than most to confront the visual wasteland and no-there places everywhere around us today. They can resist schlock and saccharine nostalgia. A friend at the Museum recently told me about a student from the Midwest who found the lush campus disorienting: It did not reflect his background. He learned that art can find value in overlooked places and took significant pleasure in Michael Kenna's photographs of the Rouge factory in Dearborn, Michigan (figs. 62, 63). Another student missed the grasslands of her home state of Montana. Did she tack a colorful calendar picture onto the wall of her room? No, she developed a relationship with the formally austere but grassily textured black-and-white photograph *Untitled (Grasses)* (1951; fig. 64), by Harry Callahan, which fortified her memory rather than dissipating her homesickness into sugary clichés. Significant form, and pleasure, can warm the mind for spiritual contemplation and, in a despairing work, add nuanced counterpoints that become devastatingly beautiful.

Students with an eye may eventually create, in ways large and small, places that brighten rather than diminish their communities. They'll be honoring Princeton's own tradition of commissioning serious architects to design its new buildings, which gives body to the conviction that good design is not a luxury but part of the way

Figs. 62, 63   Michael Kenna (born 1953, Widnes, United Kingdom; active Seattle, WA), *The Rouge, Study 96, Dearborn, Michigan*, 1995, and *The Rouge, Study 31, Dearborn, Michigan*, 1994, printed 1996. Gelatin silver prints, 50.8 × 40.6 cm (each). Princeton University Art Museum. The Ford Rouge Complex Collection, gift of the Ford Motor Company (1997-29.96, -29.31)

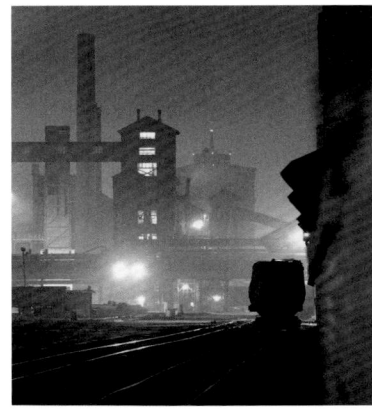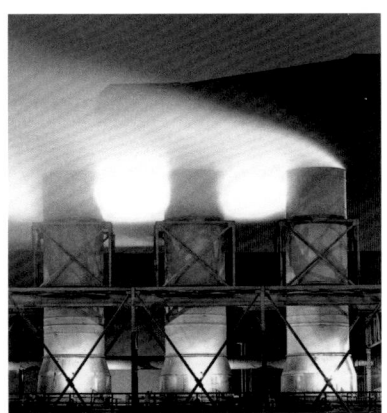

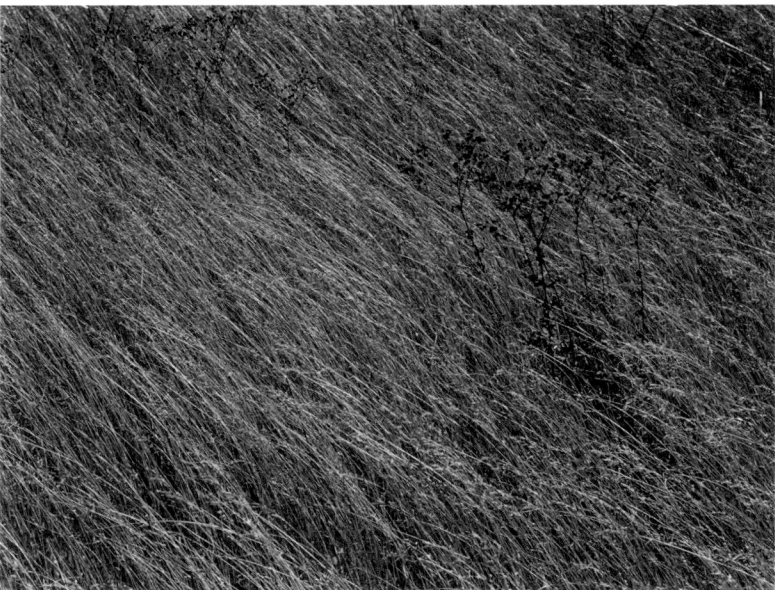

Fig. 64   Harry Callahan
(1912–1999; born Detroit, MI;
died Atlanta, GA), *Untitled
(Grasses)*, 1951. Gelatin silver
print, 8.4 × 11.2 cm. Princeton
University Art Museum. Gift
of Michael D. Francis (x1989-51)

a healthy community thrives. The University's commitment to outdoor sculpture is related to this. It does not finally matter if a piece of
sculpture—or an architectural design—is a masterpiece. What matters is that an effort is consciously made, that a place is recognized for
being a particular place, and that the community wants to enliven its
environment. The friend at the Museum who told me about the students from Montana and the Midwest mentioned another student for
whom Henry Moore's *Oval with Points* (1969–70; fig. 65) provided an
essential "grounding" on the campus. Across the changing seasons it
stood there in all its mysterious oddity, a point of permanence amid
the Princeton flux.

My other fantasy about museums is a "what if?" Imagine, for a
moment, removing the veils of careful thought, the artful arrange-
ments, and the aura of cultural beneficence (art as the highest expression of, etc.). What then? Even a museum the manageable size of
Princeton's would become a mishmash of time, place, and style. An
arena of conflict and disagreement. This kind of environment—one
without scholarly dispassion—can be useful to edgy young minds
who naturally question authority and may sometimes want to see the
museum in a confrontational light. Bitter fruit can nourish. Stale ideas
may crack. Different ways of ordering emerge. Students at Princeton
are not far removed from high school (like many of us) and know in
their bones the important role played by bad boys and bad girls in
America, memorably defined by the Shangri-Las in that 1964 classic
of delirious teenage kitsch, "Give Him a Great Big Kiss," in which one
singer pauses to say conversationally to another, "I hear he's bad,"
and the other answers, "Hmm…he's good bad, but he's not evil."*

Princeton should have some difficult boys and girls, with the
Museum itself a potential target. Isn't the Museum just a big bazaar
purveying products stamped and certified by a professor or curator? Is every tradition of equal value, a slice in the great art pie, with a

* Scholars working in bad-boy
studies should not, of course, over-
look "Leader of the Pack."

Fig. 65 Henry Moore (1898–1986; born Castleford, United Kingdom; died Perry Green, United Kingdom), *Oval with Points*, 1969–70. Bronze, 335 × 265.4 × 133.3 cm. Princeton University Art Museum. The John B. Putnam Jr. Memorial Collection, Princeton University (y1969-128)

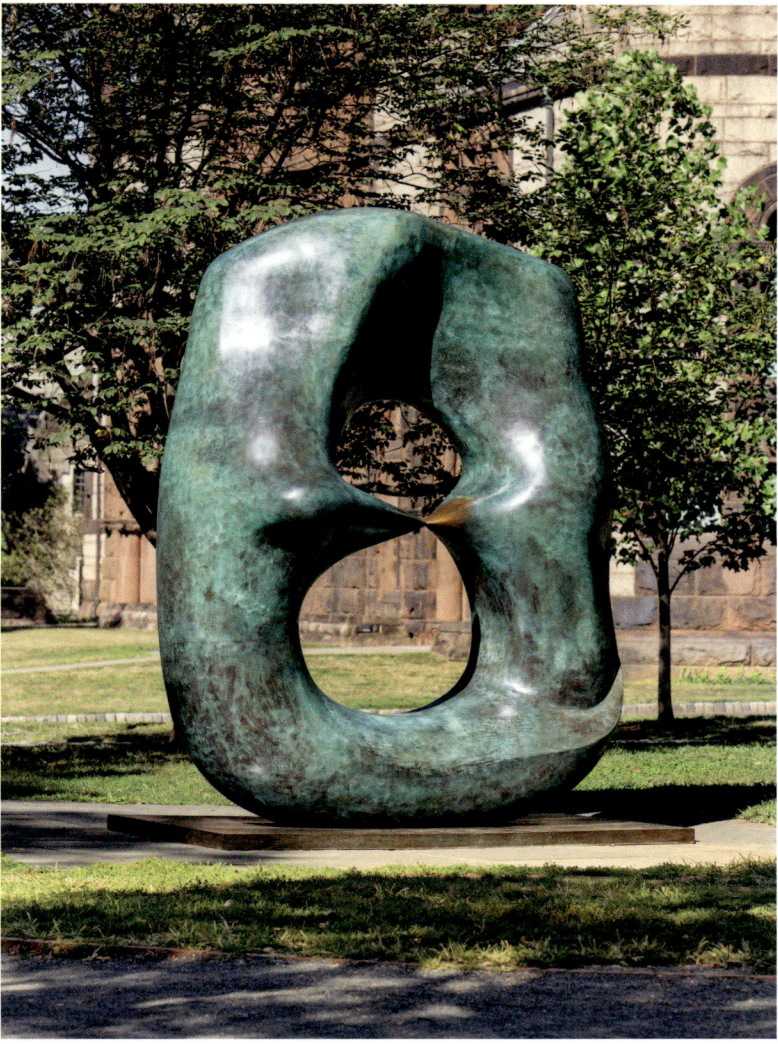

preference for one thing over another being merely a matter of taste? Aren't some works of art better than others? Perhaps rebellious minds will become generous with time, but perhaps not. Some of the greatest artists squint, leaving out much, in order to see in their own way. I like to imagine the Museum creating predicaments for students. What if a nineteen-year-old from Texas of South Asian descent does not like South Asian temple art? What if a student powerfully drawn to modernism looks and looks and looks and thinks Mark Rothko is corny?

The new Museum will embody some of the presiding tensions of our time, inviting useful argument. David Adjaye's design is highly wrought, highly controlled. Its details, having been so carefully considered, almost wink at visitors. Lovely terrazzo, granite, and wood; generous spaces that do not cramp the eye. At the same time, the Museum has commissioned an artist, Nick Cave, to do something fundamentally different: sprawl an outrageous, enormous, riotously colored figure around its main entrance (fig. 66), a concoction that, like the architecture, shimmers with exciting materials but to contrasting effect. The different outlooks may not be noticed by students as they think about an upcoming lecture at McCosh, but they will instinctively

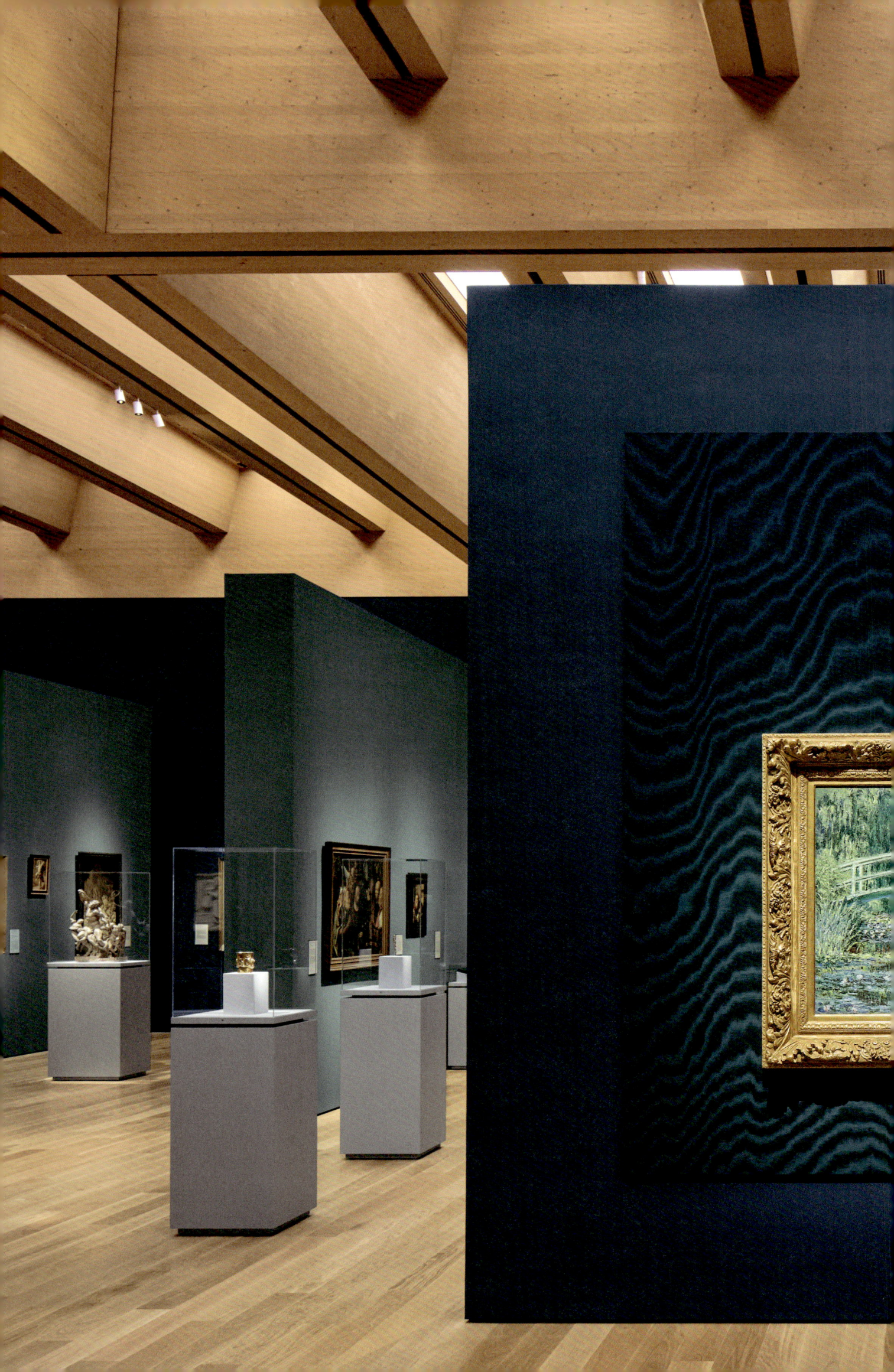

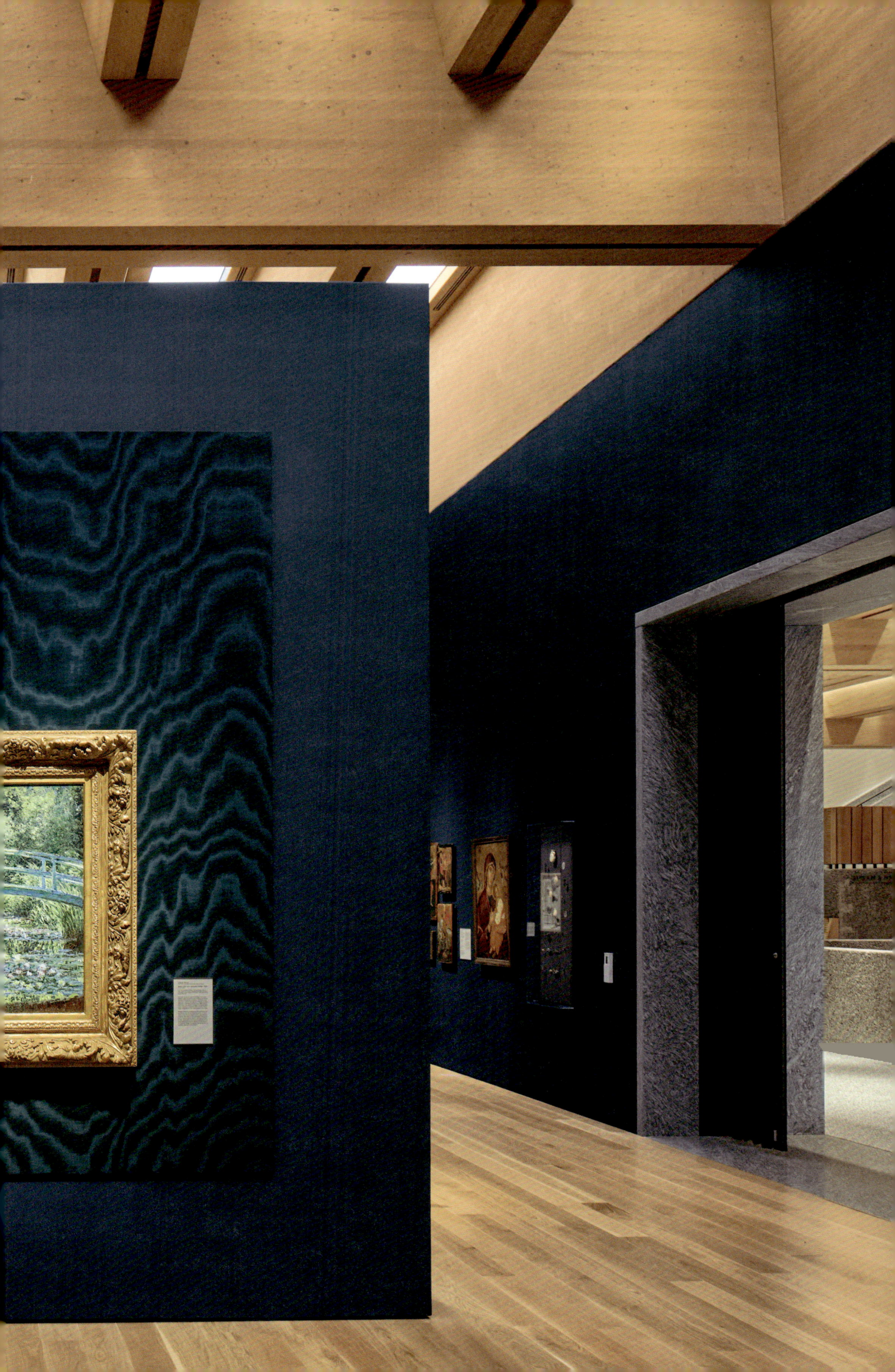

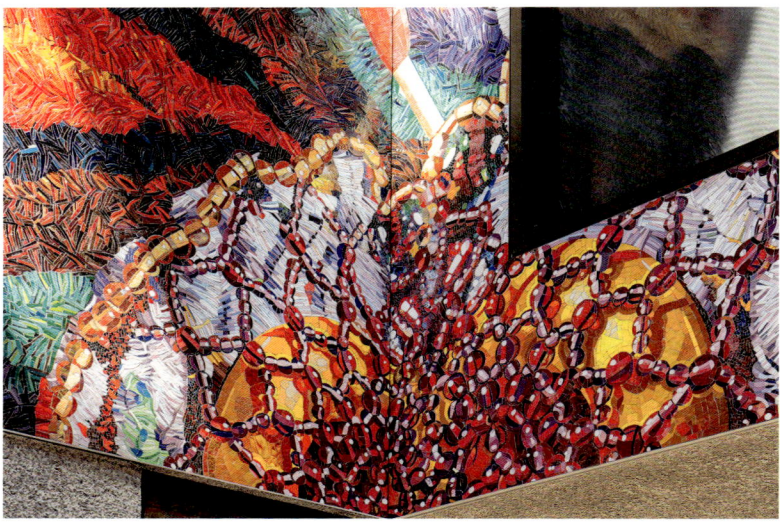

Fig. 66   Nick Cave (born 1959,
Fulton, MO; active Chicago, IL),
Let me kindly introduce myself.
They call me MC Prince Brighton.
(detail), 2025. Mosaic tile, wood,
and chrome-painted HDU inlay.
Princeton University Art
Museum. Museum commission
made possible by the John B.
Putnam Jr. Memorial Fund and
the Fowler McCormick, Class
of 1921, Fund (2025-108)

begin to understand alternatives. The lively street or the refined interior. The solace of control or the thrill of eruption.

What will artists make of AI? Will there be a tradition of… selfies? The way the Museum entwines past and present opens up the possibility of a rich conversation with the digital world. Are artists, for example, made of flesh and blood? Or are they phantoms on a screen? The Museum has long made a determined effort to bring living artists to campus whose flesh and blood can haunt young minds. Some of my friends at Princeton were students of Toshiko Takaezu, the ceramic artist who taught at the university and lived not far from campus, where her sort-of disciples gathered for conversation and to help with firings at her kiln. Her connection to ancient Japanese traditions seemed entirely alive, as did her connection to midcentury contemporary art (fig. 67). Princeton has also traditionally let students in certain courses move past the vitrine and handle art (not, of course, fragile pieces). To run your fingers along ridges made by ancient fingers is, in a way, to sit beside an artist from long ago and touch time itself— a useful exercise for students looking only at the present and the future. The old was once young.

As the past questions our present, it will find much wanting that the Museum is well equipped to address in a digital world. The first is want of physical touch. Until recently, art was steeped in tactile sensations. Even artists interested in spiritual, ethereal, or evanescent ideas depended on an atmosphere of physical touch. A Renaissance fresco, spiritually light on the wall, becomes still lighter when surrounded by stone; a Chinese ink wash painting, while seeming to fade into the mist, does not let you forget the animal-hair brush or wet spilled ink. Many artists directly embrace touch: They know the hand can be felt by the eye. ("Flesh," said Willem de Kooning, "is the reason why oil paint was invented.") On the glassy screen of a phone or computer, you may find many intimations of touch—a finely rendered image, say, of the whorls of a shell—but not the powerful thinginess of some paintings. Already in the 1950s artists were complaining that the photographs circulating of Mondrian's paintings were misleading because they could not adequately convey the presence of his hand, which was not a ruler. The walls, floors, and ceilings of the new Museum all celebrate touch.

Another great want, and loss, is slow looking. The consumption of images has been speeding up for a long time, but the speed with which images appear and disappear as you turn the pages of a magazine, when compared to flipping through a phone, seems as slow-moving as a horse and carriage. When few images existed, they were either ignored—having become blindingly familiar—or were looked at slowly and, sometimes, with extraordinary intensity. Fast looking skitters across a surface; slow looking penetrates. The new Museum will provide students with limitless opportunities to re-awaken both touch and slow looking. Of course, someone will object, "So what? There's no going back," which is true. But slow and tactile looking are their own reward, and they are especially useful for those students who are developing into artists, writers, musicians, and the like—or who want to live in this neighborhood. Their imaginations are maturing, their sensibilities struggling with form. The strongest will want to feel the pressure of the past on the present, however

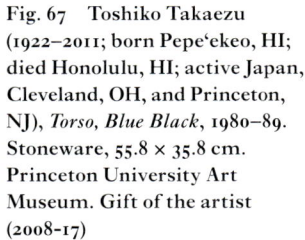

Fig. 67   Toshiko Takaezu (1922–2011; born Pepe'ekeo, HI; died Honolulu, HI; active Japan, Cleveland, OH, and Princeton, NJ), *Torso, Blue Black*, 1980–89. Stoneware, 55.8 × 35.8 cm. Princeton University Art Museum. Gift of the artist (2008-17)

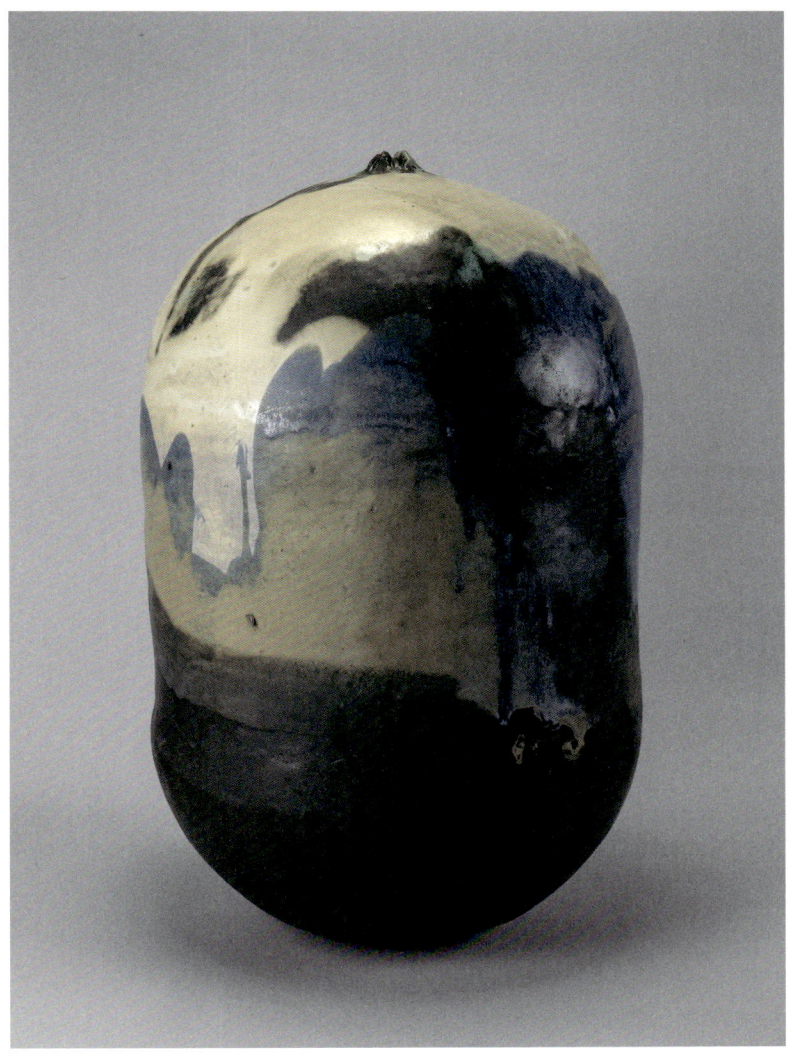

great their commitment is to the contemporary. They will want to know what is being forgotten.

Among this group there will inevitably be a subset of imaginative students who feel isolated, moody, and depressed. The impact a museum can make on such students passes mostly unnoticed, but it is not insignificant. A museum can become, for one who is alienated, a place of imagined community with friends to whom one can almost talk. A writer told me that many years ago, when she was a student living alone in London and seriously depressed, she began regularly going to the Tate. She would sit on a bench staring at one of the twentieth century's darkest works of art: Francis Bacon's triptych *Three Studies for Figures at the Base of a Crucifixion* (1944; fig. 68). She would go home cheered up. She found a friend in Bacon.

Another instance: A few years ago, in the old Museum, I noticed a young man and woman on a date who could barely look at each other. They spoke to each other sideways. He was red-faced. She had purple hair. They stood a while in front of Édouard Manet's *Woman with a Cigarette* (ca. 1878–80; fig. 69), a painting that is probably unfinished but full of touch. It was once called (not by Manet) *Gypsy with a Cigarette*, which the Museum thinks might be derogatory or condescending to the Romani people. That said, the painting has no desire to be proper. In the 1880s a woman who dangled a cigarette from her lips while standing beside a horse's head was not a lady riding in her carriage through the Bois de Boulogne. Manet admired women who were outsiders. Women who did not submit to the male gaze but looked back. This woman does not quite do that, but it appears she might at any moment. The young couple, looking straight into the painting, still spoke to each other sideways. But they were beginning to smile.

* * *

The old Princeton museum was painfully shy. Hiding behind the skirt of its library, well back from the crowd on McCosh Walk, it kept its eyes down. Much of its collection lay beneath the stairs, and its rooms rambled for no apparent reason, like someone who dresses in whatever happens to be in the closet. The old Princeton museum was one of those places about which people said, "It has some wonderful things."

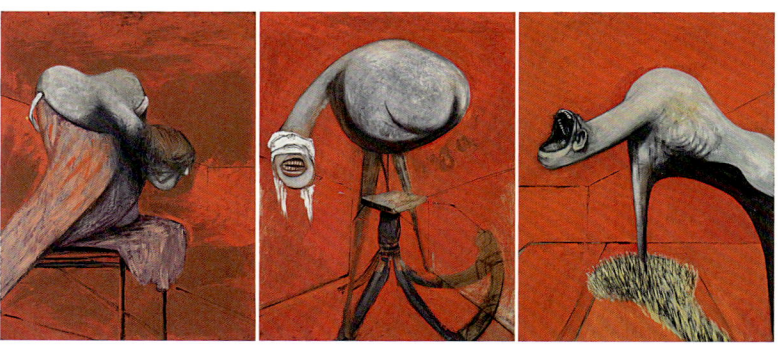

Fig. 68   Francis Bacon (1909–1992; born Dublin, Ireland; died Madrid, Spain), *Three Studies for Figures at the Base of a Crucifixion*, 1944. Triptych: oil on board, 94 × 73.7 cm (each). Tate, London. Presented by Eric Hall 1953 (N06171)

Fig. 69   Édouard Manet
(1832–1883; born and died Paris,
France), *Woman with a Cigarette*,
ca. 1878–80. Oil on canvas, 92 ×
73.5 cm. Princeton University Art
Museum. Bequest of Archibald S.
Alexander, Class of 1928
(y1979-55)

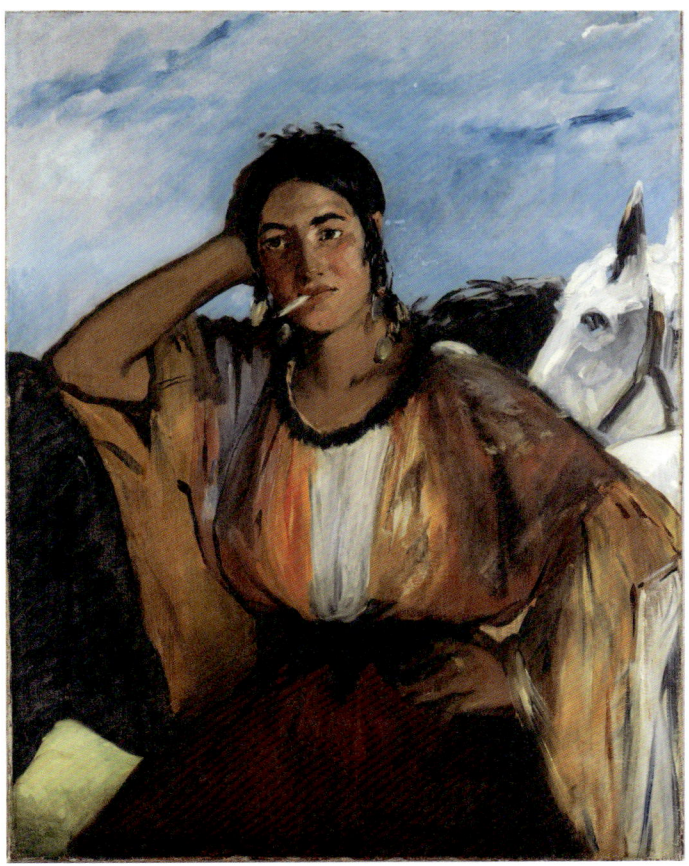

The new Princeton museum raises a window while permitting secrets. Open and light-filled but with shady and retiring corners, it is a place for professors to teach students and for students to teach themselves. A place of meditation on a Princeton crossroads: "When you come to a fork in the road," said Professor Yogi Berra, "take it." Of course, many students now avoid classes in the humanities. But it's remarkable what even the corner of the eye can accomplish. People caught by a glimpse often begin to see in new ways. They become collectors, readers, philanthropists, and mentors. Since they continue to look into art's mirror, they remain students in spirit who can tolerate difficult questions. Of what social use is an education in the humanities? A person at ease with questions can better resist the real monsters—the dinosaurs with all the answers—regularly loosed upon our world. The luckiest Princeton students, as they move into adult society, will take a museum with them.

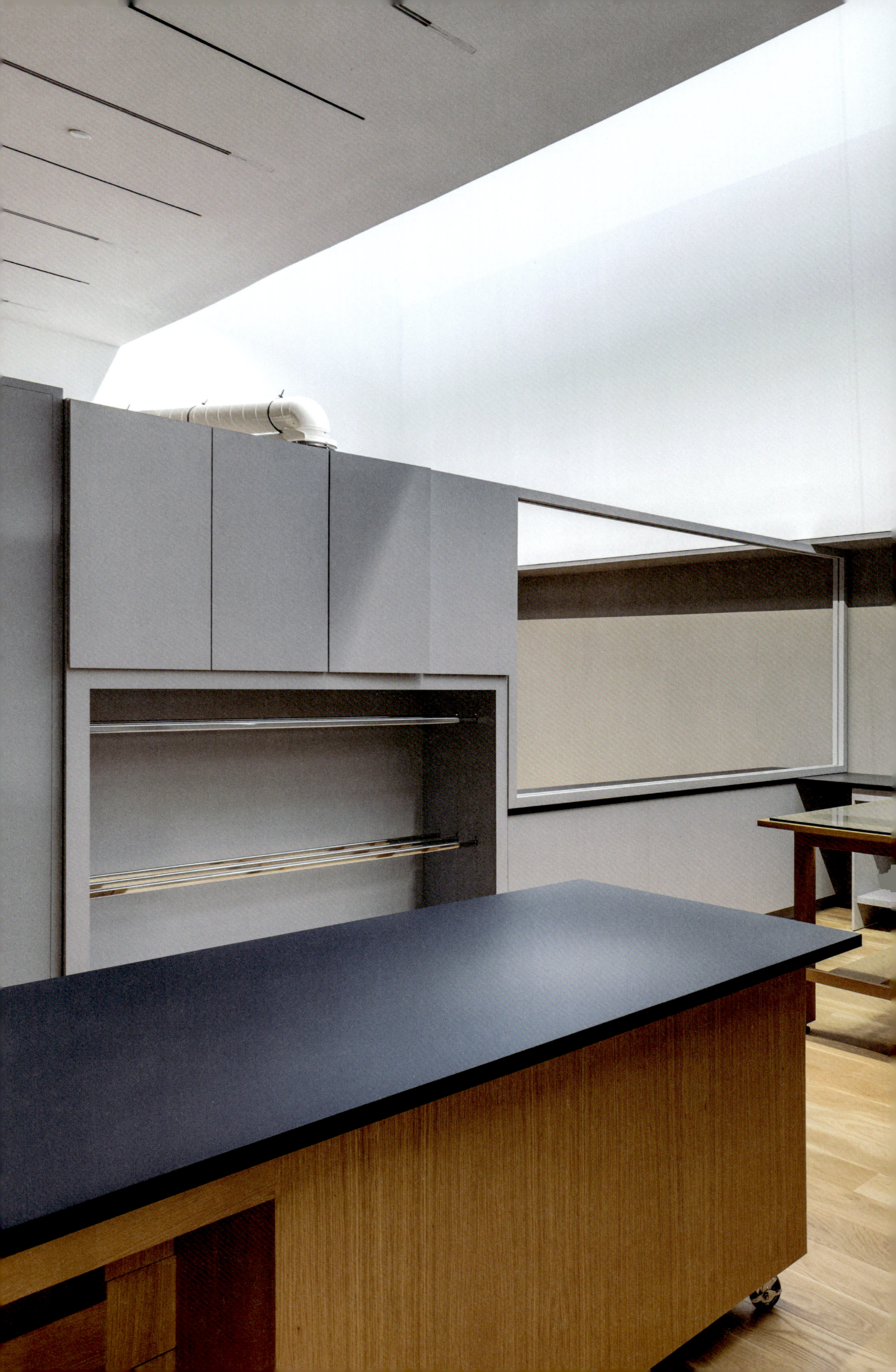

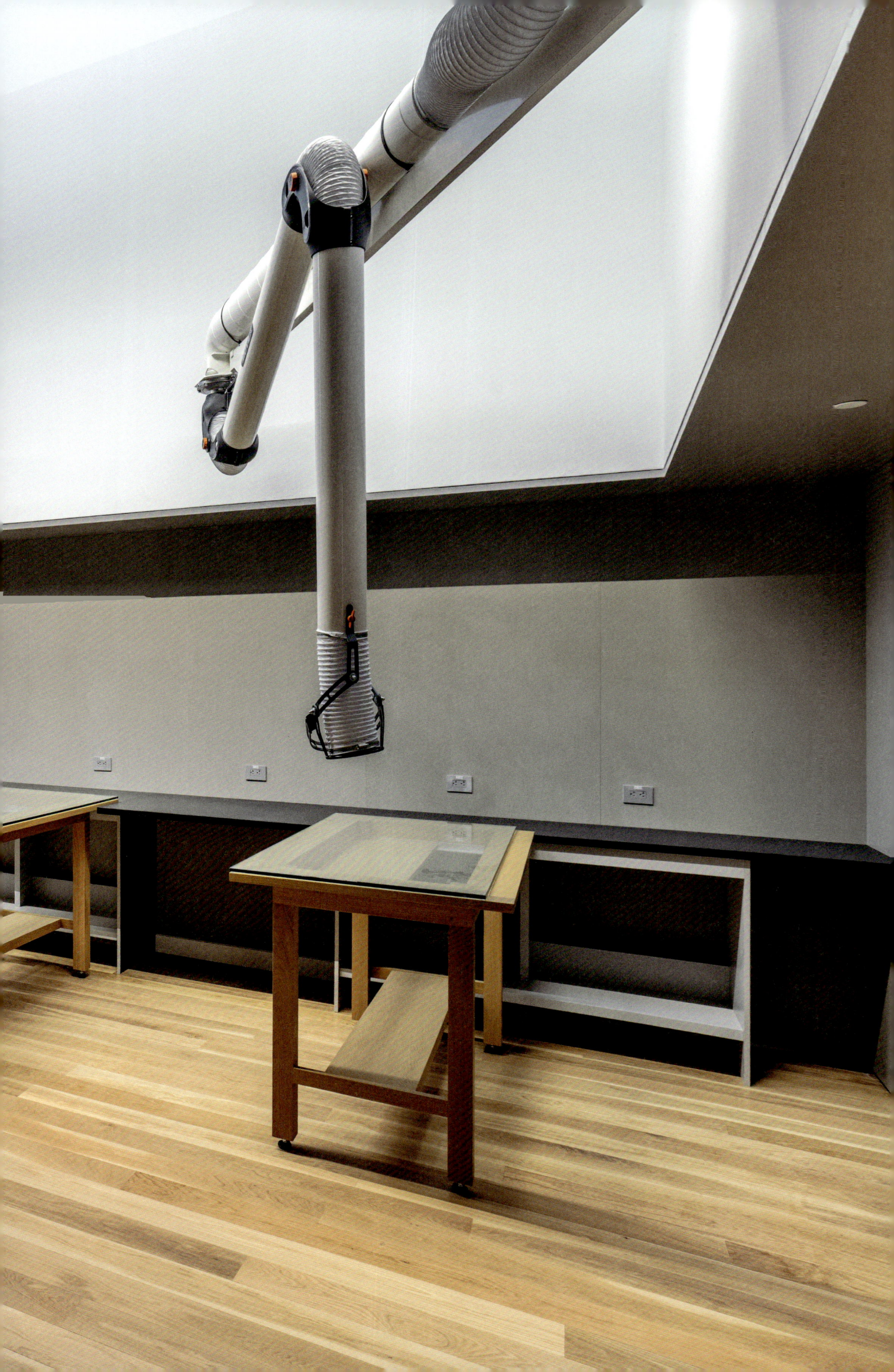

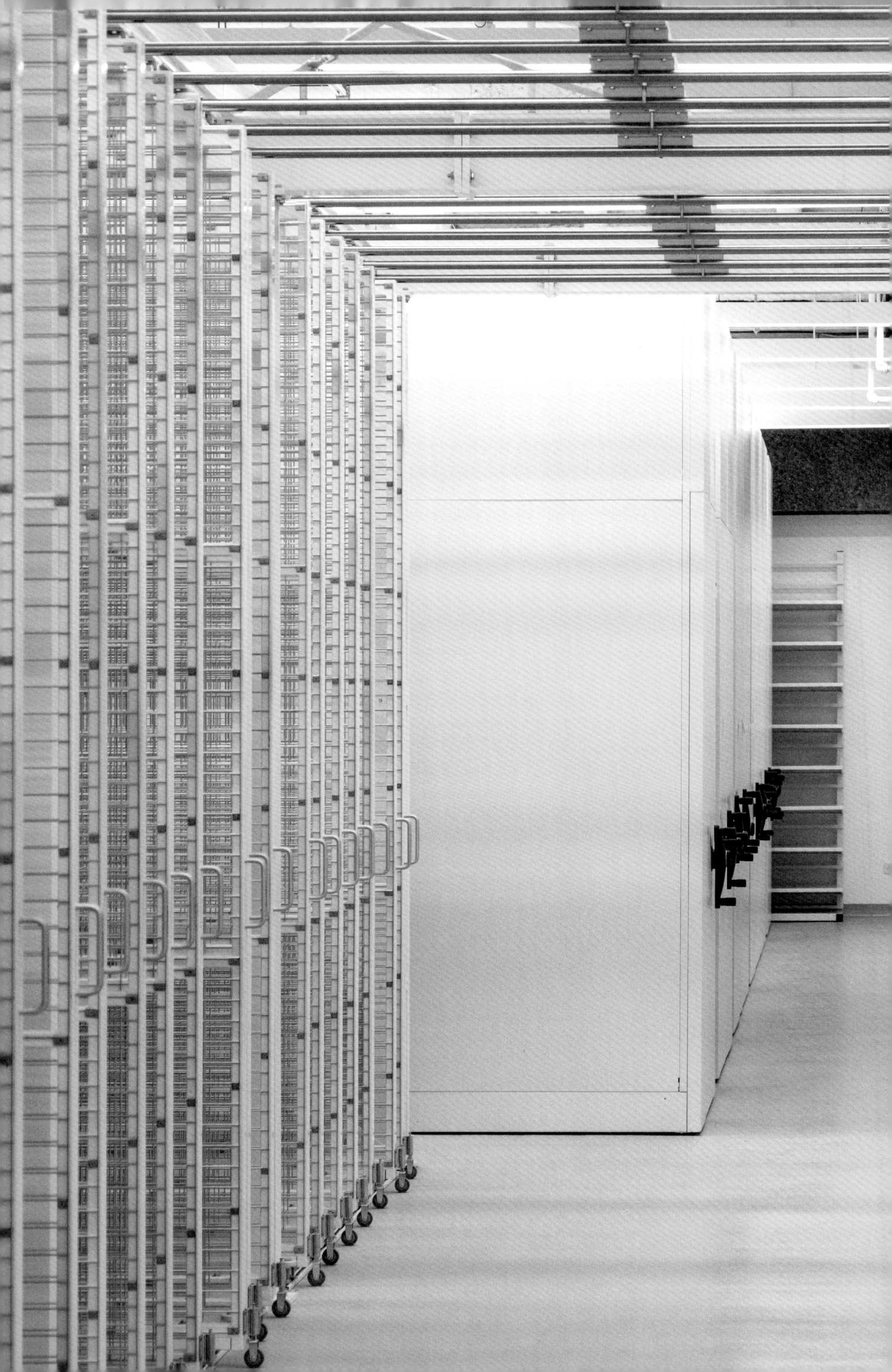

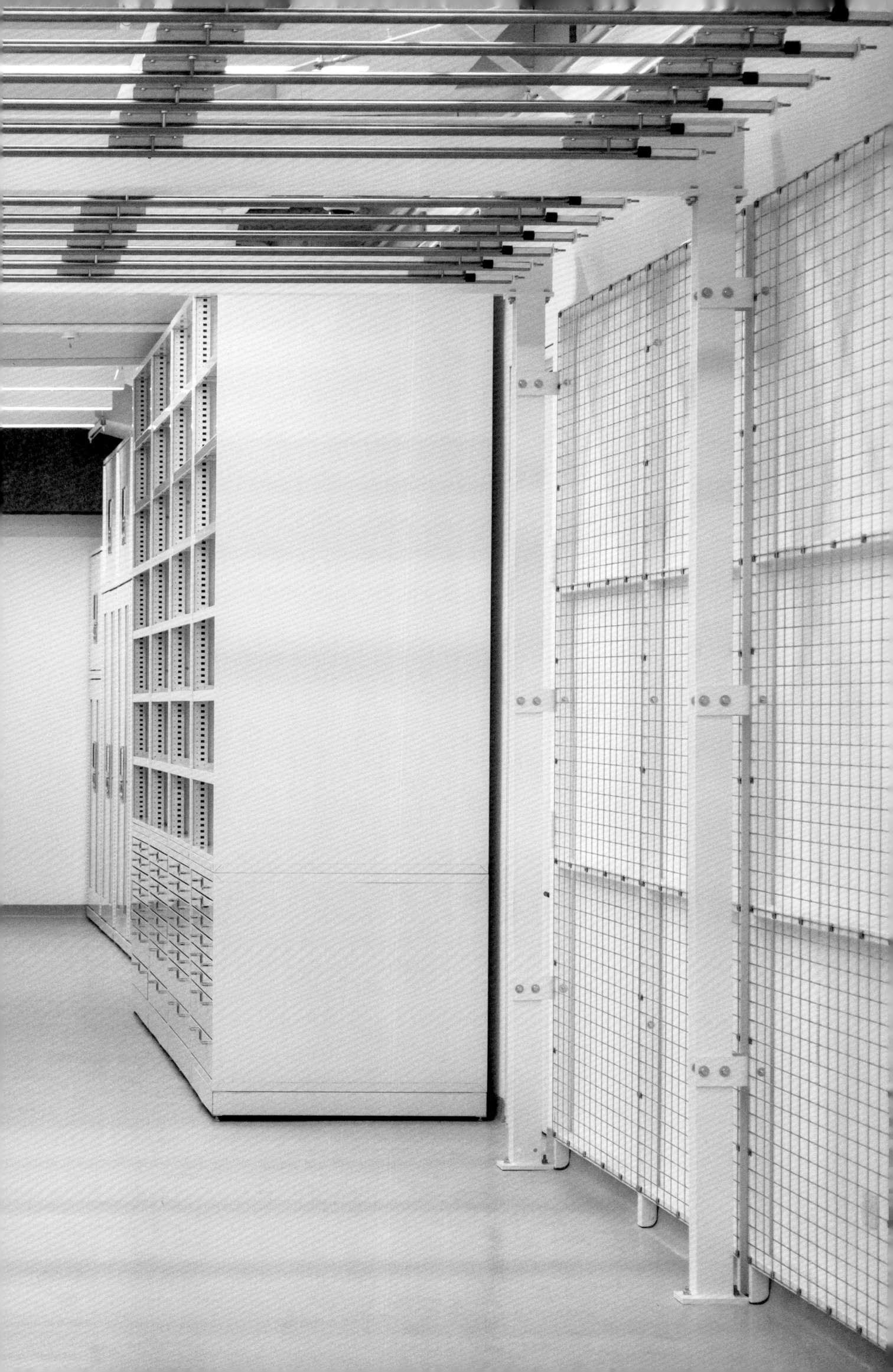

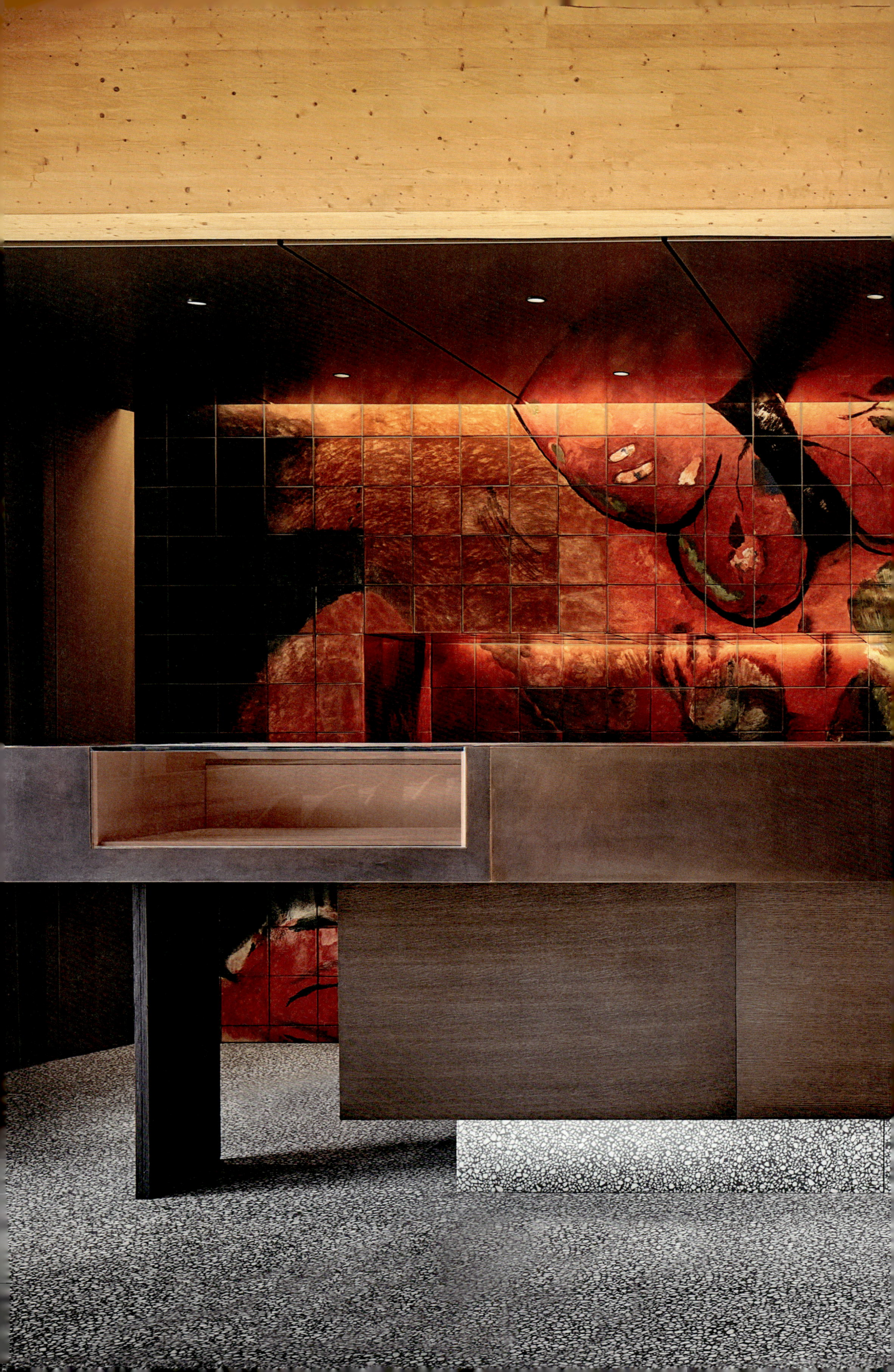

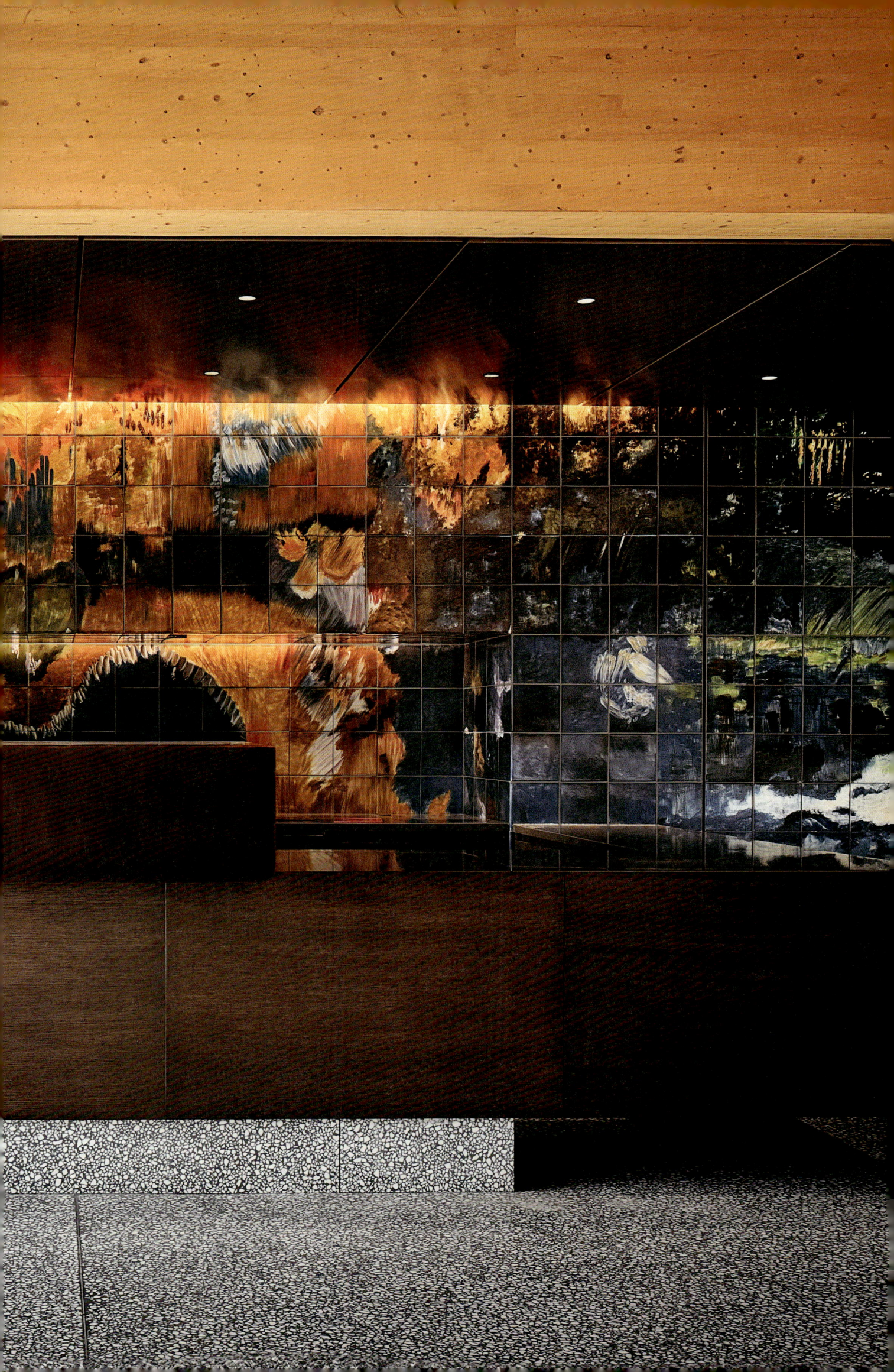

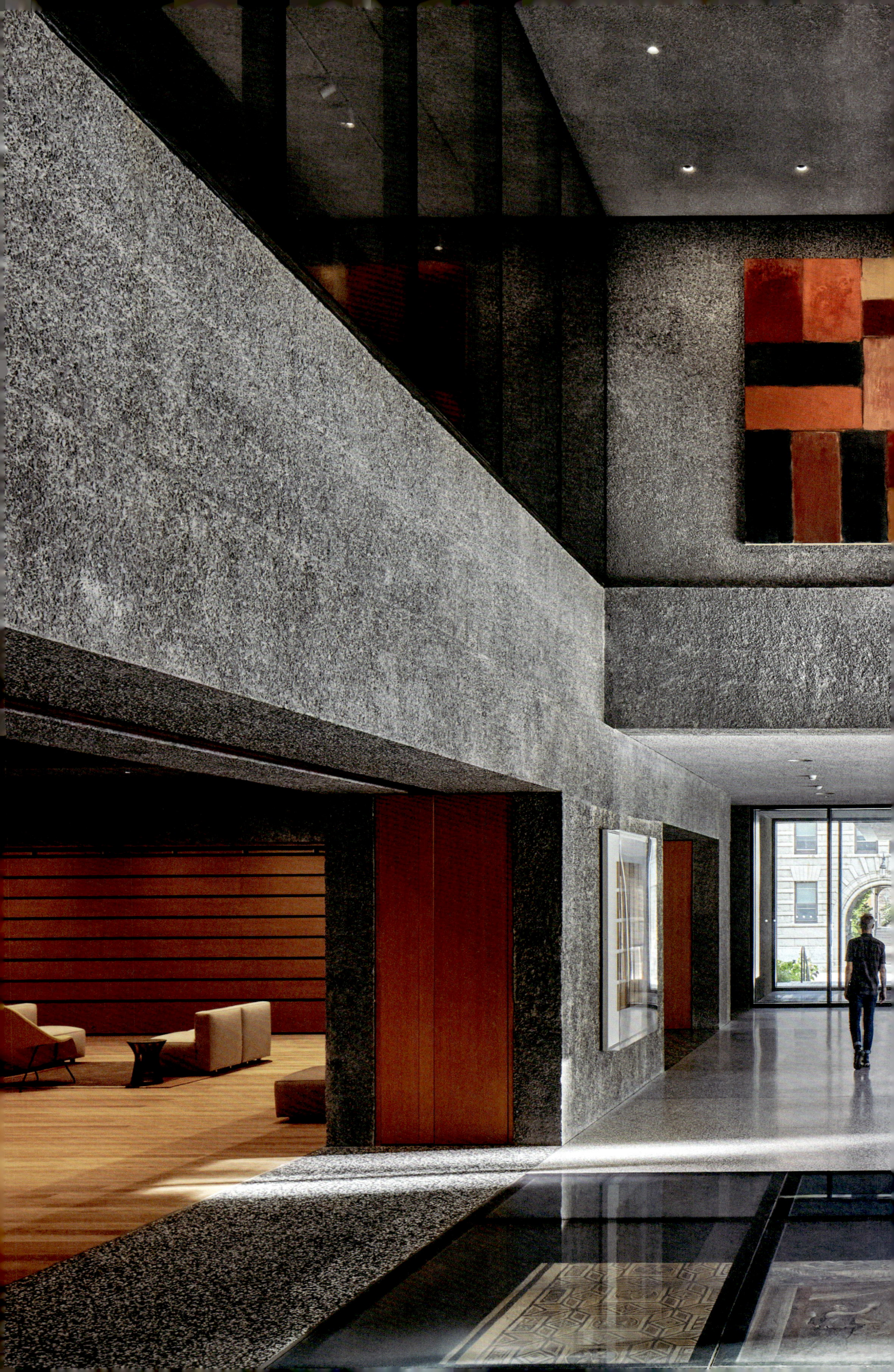

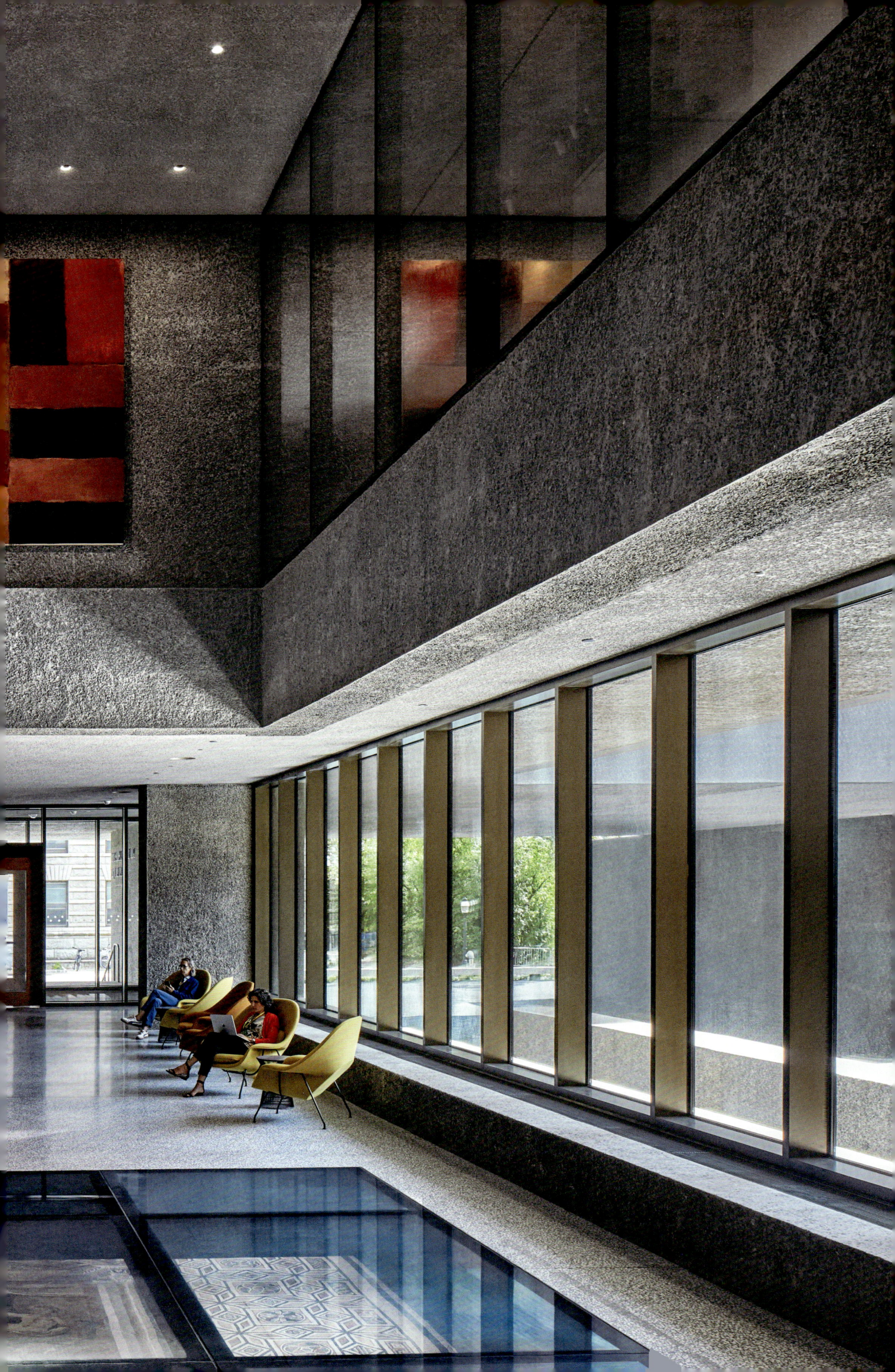

CONTRIBUTORS

JAMES STEWARD is the Nancy A. Nasher–David J. Haemisegger, Class of 1976, Director of the Princeton University Art Museum, as well as lecturer with the rank of professor in Princeton's Department of Art & Archaeology and a faculty fellow of Rockefeller College. He served as director of the University of Michigan Museum of Art from 1998 to 2009. A scholar of eighteenth- and nineteenth-century European art, Steward is a member of the Order of St. Petersburg and a Knight of the Royal House of Portugal for services to art and education.

PAUL GOLDBERGER is Joseph Urban Professor of Design at the New School and the former architecture critic for *The New Yorker* and *The New York Times*. In 1984 he received the Pulitzer Prize for Distinguished Criticism for his work at the *Times*. Goldberger is the author of several books, including *Ballpark: Baseball in the American City* (2019), *Building Art: The Life and Work of Frank Gehry* (2015), and *Why Architecture Matters* (2009). He lectures widely on architecture, planning, and historic preservation.

RON McCOY, Graduate School Class of 1960, is Princeton's university architect. Since 2018 he has provided overall guidance for the planning, architecture, and landscape of the Princeton campus, collaborating with some of the leading architects of our generation to advance the values of the institution while enhancing the unique qualities of the campus. He is an emeritus professor at Arizona State University, where he was director of the School of Architecture and university architect.

MARK STEVENS, Class of 1973, is the author, with Annalyn Swan, Class of 1973, of *De Kooning: An American Master*, which won the 2005 Pulitzer Prize for Biography or Autobiography, and of *Francis Bacon: Revelations* (2021), which *The Times of London* named the art book of the year. He has served as an art critic for *Newsweek*, *New York Magazine*, and *The New Republic*. He is currently at work, with Swan, on a biography of the Anglo-Iraqi architect Zaha Hadid.

SUSAN STEWART is the Avalon Foundation University Professor in the Humanities, emeritus. A former chancellor of the Academy of American Poets and a MacArthur Fellow, she is the author most recently of a book of poems, *Bramble*, forthcoming in 2026; her Clarendon Lectures from 2023, *Poetry's Nature*; and *The Ruins Lesson* from 2020. Her *Columbarium* (2003) won the National Book Critics Circle Award in poetry. She is a member of the American Academy of Arts and Sciences and the American Philosophical Society.

ACKNOWLEDGMENTS

Much like the complex building project it celebrates, this volume is the fruit of a long history. Initial planning for making a new museum for Princeton began in 2012, while the prehistory of that effort—described on the preceding pages—goes back decades and nestles into a history of building, demolishing, rebuilding, and expanding that dates to the nineteenth century. Both building and book have been realized only through the extraordinary contributions of many individuals, whose gracious participation bespeaks a commitment to the academic art museum as an essential laboratory for the production of new knowledge and the shaping of experience.

First, I am grateful for the leadership of Princeton University President Christopher L. Eisgruber, whose belief in the Museum as a hub for humanistic inquiry has made possible both this book and the building it commemorates—and who graciously authored the foreword to this volume. The University's senior leaders—particularly Provost Jennifer Rexford and Executive Vice President Katie Callow-Wright, as well as their predecessors, Deborah Prentice and Charlotte "Treby" Williams, respectively—are also deserving of my deepest thanks for their belief in what this work could do and their focus on doing it. My colleagues in the University's Office of Capital Projects have been exceptional partners in the planning for and making of a new museum, most notably University Architect Ron McCoy, who also agreed to write for this book. Without Ron's shared commitment to great architects and the buildings they produce, the process that led us to this moment would have had neither such integrity nor such vision; nor would it have been half so much fun.

I also cannot let the moment pass without calling out the talents and commitment of the whole of our design team, co-led from the beginning by Adjaye Associates and executive architects Cooper Robertson. Their bold but welcoming design gives us a building that amplifies the art within it—not so common as one might imagine in the business of making museum architecture—and positions the Museum not only as a vibrant gathering place for students, faculty, and the greater community but also as a continuation of the noblest museum-making of the past 150 years. To our lighting designers at Tilletson Associates, our landscape architects at Field Operations, our branding and graphic design team at 2×4, the gallery design group at Studio Joseph, the architectural casework team at Goppion in Milan, and the "loose" casework teams at Click Netherfield in Edinburgh and at Kubik Maltbie here in New Jersey, each of you has ensured that the result would be a seamless and elegant integration of form and function. Equally, as we moved from vessel to program, our colleagues at Bluecadet have been essential in working through myriad issues of interpretation and how to deliver information far more effectively through an entirely new website, just as our communications colleagues at Berlin Rosen have worked to assure that the good word would be heard.

Since 1746, when New Jersey's colonial governor Jonathan Belcher donated the first work of art to Princeton University (then called the College of New Jersey), the vitality of this Museum has been shaped by generations of philanthropists who have given selflessly to ensure that a museum at Princeton could matter. This has been especially true over the past decade, when a cadre of supporters made commitments that aggregated to nearly two-thirds of the cost of making the new Museum. Unusually for such a project, there was no single lead donor, but rather a consortium of donors helped to ensure that both the project and the Museum itself could thrive for generations to come. A list of those benefactors can be found on page 144; every one of them has my humblest and most enduring thanks, not least for their friendship.

It has been my belief that a building project of such significance warranted a volume like this that would not merely commemorate it but also interrogate it and its complex prehistory. It has been a privilege and a delight to collaborate with this book's esteemed essayists, who include two Pulitzer Prize–winning authors, Paul Goldberger and Mark Stevens, as well as my University colleagues Ron McCoy and Susan Stewart; the latter contributed an original poem. My thanks go to each of them for their compelling words and to the photographer Richard Barnes, who spent many days on-site in all weathers seeking to capture the essence of the building's spaces and materials.

As I often do on occasions less momentous than this one, I reserve my deepest and warmest gratitude to the whole of the staff at the Princeton University Art Museum, who have tolerated thirteen years of planning for and executing this project as well as five and a half years of wandering in the wilderness from the time we closed the old building in March 2020 in the face of the COVID-19 pandemic and then remained closed as we pivoted to evacuation of the collections, demolition of the old building, construction of a new one, and then the return of art that began almost a year ago. Space here does not allow me to call out everyone whose talents and fortitude have been put toward this once-in-a-lifetime project, but from the senior management team—the incomparable Caroline Harris, Stephen Kim, Chris Newth, Karen Ohland, and Shara Pollie—to our curators, educators, registrars, designers, art handlers, project managers, fundraisers, finance team, data team, facilities team, security officers, and housekeepers, every one of you has risen to the challenge. And if any reader wants to know how I've slept at night in recent months, it is thanks to all of these people and particularly to project managers Katie Getchell and Laura Hahn. You are my heroes.

In the context of this printed volume, I must call out by name those individuals who made such essential and often unsung contributions that without their efforts these pages would have remained but a directorial dream. Senior Associate Director for Education Caroline Harris provided overall project leadership. Managing Editor Anna Brouwer made essential contributions at every turn and to every page, even in the face of authors like me who failed to meet their deadlines, and with a discerning eye for word and image that truly gave us this book. Museum writer Christine Minerva tracked down endless seemingly impossible attributions and contributed in many other ways; former research intern Oskar Pezalla-Granlund mined the archives to find many nuggets of previously unpublished historical information. Photographer Richard Barnes brought his masterful eye and a lot of patience to the images that dominate the pages that follow, and my colleagues Jeff Evans, Joseph Hu, and Kristina Giasi both coordinated and supplemented that work in remarkable ways. Kate Justement and Sarah Brown provided valuable assistance with sourcing images. Finally, warmest thanks go to the designers, editors, and printers whose talents brought all this raw data to life, including our new partners Takumi Akin and Wesley Chou at Folder Studio for their immensely thoughtful response to the building's design and the challenge of producing a book that complements it; Karen Jacobson and Dianne Woo for their expert copyediting and proofreading, respectively; and Massimo Tonolli and his team at Trifolio, who produced this beautiful publication.

In the age of AI, making a new museum and, for that matter, making a book are acts of audacity. They are acts worth undertaking when one is surrounded by such humanity, generosity, and talent. I hope the pages herein persuade the reader that our collective efforts have left the world a richer place.

James Christen Steward
Nancy A. Nasher–David J. Haemisegger, Class of 1976, Director

DONORS TO THE NEW PRINCETON
UNIVERSITY ART MUSEUM

The Fisher Family
Preston H. Haskell III, Class of 1960
Nancy A. Nasher, Class of 1976; David J. Haemisegger, Class of 1976;
    David N. Haemisegger, Class of 2022; Isabelle N. Haemisegger; and Sarah N.
    Haemisegger

Philip Anschutz, parent, Class of 1993 & 1996; Nancy Anschutz, parent, Class of
    1993 & 1996; Sarah Shaw Anschutz, Class of 1993; Libby Anschutz, Class of 1996;
    William P. A. Hunt, Class of 2021; and Eleanor Marie Hunt, Class of 2025
Yan Huo, Graduate School Class of 1994
Louisa Stude Sarofim, parent, Class of 1986
William H. Walton III, Class of 1974; Theodora D. Walton, Class of 1978; Francesca S.
    Walton, Class of 2021; and William H. Walton IV

Susan Diekman and John Diekman, Class of 1965
Heather Sturt Haaga and Paul G. Haaga Jr., Class of 1970
Catherine Loevner and David Loevner, Class of 1976

Allen R. Adler, Class of 1967, and Frances Beatty Adler
Stephanie Bernheim, in memory of Leonard H. Bernheim, Class of 1954
John Cecil, Class of 1976, and Celia Felsher, Class of 1976
Joel L. Cohen, in memory of Kermit A. Brandt, Class of 1956
The Elfers Family, in memory of William R. Elfers, Class of 1971
Stacey Goergen, Class of 1990, and Robert Goergen Jr.
The Laporte Family, in memory of John H. Laporte Jr., Class of 1967
Nancy C. Lee, parent, Class of 2013 & 2018
Sharon and Anthony H. P. Lee, Class of 1979, in memory of Christina Lee, parent,
    Class of 1979
Alan Y. K. Lo, Class of 2003; Yenn Wong Lo; and Victor Lo, parent, Class of 2003
Gene Locks, Class of 1959, and Sueyun Locks
Shelly Belfer Malkin, Class of 1986, and Tony Malkin
Jennifer Maritz and Philip Maritz, Class of 1983
Grace Mele, in memory of Howard Mele, Class of 1949
Annette Merle-Smith
The Sherrerd Family, in memory of Kathleen Compton Sherrerd
Thomas Tuttle, Class of 1988
Duane Wilder, Class of 1951
Anonymous

Edward E. Matthews, Class of 1953
Morley G. Melden and Jean Z. Melden
Louise Sams, Class of 1979, and Jerome Grilhot
Hans J. Sternberg, Class of 1957, and Donna W. Sternberg

Frank S. Accetta, Class of 1982, and Carol Wilcox Accetta
Cionna Mary Buckley
Peter C. Bunnell
Julie Neuffer Callaghan and Kevin T. Callaghan, Class of 1983
Melanie Clarke, parent, Class of 2011, and John Clarke, parent, Class of 2011
Lloyd E. Cotsen, Class of 1950, and Margit Sperling Cotsen
Sarah Lee Elson, Class of 1984
Barbara Essig, parent, Class of 1983, and Gerald Essig, parent, Class of 1983
Andrea Fessler and Davide Erro, Class of 1991
Helen Frankenthaler Foundation and the Frankenthaler Climate Initiative
M. Robin Krasny, Class of 1973
William Martin and Geniva Martin
Peter M. Ochs, Class of 1965, and Gail J. Ochs
Christopher E. Olofson, Class of 1992
Ellen Peck and Bob Peck, Class of 1988
Peter Jay Sharp Foundation
Juan A. Sabater, Class of 1987, and Marianna Nunez Sabater
Mark Stevens, Class of 1973
James Christen Steward, Honorary Class of 1967 & 1970
Anne Robinson Woods, Class of 1988

...CY

...NEROSITY HAS LEFT A LASTING MARK

WALL HONORS PAST BENEFACTORS

WILLIAM COWPER PRIME, CLASS OF 1843, & MAR...

ROBERT GARRETT, CLASS OF 1867

T. HARRISON GARRETT, CLASS OF 1868

ALLAN MARQUAND, CLASS OF 1874

MRS. CYRUS H. MCCORMICK SR.

CYRUS H. MCCORMICK JR., CLASS OF 1879

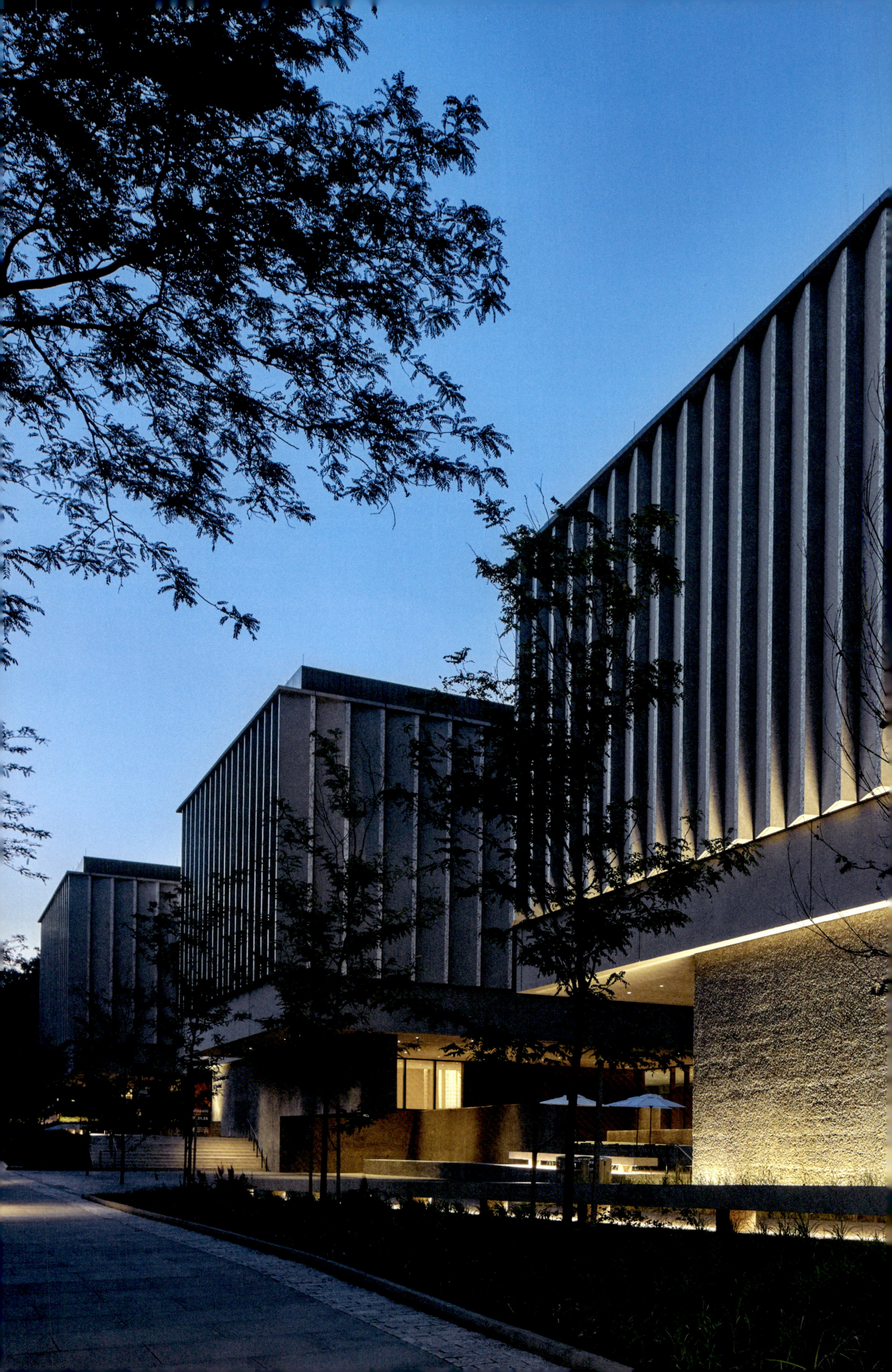

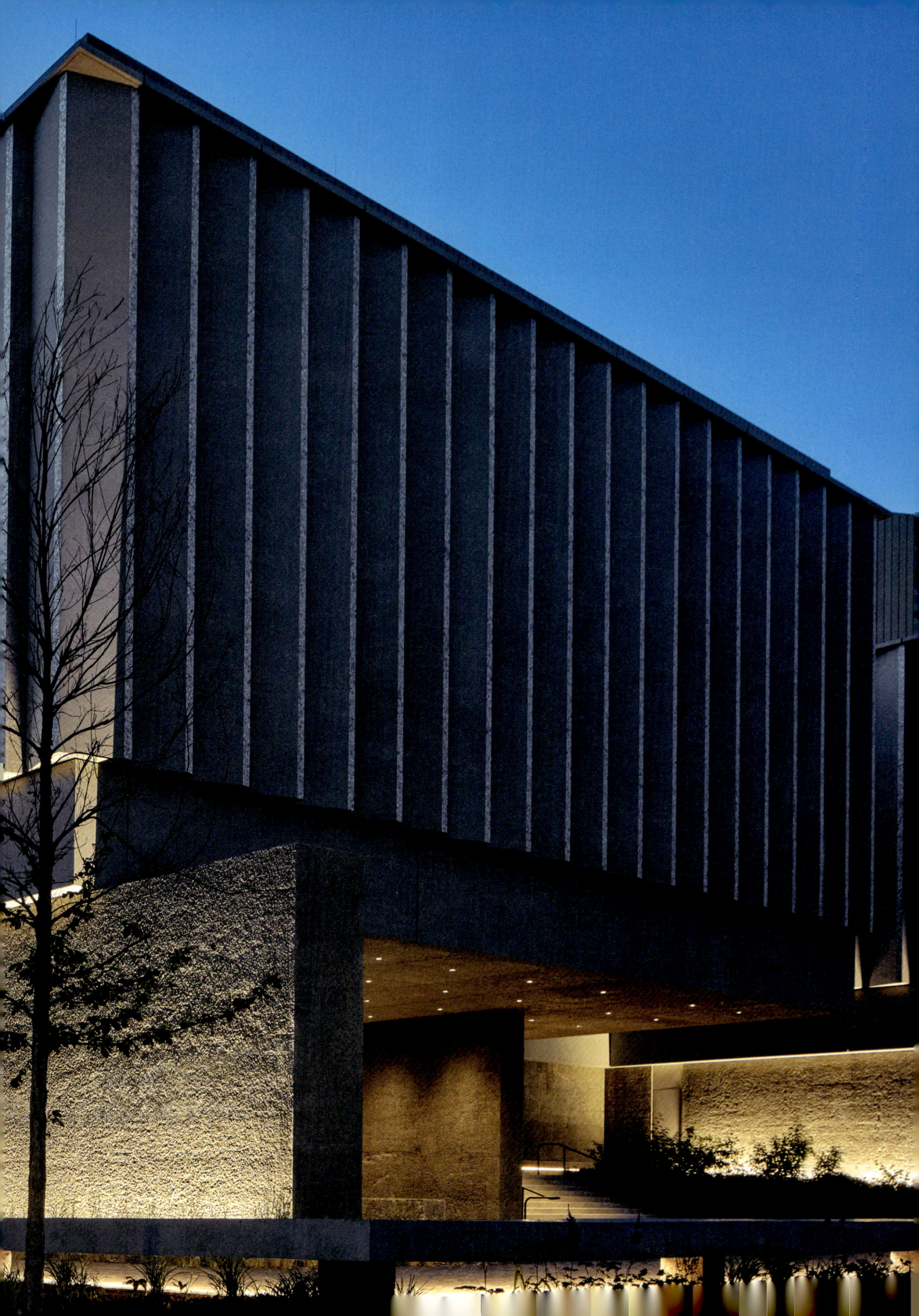

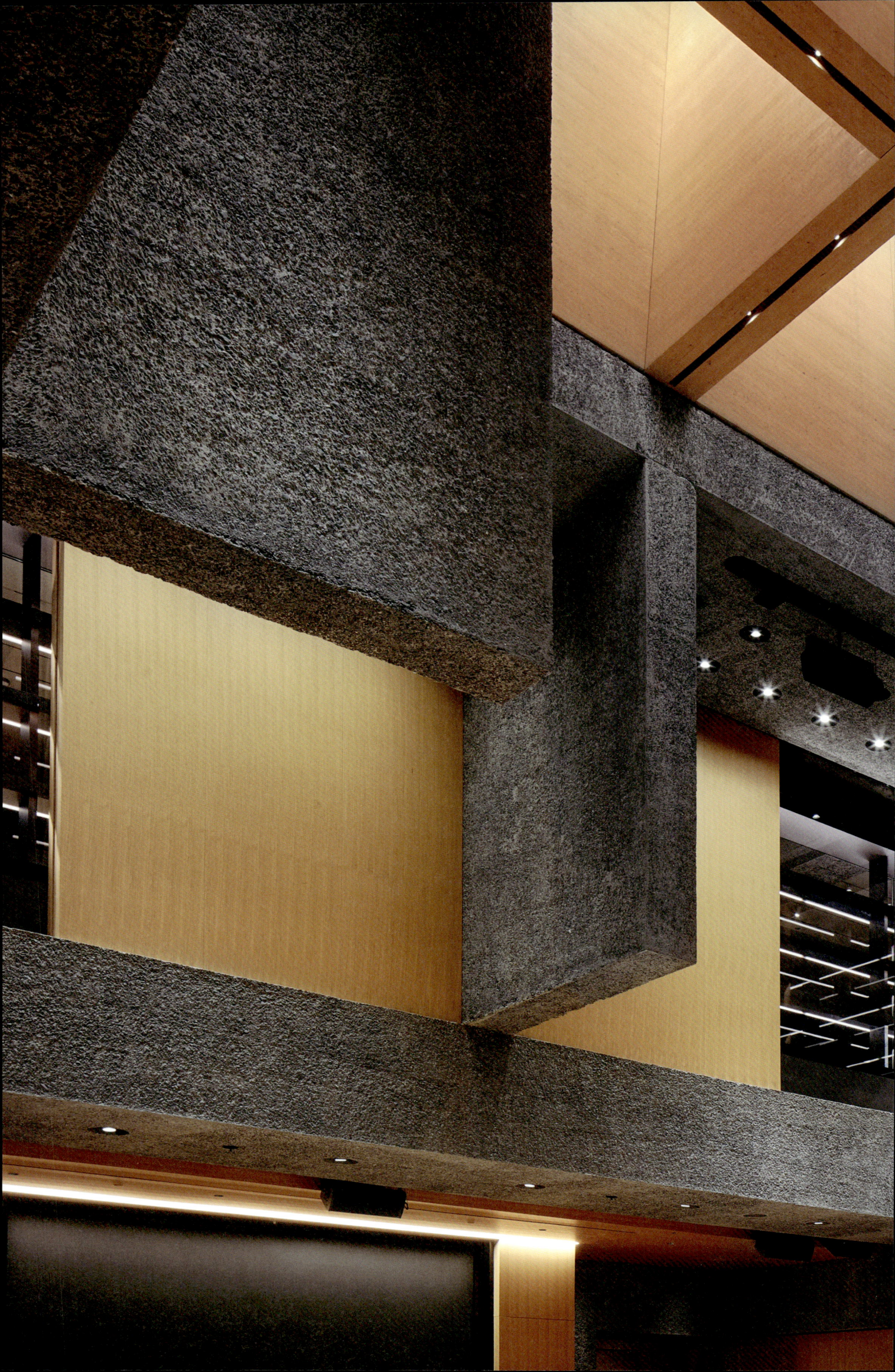

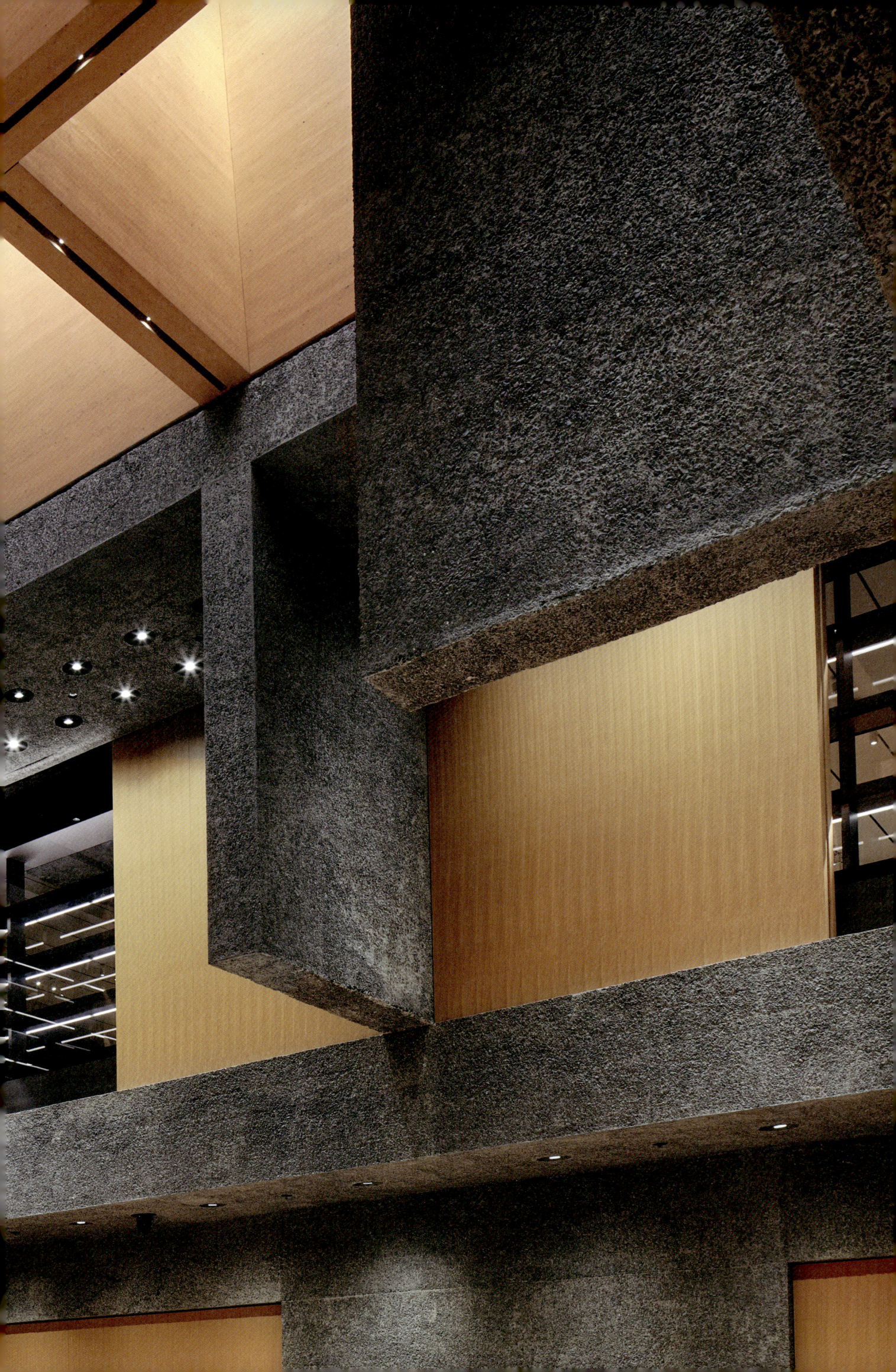

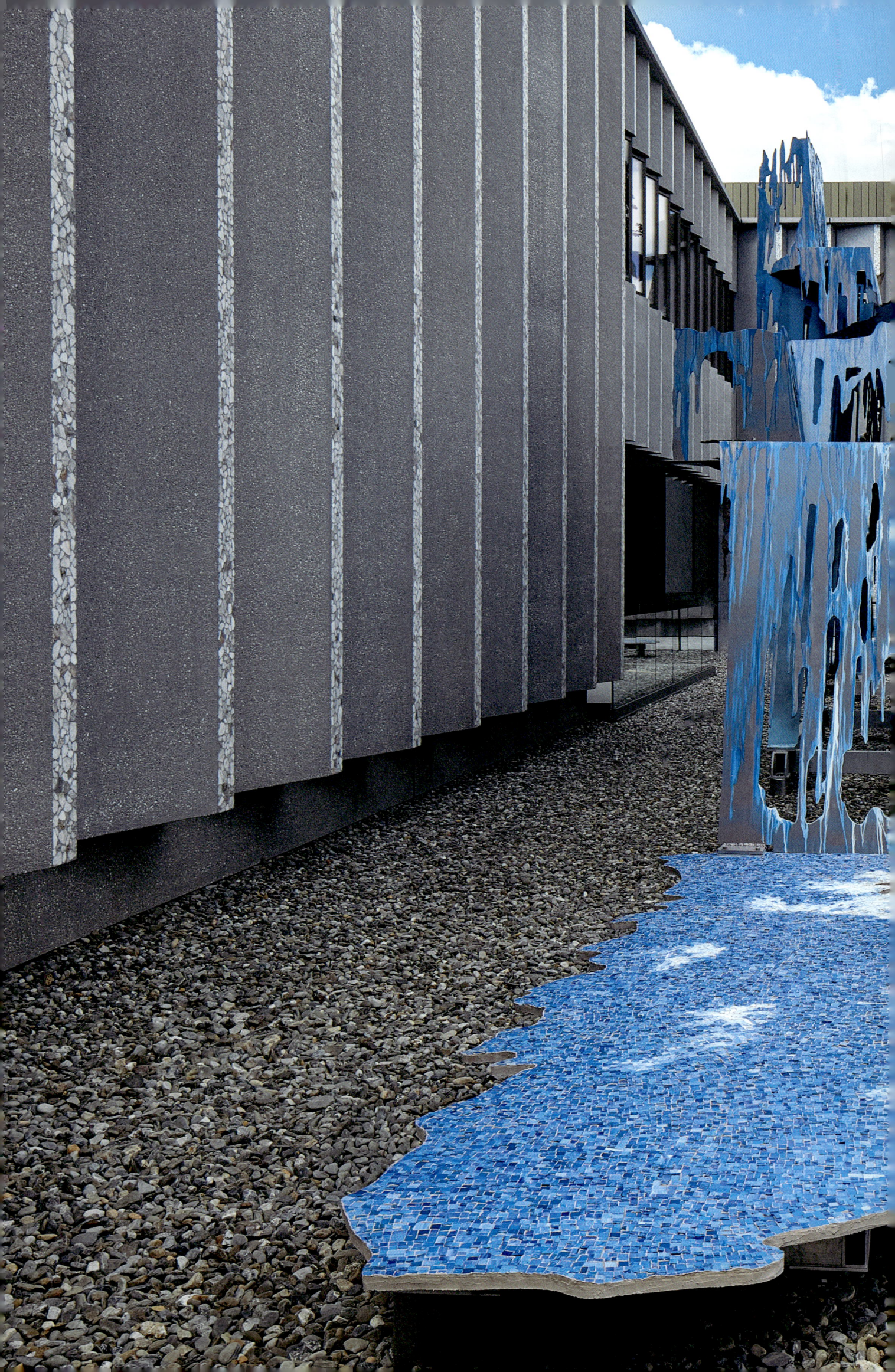

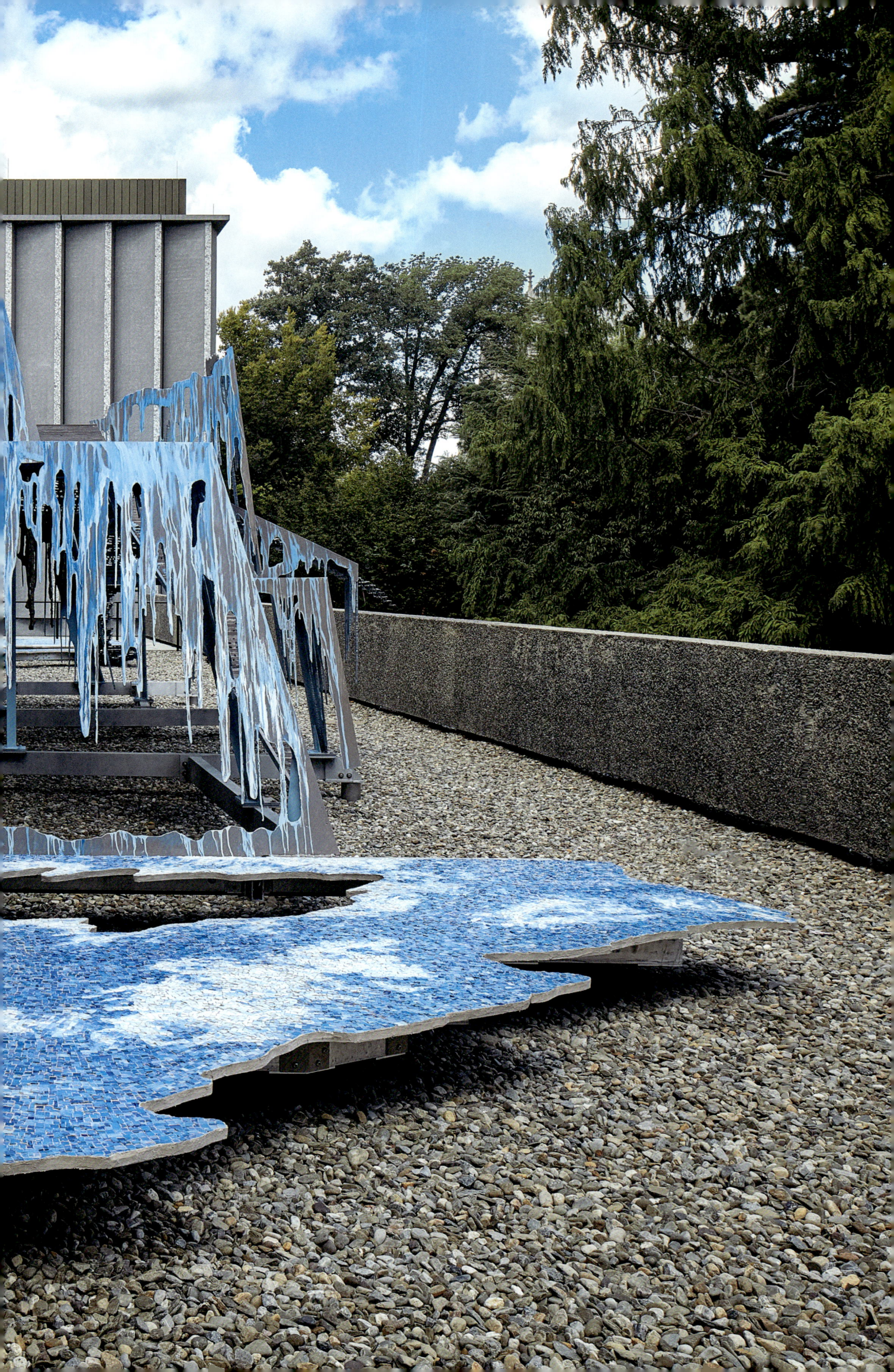

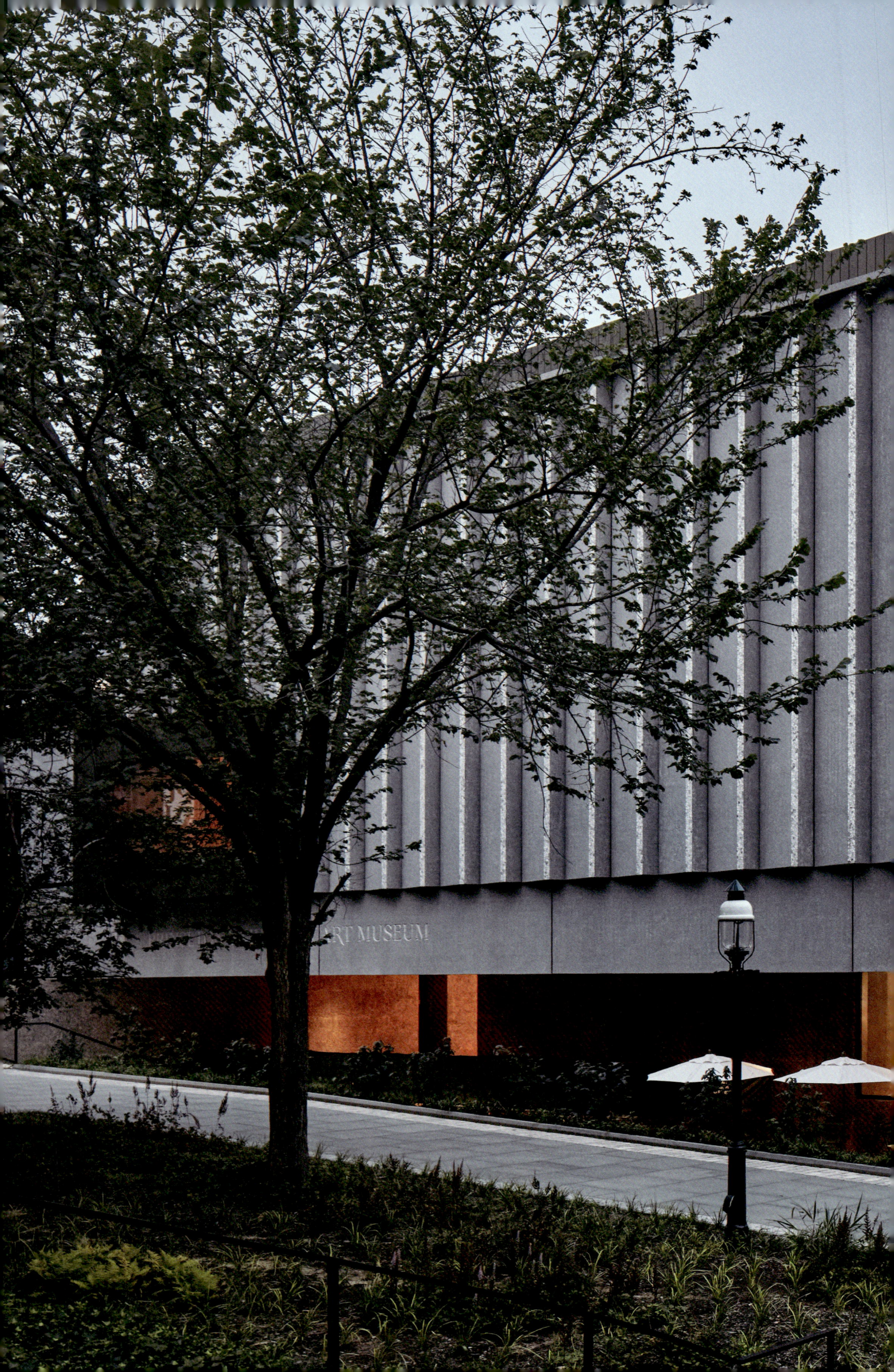

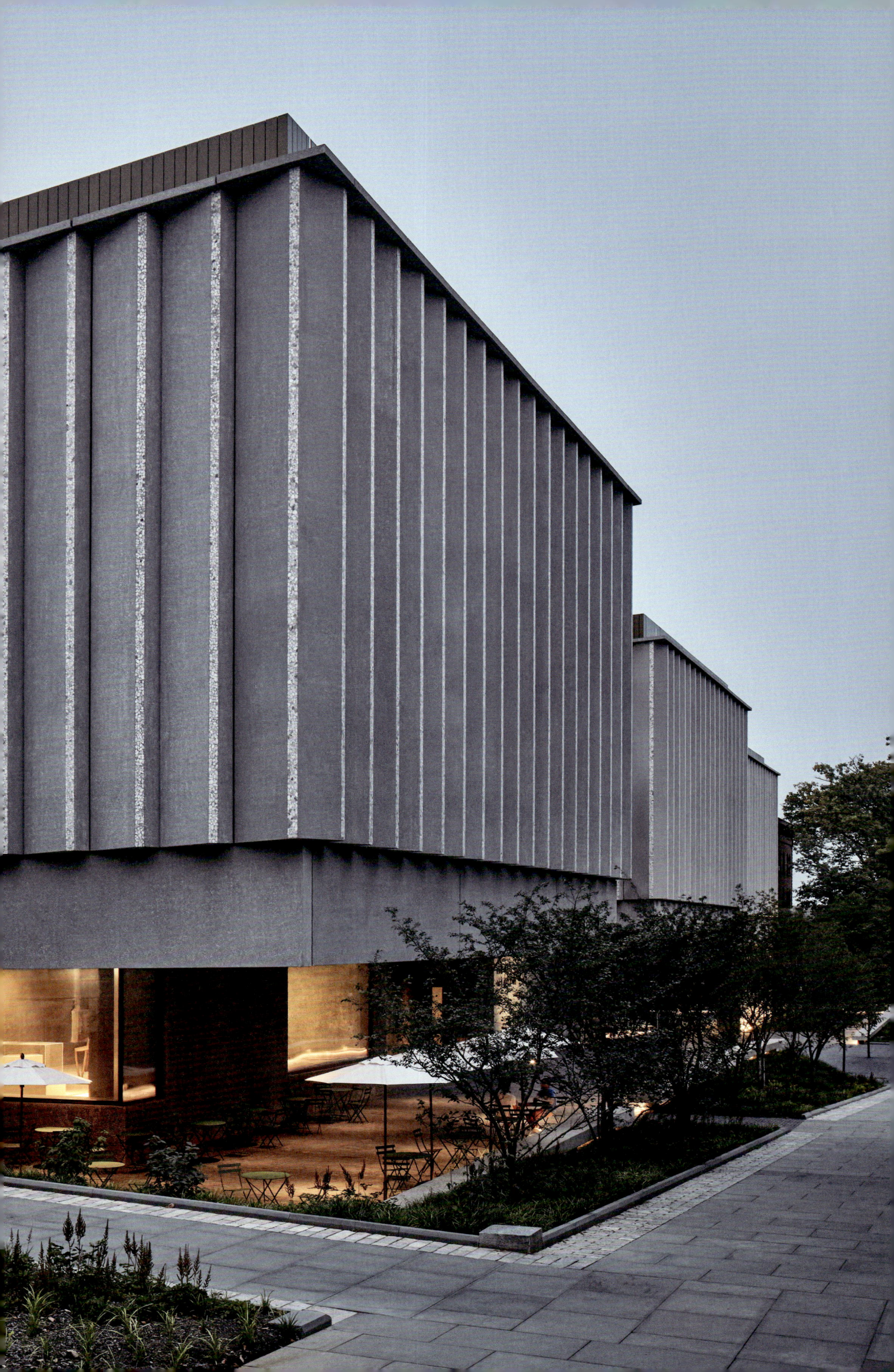

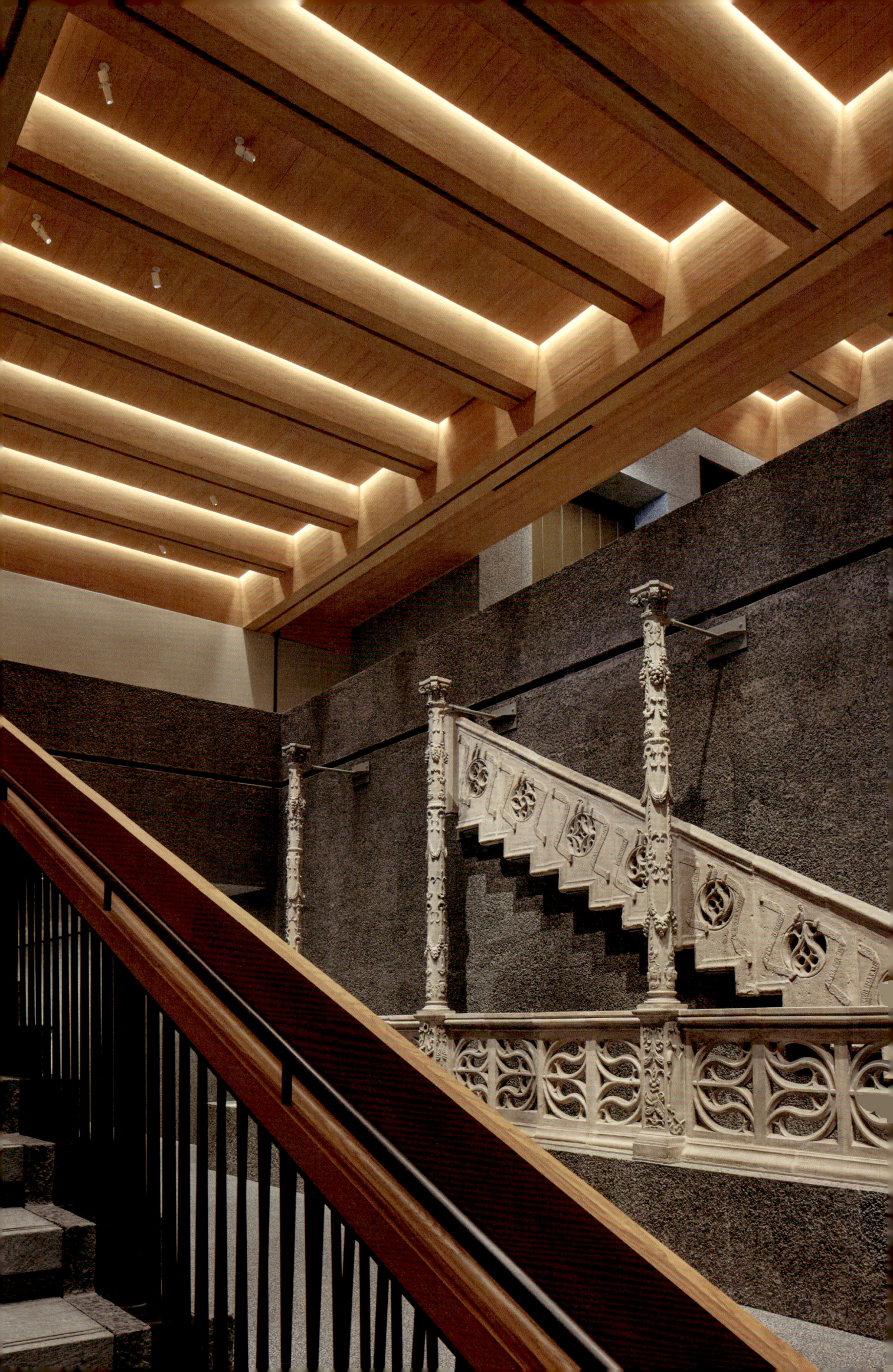

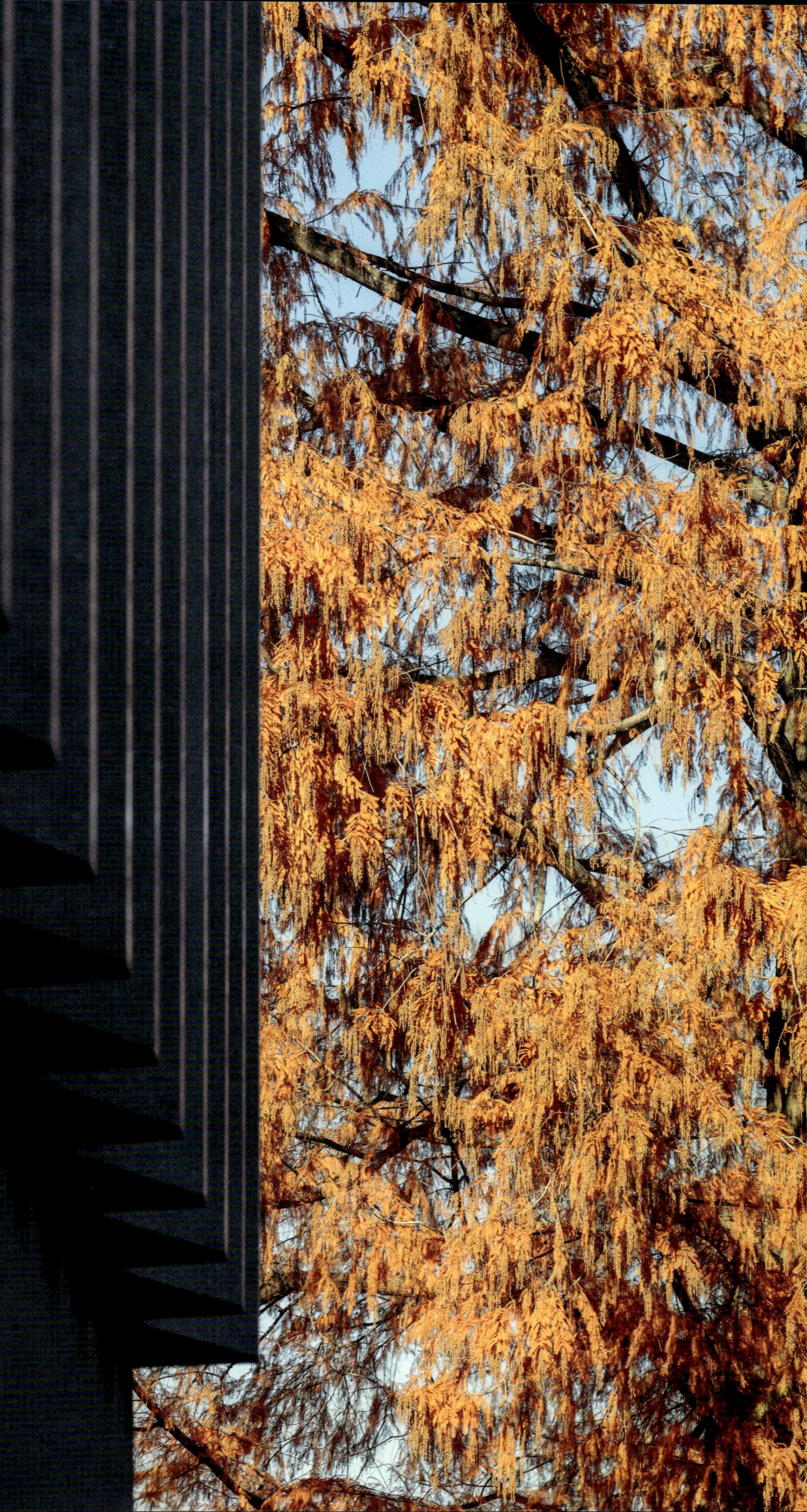

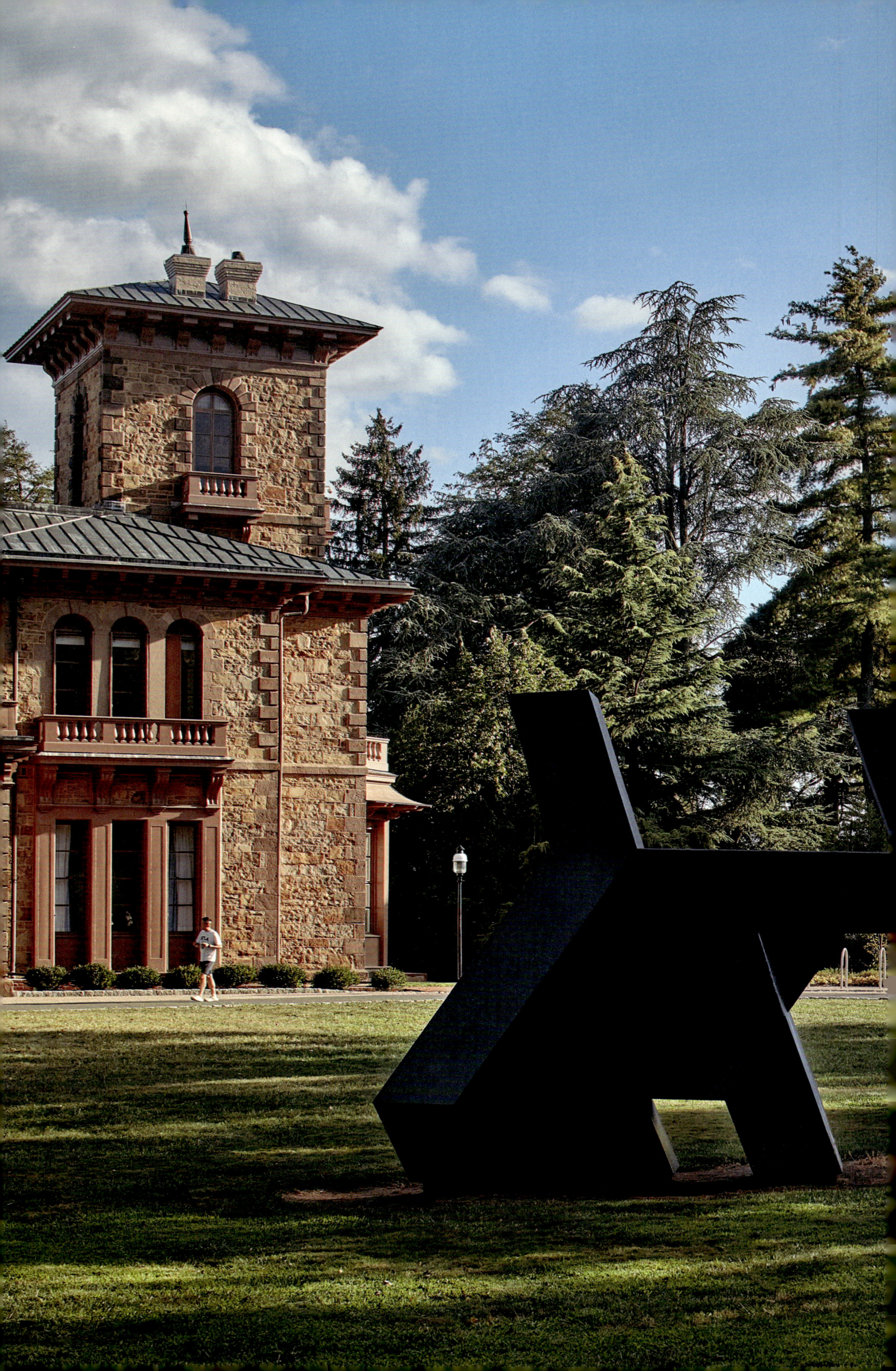

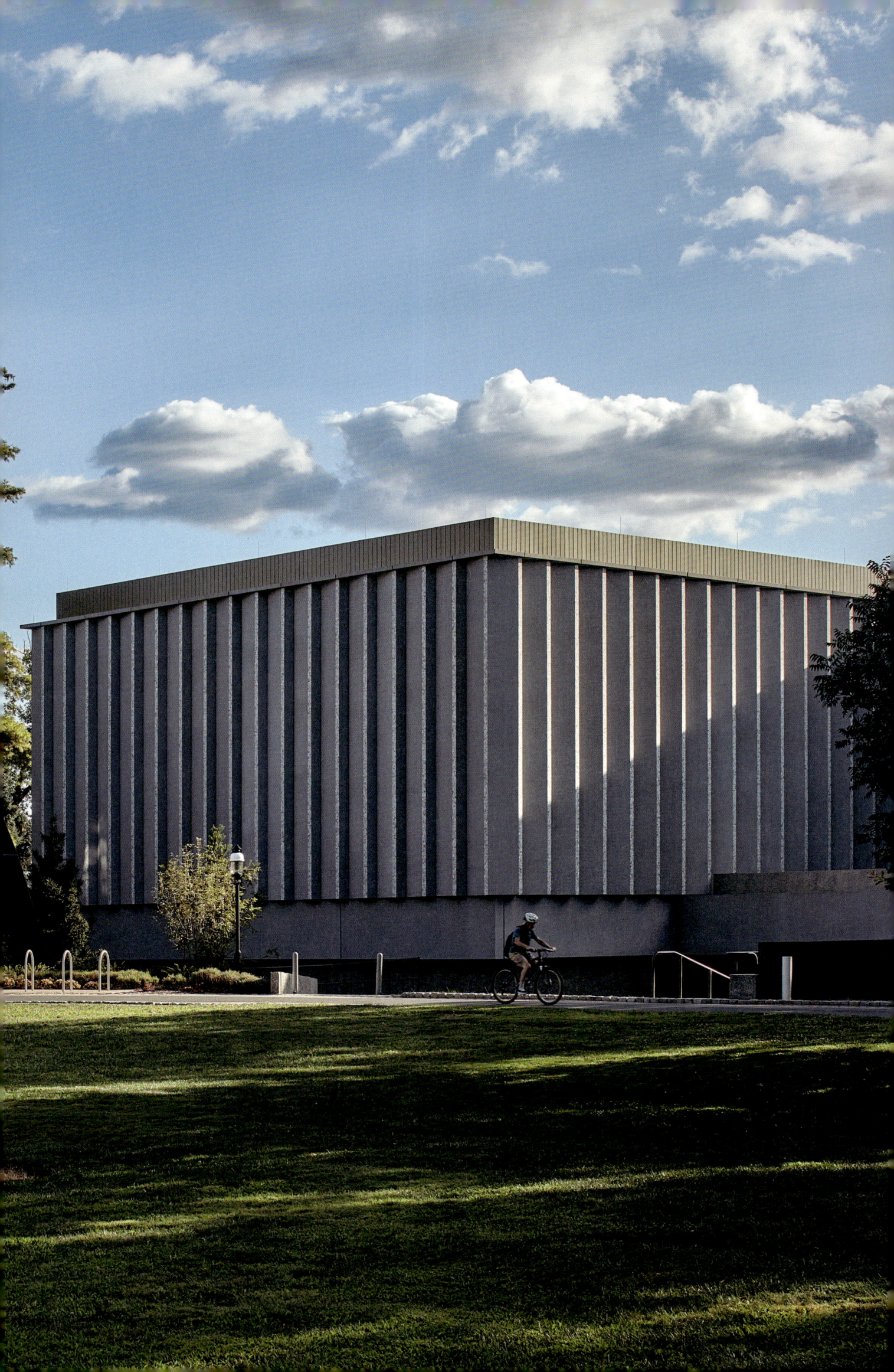

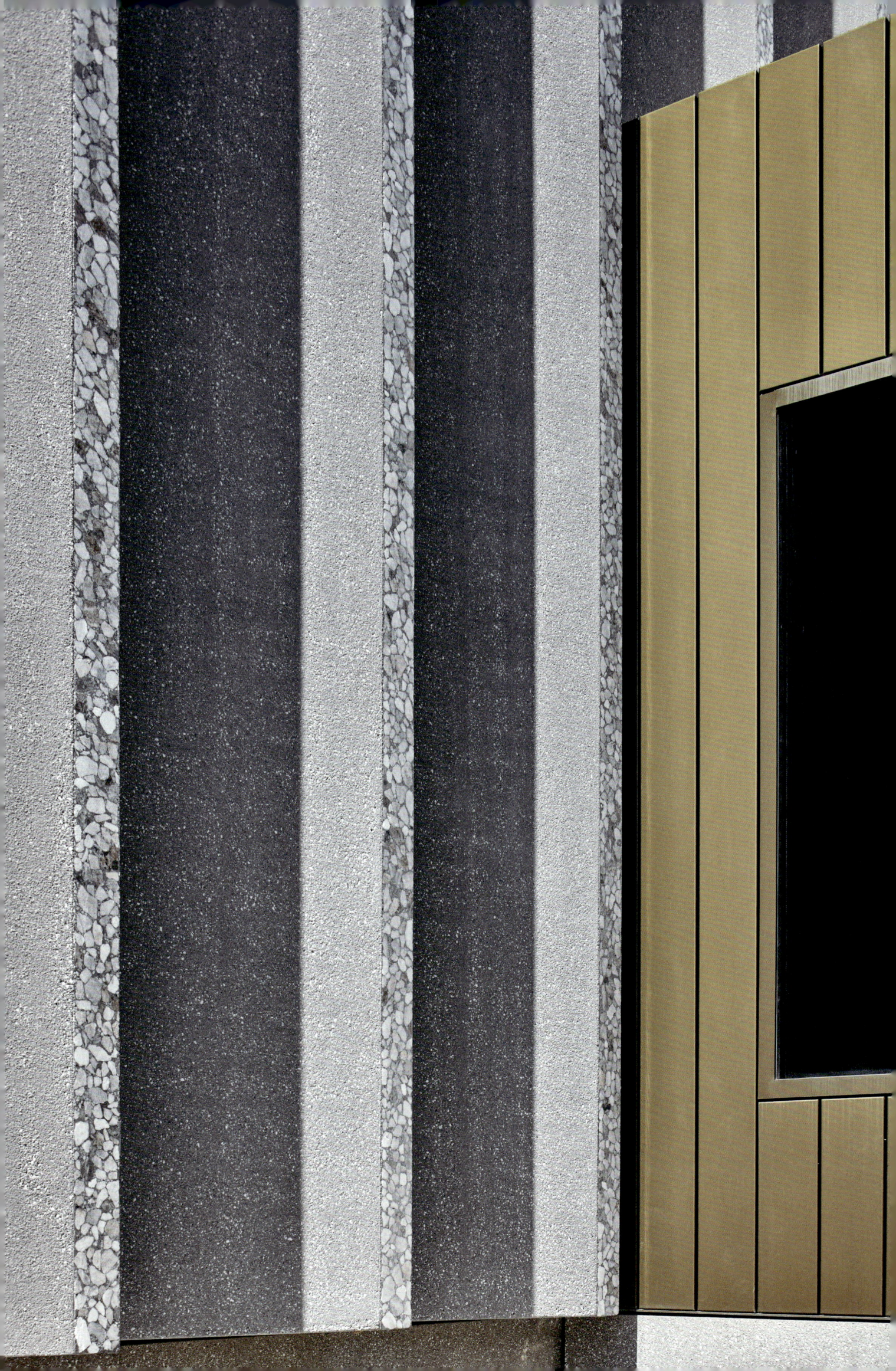

IMAGE CREDITS

Published by the Princeton University Art Museum
Princeton, NJ 08544-1018
artmuseum.princeton.edu

Project editor: Anna Brouwer
Copyedited by Karen Jacobson
Proofread by Dianne Woo
Designed by Folder Studio
Printing and color separations by Trifolio SRL, Verona, Italy
Printed on Symbol Tatami 150 gsm
Typeset in Intervogue and Ehrhardt MT

Distributed by Princeton University Press
41 William Street, Princeton, NJ 08540-5237
99 Banbury Road, Oxford OX2 6JX
press.princeton.edu

GPSR Authorized Representative: Easy Access System Europe - Mustamäe tee 50, 10621 Tallinn, Estonia, gpsr.requests@easproject.com

Library of Congress Control Number: 2025941865
ISBN: 978-0-691-97891-8
E-book ISBN: 978-0-691-97893-2
British Library Cataloging-in-Publication Data is available

Cover design by Folder Studio

Printed and bound in Italy
10 9 8 7 6 5 4 3 2 1